NORTHSTAR 5
LISTENING & SPEAKING

FOURTH EDITION

Author **SHERRY PREISS**

Series Editors **FRANCES BOYD**

CAROL NUMRICH

NorthStar: Listening & Speaking Level 5, Fourth Edition

Pearson Education, 10 Bank Street, White Plains, NY 10606

Staff credits: The people who made up the *NorthStar: Listening & Speaking Level 5, Fourth Edition* team, representing editorial, production, design, and manufacturing, are Kimberly Casey, Tracey Cataldo, Rosa Chapinal, Aerin Csigay, Mindy DePalma, Dave Dickey, Nancy Flaggman, Niki Lee, Amy McCormick, Mary Perrotta Rich, Robert Ruvo, Christopher Siley, and Debbie Sistino

Text composition: ElectraGraphics, Inc.
Development Editing: Barefoot Editorial Services

Library of Congress Cataloging-in-Publication Data

Frazier, Laurie.
  Northstar 2 : Listening and speaking / Authors : Laurie Frazier, Robin Mills. — Fourth Edition. / Frazier, Laurie.
       pages cm
  ISBN-13: 978-0-13-338213-6 (Level 2) – ISBN 978-0-13-294040-5 (Level 3) –
ISBN 978-0-13-338207-5 (Level 4) – ISBN 978-0-13-338214-3 (Level 5)
1. English language—Textbooks for foreign speakers. 2. English language—Spoken English—Problems, exercises, etc. 3. Listening—Problems, exercises, etc. I. Mills, Robin, 1962– II. Title.
III. Title: Northstar two. IV. Title: Listening and speaking.
  PE1128.M586 2015
  428.2'4—dc23

                                                                                    2013050585

Printed in the United States of America

ISBN-10: 0-13-338214-1
ISBN-13: 978-0-13-338214-3

ISBN-10: 0-13-404983-7 (International Edition)
ISBN-13: 978-0-13-404983-0 (International Edition)

CONTENTS

WELCOME TO

NORTHSTAR

A BLENDED-LEARNING COURSE FOR THE 21ST CENTURY

Building on the success of previous editions, *NorthStar* continues to engage and motivate students through new and updated contemporary, authentic topics in a seamless integration of print and online content. Students will achieve their academic as well as language and personal goals in order to meet the challenges of the 21st century.

New for the FOURTH EDITION

★ Fully Blended MyEnglishLab

NorthStar aims to prepare students for academic success and digital literacy with its fully blended online lab. The innovative new MyEnglishLab: *NorthStar* gives learners immediate feedback—anytime, anywhere—as they complete auto-graded language activities online.

★ NEW and UPDATED THEMES

Current and thought-provoking topics presented in a variety of genres promote intellectual stimulation. The authentic content engages students, links them to language use outside of the classroom, and encourages personal expression and critical thinking.

★ EXPLICIT SKILL INSTRUCTION and PRACTICE

Language skills are highlighted in each unit, providing students with systematic and multiple exposures to language forms and structures in a variety of contexts. Concise presentations and targeted practice in print and online prepare students for academic success.

★ LEARNING OUTCOMES and ASSESSMENT

A variety of assessment tools, including online diagnostic, formative and summative assessments, and a flexible gradebook, aligned with clearly identified unit learning outcomes, allow teachers to individualize instruction and track student progress.

THE NORTHSTAR APPROACH TO CRITICAL THINKING

What is critical thinking?

Most textbooks include interesting questions for students to discuss and tasks for students to engage in to develop language skills. Often these questions and tasks are labeled critical thinking. Look at this question as an example:

When you buy fruits and vegetables, do you usually look for the cheapest price? Explain.

The question may inspire a lively discussion with students exploring a variety of viewpoints—but it doesn't necessarily develop critical thinking. Now look at another example:

When people in your neighborhood buy fruits and vegetables, what factors are the most important: the price, the freshness, locally grown, organic (without chemicals)? Make a prediction and explain. How can you find out if your prediction is correct? This question does develop critical thinking. It asks students to make predictions, formulate a hypothesis, and draw a conclusion—all higher-level critical thinking skills. Critical thinking, as philosophers and psychologists suggest, is a sharpening and a broadening of the mind. A critical thinker engages in true problem solving, connects information in novel ways, and challenges assumptions. A critical thinker is a skillful, responsible thinker who is open-minded and has the ability to evaluate information based on evidence. Ultimately, through this process of critical thinking, students are better able to decide what to think, what to say, or what to do.

How do we teach critical thinking?

It is not enough to teach "about" critical thinking. Teaching the theory of critical-thinking will not produce critical thinkers. Additionally, it is not enough to simply expose students to good examples of critical thinking without explanation or explicit practice and hope our students will learn by imitation.

Students need to engage in specially designed exercises that aim to improve critical-thinking skills. This approach practices skills both implicitly and explicitly and is embedded in thought-provoking content. Some strategies include:

- subject matter that is carefully selected and exploited so that students learn new concepts and encounter new perspectives.
- students identifying their own assumptions about the world and later challenging them.
- activities that are designed in a way that students answer questions and complete language-learning tasks that may not have black-and-white answers. (Finding THE answer is often less valuable than the process by which answers are derived.)
- activities that engage students in logical thinking, where they support their reasoning and resolve differences with their peers.

Infused throughout each unit of each book, *NorthStar* uses the principles and strategies outlined above, including:

- Make Inferences: inference comprehension questions in every unit
- Vocabulary and Comprehension: categorization activities
- Vocabulary and Synthesize: relationship analyses (analogies); comparisons (Venn diagrams)
- Synthesize: synthesis of information from two texts teaches a "multiplicity" approach rather than a "duality" approach to learning; ideas that seem to be in opposition on the surface may actually intersect and reinforce each other
- Focus on the Topic and Preview: identifying assumptions, recognizing attitudes and values, and then re-evaluating them
- Focus on Writing/Speaking: reasoning and argumentation
- Unit Project: judgment; choosing factual, unbiased information for research projects
- Focus on Writing/Speaking and Express Opinions: decision making; proposing solutions

THE NORTHSTAR UNIT

1 FOCUS ON THE TOPIC

* **CT** Each unit begins with a photo that draws students into the topic. Focus questions motivate students and encourage them to make personal connections. Students make inferences about and predict the content of the unit.

UNIT **1**

THE FANTASTIC PLASTIC
Brain

1 FOCUS ON THE TOPIC

1. For years, scientists thought that the brain's structure could not be changed—that the brain we were born with was the brain we were going to have forever. In recent years, a new science emerged, neuroplasticity, which confirmed that our brains are not fixed, or hard-wired; rather they are "plastic," meaning flexible. Look at the picture and the title of the unit. Why is this discovery important? How might it change our lives?

2. Look at the picture again. What is the artist trying to tell us about the way our brains work? How does the image reflect or not reflect the new science of neuroplasticity?

3. Working with a partner, decide if each statement is a fact (**F**) or a myth (**M**). Read the article on pages 4–5 to check your answers.
   a. _____ We only use 10% of our brain.
   b. _____ Brain damage is always permanent.
   c. _____ Our working memory can only store seven digits.

MyEnglishLab

CT A short self-assessment based on each unit's learning outcomes helps students check what they know and allows teachers to target instruction.

MyEnglishLab

Home | Help | Test student, reallylongname@emailaddress.com | Sign out

NORTHSTAR 5 LISTENING & SPEAKING

1 Unit 1

Check What You Know

Read the list of skills. You may already use some of them. Don't worry if you don't know about some or all of these skills. You will learn and practice them in this unit.

Check what you know. Put an *X* by the number of each skill that you already use.

If this activity was not assigned by your teacher, it will not be checked. You can still do this activity for practice.

Vocabulary	Vocabulary
1 Infer word meaning from context	1
2 Recognize synonyms	2
3 Recognize and use commonly confused words	3
Listening	**Listening**
4 Identify and take notes on main ideas and details	4
5 Identify a speaker's point of view	5
6 Infer a speaker's degree of certainty	6
7 Recognize language that signals a revision of previously held beliefs	7
Speaking	**Speaking**
8 Express and support opinions	8
9 Paraphrase a speaker's ideas	9
10 Connect statements to specific speakers	10
11 Interpret graphs	11
12 Use expressions to correct a myth or misconception	12
13 Prepare and deliver an oral presentation using "rich pictures"	13
Pronunciation	**Pronunciation**
14 Recognize emphasis through stress	14
	Grammar
	15

ALWAYS LEARNING

PEARSON

---

*indicates Critical Thinking

Two contrasting, thought-provoking listening selections, from a variety of authentic genres, stimulate students intellectually.

CT Students predict content, verify their predictions, and follow up with a variety of tasks that ensure comprehension.

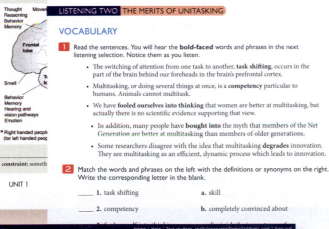

LISTENING ONE AN INTERVIEW WITH A BRAIN RESEARCHER

VOCABULARY

🎧 Read and listen to the article published in a popular science magazine. Pay attention to the **bold-faced** words and phrases. Then read the list of definitions that follows. Work with a partner. Write the number of the bold-faced word or phrase next to its definition.

THE BRAIN: MYTH AND FACT

1. **We only use 10% of our brains.**

   This **(1) astounding** myth has been around for a long time. This myth has persisted because, at any given time, people may **(2) perceive** they are using 10% of their brains, especially when they are resting, thinking, or taking a walk. It turns out, however, that with the advent of brain imaging technology, neuroscientists have proven that most parts of our brains are continually active over a 24-hour period.

   This fact has now been **(3) authenticated** in numerous studies.

2. **Brain damage is always permanent.**

   Not so, say neuroscientists. It is simply not true that a brain injury resulting in brain damage **(4) renders** the brain permanently damaged in every case. In some cases, the **(5) affected** brain cells, or neurons, may be permanently damaged. In other cases, these neurons connect to other neurons to form networks. The new connections, or networks,

LISTENING TWO THE MERITS OF UNITASKING

VOCABULARY

1 Read the sentences. You will hear the **bold-faced** words and phrases in the next listening selection. Notice them as you listen.

- The switching of attention from one task to another, **task shifting**, occurs in the part of the brain behind our foreheads in the brain's prefrontal cortex.
- Multitasking, or doing several things at once, is a **competency** particular to humans. Animals cannot multitask.
- We have **fooled ourselves into thinking** that women are better at multitasking, but actually there is no scientific evidence supporting that view.
- In addition, many people have **bought into** the myth that members of the Net Generation are better at multitasking than members of older generations.
- Some researchers disagree with the idea that multitasking **degrades** innovation. They see multitasking as an efficient, dynamic process which leads to innovation.

2 Match the words and phrases on the left with the definitions or synonyms on the right. Write the corresponding letter in the blank.

_____ 1. task shifting   a. skill

_____ 2. competency   b. completely convinced about

4 UNIT 1

CONNECT THE LISTENINGS

STEP 1: Organize

Both speakers, Dr. Doidge and Dr. Turkle focus on brain functioning. Yet each addresses the topic from a slightly different perspective. Review your notes on page 6.

Imagine that you have interviewed both Doidge and Turkle for a variety of tips (see page 7) for effective brain functioning. Unfortunately, your notes are a mess and now you can't remember who said what. Kick your frontal lobe into action and use your best analytical and problem solving skills to figure out who said what! Write the appropriate tip in the speech bubble above the appropriate photo.

STEP 2: Synthesize

Work with a partner. Imagine you are either Dr. Doidge or Dr. Turkle. You are giving a talk together about effective brain functioning to 200 professionals between the ages of 65–85 years old.

Below are two slides both of you will use. Practice by telling each other what you intend to say about each of the slides. Use tips from Step 1 on the previous page. Ask each other questions to get further information. Use these expressions:

Student A: On this slide you see . . . the point I would like to make here is . . .

Student B: Could you be a bit more specific . . . I think you need to give an example . . . so what you are saying is . . .

CT Students are challenged to take what they have learned and organize, integrate, and synthesize the information in a meaningful way.

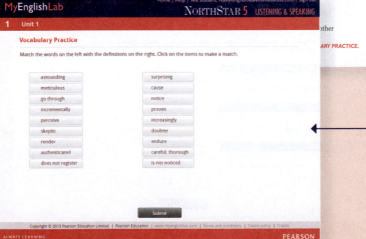

MyEnglishLab

Auto-graded vocabulary practice activities reinforce meaning and pronunciation.

EXPLICIT SKILL INSTRUCTION AND PRACTICE

CT Step-by-step instructions and practice guide students to exercise critical thinking and to dig deeper by asking questions that move beyond the literal meaning of the text.

MAKE INFERENCES

RECOGNIZING DEGREES OF CERTAINTY

An **inference** is an **educated guess** about something that is **not directly stated**, but which you believe is true based on the intention, attitude, voice, pausing, and word choices of the speaker.

Dr. Norman Doidge, a neuroscientist speaking to laypeople on the radio, presents surprising and important information about our brains. He expresses varying degrees of certainty about the results of scientific practices.

🎧 Listen to and read the example. Then answer the question and read the explanation.

Example

DOIDGE: And it turns out that that metaphor was actually just spectacularly wrong.

Think about the way in which Dr. Doidge expresses certainty about this claim about the brain. What is Doidge's degree of certainty about his assertion? What are the clues that helped you decide?

a. not very certain

b. certain

c. absolutely certain

The answer is *c*. There are two clues which indicated his absolute certainty: **1)** use of the word ~~ularly~~" meaning "totally" and **2)** tone of voice. Doidge places emphasis and stress on the ~~pectacularly~~" to convey he is completely convinced that the mechanistic view of the brain

~~en~~ to each excerpt. Decide how certain Doidge is about his assertions and note the ~~: helped~~ you decide.

One

What is Doidge's degree of certainty? What are the clues?

. not very certain

. certain

. absolutely certain

LISTENING SKILL

REVIEWING ASSUMPTIONS AND LISTENING FOR REVISIONS

In the second listening, Professor Sherry Turkle debunks the myth that multitasking—doing several things at once—is a skill that promotes effective performance. She believes that we need to value unitasking—the art of doing one thing at a time—over multitasking. She supports her thesis with statements that revise previously held beliefs and assumptions.

🎧 Read and listen to the example. Then answer the questions and read the explanation.

Example

TURKLE: We believed for so long that multitasking was a 21st century alchemy, that we could make more time by doing all of these things together. . . . And now we know—the research is clear—that we can multitask, but we degrade our performance for every task we multitask.

The earlier belief is that multitasking was efficient and effective.

1. What language does Turkle use to introduce the revised belief?_____

2. What is the revised belief?_____

Turkle introduced the revised belief by saying, "And now we know."

The revised belief is multitasking is not effective and in fact our performance worsens when we multitask.

🎧 Listen to Turkle's comments. Identify the language used to introduce the revised belief and then paraphrase the new belief in a single sentence.

Excerpt One

The earlier belief is that people can look like they are multitasking in certain situations.

Language used to introduce the revised belief: _____

Revised belief: _____

Excerpt Two

The earlier belief is that you can think you are multitasking and you think
because the brain is producing chemicals that make you feel like you are ⌐

Explicit skill presentation and practice lead to student mastery and success in an academic environment.

MyEnglishLab

Key listening skills are reinforced and practiced in new contexts. Meaningful and instant feedback provides students and teachers with essential information to monitor progress.

Using models from the unit listening selections, the pronunciation and speaking skill sections expose students to the sounds and patterns of English, as well as to functional language that prepares them to express ideas on a higher level.

6. **a.** The boxer finally **quit** competing. The latest jolt to his brain felt like a 15 pound bowling ball traveling at 20 miles per hour.

   b. He **quit** to teach young people about the dangers of certain sports like football, soccer, boxing, cycling, and horseback riding, and to teach them how to protect themselves from injury.

   _____ stopped

   _____ stopped doing something in order to do something else

7. **a.** The professional football player knew that playing the game **meant** risking long-term mental health, so he refused to let his son play.

   b. The coach **meant** to remind the young player to wear his helmet, but forgot. The child suffered a traumatic brain injury and his parents are now suing the coach for millions of dollars.

   _____ intended; planned

   _____ signified; involved

GO TO MyEnglishLab *FOR MORE GRAMMAR PRACTICE.*

PRONUNCIATION

STRESSING IMPORTANT WORDS

In a sentence, one or two words usually express the most important information. These are words that the speaker wants the listener to notice.

🎧 Listen to how the capitalized words are stressed in these sentences.

Example One

I've GOT to get some more sleep.
I REALLY need to check my email again.

We stress the most important words by saying them on a high pitch, or with strong stress: the stressed vowel is long and loud. When you speak, make sure your voice is high enough when you stress an important word.

In English, we emphasize new information (usually the last important word of the sentence), and we emphasize information that contrasts or corrects.

Example Two

Today we're going to talk about MULTItasking.
The kids are doing email instead of HOMEwork.

24   UNIT 1

SPEAKING SKILL

DEBUNKING MYTHS AND REVISING MISCONCEPTIONS

When research actually creates new knowledge, we have to change our ideas. We often call this process "debunking myths" or "revising misconceptions." It can take a long time for people to learn about and accept the new science. Doidge and Turkle are involved in spreading the new research and debunking myths.

🎧 Read and listen to the conversation. Notice how the underlined expressions are used (in conversation) to correct a myth or misconception.

Example

A: Our brains shut down when we sleep.

B: Actually, that's not true. For the longest time, we thought our brains shut down when we slept, but it turns out our brains never shut down.

A: Our brains stop developing after we are about 7 or 8 years old.

B: Sorry, but that's no longer an accepted fact. We used to believe that brain development stopped during childhood, but now we know our brains continue to grow and change throughout our life span.

A: We only use 10% of our brains.

B: Actually, that's been proven false. A while ago, people thought we used only 10% of our brains, but now it's widely known that all parts of our brains are continually active.

Useful Expressions for Debunking Myths and Revising Misconceptions
• Actually, that's not true . . . For the longest time, we thought . . . but it turns out . . .
• Sorry, but that's no longer an accepted fact. We used to believe . . . but now we know . . .
• Actually, that's been proven false. A while ago, people thought . . . , but now it's widely known that . . .
• That's a myth. For centuries people believed . . . but now we have clear proof that . . .

Work with a partner.

Student A: Read each of the three myths on the next page aloud.

Student B: Cover the left column. Correct each myth using one of the expressions listed above and the information provided. Switch roles after item 3.

Example

A: (Myth) Genes determine the fate of our brains.

B: (Correcting the myth) That's a myth. For centuries people believed that, but we now have clear proof that our experiences can shape our brains' capabilities.

26   UNIT 1

MyEnglishLab

Students continue online practice of key pronunciation and speaking skills with immediate feedback and scoring.

MyEnglishLab

Home | Help | Test student, reallylongname@emailaddress.com | Sign out

NORTHSTAR 5   LISTENING & SPEAKING

1   Unit 1

Speaking Skill: Debunking Myths and Revising Misconceptions

Type in the correct word to debunk each of the myths and revise the misconception. Use the letters in each blank as hints.

1   Myth: People in their 80's cannot sharpen their brain functioning

Revision: A c t [ ] [ ] [ ] [ ] , that's not true. F [ ] [ ] t [ ] I [ ] [ ] [ ] [ ] [ ] t time we thought older people couldn't learn new things, but research shows we can make older people cognitively younger through brain training.

2   Myth: Computers provide a surefire, absolute way to get smarter.

Revision: Sorry, that's not an a c c [ ] [ ] [ ] fact. We u [ ] [ ] to believe that there was some benefit, but now we k [ ] [ ] that we need more evidence.

3   Myth: Brain damage is permanent.

Revision: That idea has been p [ ] [ ] [ ] n f [ ] [ ] [ ] e Now, it is w [ ] [ ] y known that the brain can often heal itself over time and form new connections.

ALWAYS LEARNING   PEARSON

Welcome to *NorthStar*   ix

FOCUS ON SPEAKING

3 FOCUS ON SPEAKING

VOCABULARY

REVIEW

Taxi drivers in London are known as the "Olympic athletes" of memory according to Joshua Foer, author of the bestselling book *Moonwalking with Einstein: The Art and Science of Remembering Everything*. Dr. Janet Alcalde, professor of neuroscience, recently spoke about the book to an audience at a community event for senior citizens. Alcalde discusses a well-known study detailed in Foer's book.

1 🎧 Read and listen to a transcript of the discussion. Notice the **bold-faced** words.

AUDIENCE MEMBER 1: Tell us . . . do London taxi drivers really grow bigger brains simply by navigating their routes? It's tough for me to **buy into** the idea that we can **rewire** our brains just by driving a taxi!

ALCALDE: Yes, I know. There are a lot of **skeptics** out there who don't buy into this conclusion. But listen. **Meticulous** research was conducted by a British neuroscientist named Ellen Maguire who wanted to find out what effect all the driving around the spaghetti-like, higgledy-piggledy London streets might have on the cabbies' brains. A few years later, this initial study was **authenticated**, and it **rendered** the same conclusion. The results are simply **astounding**.

Street Map of London

14   UNIT 1

GRAMMAR

1 Work with a partner. Examine the sentences and discuss the questions that follow.

- He **stopped recalling** important memories after a serious concussion on the soccer field.
- He **stopped to recall** some of his favorite childhood memories.

1. What is the difference in meaning of the verb *stop* in the two sentences?

2. What other verbs can be followed by either a gerund or infinitive with a change in meaning?

VERBS FOLLOWED BY GERUNDS OR INFINITIVES WITH A CHANGE IN MEANING

Some verbs must always be followed by a **gerund** (base form of verb + *ing*). Other verbs must be followed by an **infinitive** (*to* + base form of verb). Others can be followed by either a gerund or an infinitive with no change in meaning.

However, certain verbs that can be followed by either a gerund or an infinitive do have a change in meaning. Sometimes the change is subtle; sometimes it is very obvious. Look at the verbs *forget* and *stop*.

Verb	Meaning
Forget + gerund He will never **forget winning** the championship even though he ended up in the hospital with a traumatic brain injury (TBI).	To forget an experience—usually one that is particularly good or bad
Forget + infinitive After his TBI, which was caused by heading the ball in the soccer match, he often **forgot to do** simple daily tasks.	To forget to perform an action
Stop + gerund He **stopped playing** soccer after the injury.	To stop doing something for an extended period time
Stop + infinitive When he realized how much his head hurt, he **stopped to get** medical help.	To stop doing something for a short period of time in order to do something else

NOTE: Some other verbs like this are *mean, quit, regret, remember,* and *try*.

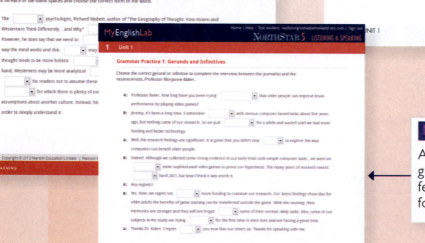

A final speaking task gives students an opportunity to exchange ideas and express opinions in sustained speaking contexts using the vocabulary, grammar, pronunciation, listening, and speaking skills presented in the unit.

FINAL SPEAKING TASK

In this task, you will use "Rich Pictures" to discuss case studies. During the Middle Ages, people seemed to know that words accompanied by imagery are much more memorable. Nowadays, brain scientists have proven that associating images and pictures with words enhances memory and learning. One technique used by students and professionals in all disciplines is the "rich picture technique." A Rich Picture is a picture that uses symbols, sketches, or "doodles" to present a problem or situation. Rich Pictures are an illustrative and creative way of conveying an understanding of a particular situation. Try to use the vocabulary, grammar, pronunciation, and listening and speaking skills that you learned in this unit.*

Example

Case Study: Michael's Story

Michael Bernstein was an eye surgeon, classical pianist, and tennis player. One day while playing tennis, half of his body was rendered completely immovable. He was given 6 weeks of rehabilitation and then sent home, but he was still not able to move half of his body. Another doctor had the ingenuity to try something different. He put the good limb in a sling or cast so Michael couldn't use it and then incrementally trained the affected limb. It worked. Dr. Bernstein is now practicing medicine and playing tennis.

Work in groups of 3. Imagine that you are in a science class studying the brain. Read Case A, B, or C on pages 29–31. Follow the steps to create a brief oral presentation using the Rich Picture technique. In your presentation, be sure to include 1) the problem; 2) the solution; 3) the science behind the solution. Use the vocabulary, grammar, and speaking skills you have learned in the unit.

STEP 1: Study the case.

- Read and discuss the case with your group.
- Discuss the problem, the solution, and the science behind the solution.

STEP 2: Draw

- Draw a Rich Picture that depicts the problem.
- Use any symbols, sketches, or doodles that you think will clearly illustrate the problem.

_____

* For Alternative Speaking Topics, see page 32.

A group unit project inspires students to inquire further and prepares students to engage in real-world activities. Unit projects incorporate Internet research, helping to build students' digital literacy skills.

C.

Ben's Story

At the age of two, Ben was diagnosed with cancer of the retina. He had his eyes removed at the age of 3. When he turned 5, he discovered that he was able to identify the location of objects simply by making clicking noises with his tongue and then listening for the returning echo. Using this technique Ben was able to play basketball, cycle, rollerblade, skateboard, and play football.

Other blind individuals have mastered this technique now known as echolocation. Echolocation is a way of locating sounds that reflect off surrounding objects in order to identify their location. Dolphins, whales, and bats are expert echolocators.

Remarkably though, researchers have discovered that these blind human echolocation experts do not use the "auditory" part of the brain to register the echos. Rather they use the "visual" parts of the brain, those areas that normally process visual information in sighted individuals. The brain areas used to process auditory information are not activated. The brain seems to be able to perceive information from a variety of sources of which we are not aware.

UNIT PROJECT

Topic 1

STEP 1: Choose one of these topics:

1. Hyperthymesia—total recall disease
2. Hoarding and the brain
3. Asperger's Syndrome
4. The teenage brain

STEP 2: Research the topic using the Internet or the library. Organize your research into three parts:

1. Definition and explanation of the topic
2. A story or example of the topic
3. Information about the brain as it relates to the topic

STEP 3: Present your research to the class.

(continued on next page)

With instant access to a wide range of online content and diagnostic tools, teachers can customize learning environments to meet the needs of every student.

USING MyEnglishLab, NORTHSTAR TEACHERS CAN:

Deliver rich online content to engage and motivate students, including:

- student audio to support listening and speaking skills.
- engaging, authentic video clips, including reports adapted from ABC, NBC, and CBS newscasts, tied to the unit themes.
- opportunities for written and recorded reactions to be submitted by students.

Use a powerful selection of diagnostic reports to:

- view student scores by unit, skill, and activity.
- monitor student progress on any activity or test as often as needed.
- analyze class data to determine steps for remediation and support.

Use Teacher Resource eText* to access:

- a digital copy of the student book for whole class instruction.
- downloadable achievement and placement tests.
- printable student resources including lesson planners, videoscripts, and video activities.
- classroom audio.
- unit teaching notes and answer keys.

---

* Teacher Resource eText is accessible through MyEnglishLab: *NorthStar*

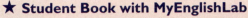

STUDENT BOOK and

★ Student Book with MyEnglishLab

The two strands, Reading & Writing and Listening & Speaking, for each of the five levels, provide a fully blended approach with the seamless integration of print and online content. Students use MyEnglishLab to access additional practice online, view videos, listen to audio selections, and receive instant feedback on their work.

eTEXT and

★ eText with MyEnglishLab

Offering maximum flexibility for different learning styles and needs, a digital version of the student book can be used on iPad® and Android® devices.

★ Instructor Access: Teacher Resource eText and MyEnglishLab (Listening & Speaking 1–5)

Teacher Resource eText

Each level and strand of *NorthStar* has an accompanying Teacher Resource eText that includes: a digital student book, unit teaching notes, answer keys, downloadable achievement tests, classroom audio, lesson planners, video activities, videoscripts, and a downloadable placement test.

MyEnglishLab

Teachers assign MyEnglishLab activities to reinforce the skills students learn in class and monitor progress through an online gradebook. The automatically-graded exercises in MyEnglishLab *NorthStar* support and build on academic skills and vocabulary presented and practiced in the Student Book/eText. The teacher-graded activities include pronunciation, speaking, and writing, and are assigned by the instructor.

★ Classroom Audio CD

The Listening & Speaking audio contains the recordings and activities, as well as audio for the achievement tests. The Reading & Writing strand contains the readings on audio.

Welcome to *NorthStar*   xiii

SCOPE AND SEQUENCE

UNIT OUTCOMES	1 THE BRAIN **THE FANTASTIC PLASTIC BRAIN** pages 2–33 *Listening 1: An Interview with a Brain Researcher* *Listening 2: The Merits of Unitasking*	2 LYING **IS HONESTY THE BEST POLICY?** pages 34–61 *Listening 1: Interview with a Psychiatrist* *Listening 2: Family Secrets*
LISTENING	• Make and confirm predictions • Identify and take notes on main ideas and details • Identify a speaker's point of view • Recognize language that signals a revision of previously held beliefs MyEnglishLab Vocabulary and Listening Skill Practice	• Make and confirm predictions • Summarize main ideas and details • Support ideas from one listening with reasons from a second listening • Identify a speaker's attitude MyEnglishLab Vocabulary and Listening Skill Practice
SPEAKING	• Express and support opinions • Paraphrase a speaker's ideas • Connect statements to specific speakers • Interpret graphs • Use expressions to correct a myth or misconception **Task:** Prepare and deliver an oral presentation using "rich pictures" MyEnglishLab Speaking Skill Practice and Speaking Task	• Express and support opinions • Recognize and use expressions to introduce, defend, and express multiple sides of an issue **Task:** Plan a group discussion, summarize an ethical dilemma, and present various solutions MyEnglishLab Speaking Skill Practice and Speaking Task
INFERENCE	• Infer a speaker's degree of certainty	• Infer meaning from language that signals hedging or hesitation
PRONUNCIATION	• Recognize emphasis through stress MyEnglishLab Pronunciation Skill Practice	• Recognize reductions of the auxiliary verb *have* MyEnglishLab Pronunciation Skill Practice
VOCABULARY	• Recognize synonyms • Recognize and use commonly confused words MyEnglishLab Vocabulary Practice	• Infer word meaning from context MyEnglishLab Vocabulary Practice
GRAMMAR	• Recognize and use verbs + gerund or infinitive with a change of meaning MyEnglishLab Grammar Practice	• Recognize and use modals to express degrees of certainty MyEnglishLab Grammar Practice
VIDEO	MyEnglishLab *Memory Boost*, ABC News, Video Activity	MyEnglishLab *Why Do Kids Lie?* ABC News, Video Activity
ASSESSMENTS	MyEnglishLab Check What You Know, Checkpoints 1 and 2, Unit 1 Achievement Test	MyEnglishLab Check What You Know, Checkpoints 1 and 2, Unit 2 Achievement Test

3 PERSONALITY	4 CROSS-CULTURAL INSIGHTS
• Make and confirm predictions • Summarize main ideas • Identify supporting details • Connect problems and solutions • Identify creative and effective examples MyEnglishLab Vocabulary and Listening Skill Practice	• Make and confirm predictions • Summarize main ideas and details • Identify a speaker's viewpoints and attitudes • Organize information using a bagua chart • Identify subtle ways to ask for and give advice MyEnglishLab Vocabulary and Listening Skill Practice
• Express and support opinions • Interpret cartoons • Describe personality • Express and defend preferences • Initiate and maintain a conversation **Task:** Prepare and dramatize a group presentation about sleep deprivation MyEnglishLab Speaking Skill Practice and Speaking Task	• Express and support opinions • Emphasize a point in a conversation **Task:** Present an argument MyEnglishLab Speaking Skill Practice and Speaking Task
• Infer meaning from language that presents a balanced point of view	• Infer a speaker's intention
• Recognize thought groups and formulate meaning MyEnglishLab Pronunciation Skill Practice	• Recognize pauses and intonation with discourse connectors MyEnglishLab Pronunciation Skill Practice
• Infer word meaning from context MyEnglishLab Vocabulary Practice	• Infer word meaning from context • Recognize and use word forms (nouns, verbs, adjectives, and adverbs) MyEnglishLab Vocabulary Practice
• Recognize and use identifying and non-identifying adjective clauses MyEnglishLab Grammar Practice	• Identify and use discourse connectors MyEnglishLab Grammar Practice
MyEnglishLab *Dale Carnegie Training Institute*, Video Activity	MyEnglishLab *Japanese Gardens*, Video Activity
MyEnglishLab Check What You Know, Checkpoints 1 and 2, Unit 3 Achievement Test	MyEnglishLab Check What You Know, Checkpoints 1 and 2, Unit 4 Achievement Test

SCOPE AND SEQUENCE

UNIT OUTCOMES	5 BUSINESS **BUSINESS NOT AS USUAL** pages 120–151 *Listening 1: The Story of Zappos* *Listening 2: The Progress Principle*	6 SOCIAL MEDIA **TOGETHER ALONE** pages 152–183 *Listening 1: An Interview with Sherry Turkle* *Listening 2: Online Identity: Authenticity or Anonymity?*
LISTENING	• Make and confirm predictions • Summarize main ideas • Identify supporting details • Recognize language to concede a point and present a counterargument **MyEnglishLab** Vocabulary and Listening Skill Practice	• Make and confirm predictions • Identify and complete main ideas • Identify supporting details • Recognize language that signals opposing perspectives of an issue • Connect statements to specific speakers **MyEnglishLab** Vocabulary and Listening Skill Practice
SPEAKING	• Agree and disagree with opinions • Make concessions to introduce counterarguments **Task:** Prepare and deliver an oral presentation **MyEnglishLab** Speaking Skill Practice and Speaking Task	• Agree and disagree with opinions • Interpret cartoons • Prepare for and engage in a debate • Recognize and use language that builds and expands on others' ideas **Task:** Participate in a group discussion and report on the groups' recommendations **MyEnglishLab** Speaking Skill Practice and Speaking Task
INFERENCE	• Infer meaning from expressive intonation	• Infer meaning and recognize techniques a speaker uses to take a stance on an issue
PRONUNCIATION	• Recognize and distinguish between /æ/, /ɑ/, and /ə/ **MyEnglishLab** Pronunciation Skill Practice	• Infer a speaker's attitude from intonation and stress **MyEnglishLab** Pronunciation Skill Practice
VOCABULARY	• Infer word meaning from context • Recognize and use synonyms • Recognize and use idioms connected to business **MyEnglishLab** Vocabulary Practice	• Infer word meaning from context • Recognize and use synonyms and antonyms **MyEnglishLab** Vocabulary Practice
GRAMMAR	• Recognize and use direct and indirect speech **MyEnglishLab** Grammar Practice	• Recognize and use wish statements, expressing unreality **MyEnglishLab** Grammar Practice
VIDEO	**MyEnglishLab** *Giving Back,* ABC News, Video Activity	**MyEnglishLab** *Making the Grade,* ABC News, Video Activity
ASSESSMENTS	**MyEnglishLab** Check What You Know, Checkpoints 1 and 2, Unit 5 Achievement Test	**MyEnglishLab** Check What You Know, Checkpoints 1 and 2, Unit 6 Achievement Test

7 THE ARTS
LEARNING THROUGH THE ARTS
pages 184–213

Listening 1: Brain Waves: This is Your Brain on Art

Listening 2: El Sistema: Music Education Changing Lives

8 POVERTY
CHANGING LIVES FOR $50
pages 214–247

Listening 1: Promises and Pitfalls of Microfinance

Listening 2: Interview with a Microfinance Director

• Make and confirm predictions • Summarize main ideas and details • Recognize persuasion with parallel structure **MyEnglishLab** Vocabulary and Listening Skill Practice	• Make and confirm predictions • Summarize main ideas and details • Recognize summary statements • Identify examples from listenings **MyEnglishLab** Vocabulary and Listening Skill Practice
• Express and support opinions • Summarize others' opinions • Prepare and deliver a mini-lecture • Incorporate parallel structure to speak persuasively **Task:** Prepare for and participate in a simulation of a public meeting **MyEnglishLab** Speaking Skill Practice and Speaking Task	• Express and support opinions • Paraphrase a speaker's key points • Summarize examples from the listenings • Use summary statements to demonstrate understanding **Task:** Prepare for and participate in a simulation of a policy meeting **MyEnglishLab** Speaking Skill Practice and Speaking Task
• Infer a speaker's purpose for examples	• Infer meaning by recognizing a speaker's assumptions about the listeners
• Recognize variations in how final consonants are joined **MyEnglishLab** Pronunciation Skill Practice	• Recognize word stress in two-word compound expressions **MyEnglishLab** Pronunciation Skill Practice
• Infer word meaning from context • Recognize and use synonyms • Distinguish between literal and figurative language **MyEnglishLab** Vocabulary Practice	• Infer word meaning from context • Recognize and use synonyms **MyEnglishLab** Vocabulary Practice
• Recognize and use the passive voice and the passive causative **MyEnglishLab** Grammar Practice	• Recognize and use present, past, and mixed unreal conditionals **MyEnglishLab** Grammar Practice
MyEnglishLab *Interlochen Arts Academy*, Video Activity	**MyEnglishLab** *Young Innovators, CBS News*, Video Activity
MyEnglishLab Check What You Know, Checkpoints 1 and 2, Unit 7 Achievement Test	**MyEnglishLab** Check What You Know, Checkpoints 1 and 2, Unit 8 Achievement Test

ACKNOWLEDGMENTS

The fourth edition of this book could not have been written without the support and assistance of my colleagues, friends, and family.

I would like to thank Frances Boyd and Carol Numrich, the architects of the *NorthStar* series, for their extraordinary vision of combining innovative language learning with topics of high interest to students. Once again, I am grateful to Frances Boyd, my series editor, for her imaginative insights, her sense of humor, and her passionate dedication to ensuring that students learn not only with their minds but also with their hearts. For the fourth time, Frances' exceptional creativity and intelligence motivated and inspired my writing.

I also owe an enormous debt of gratitude to the following people at Pearson: Mary Perrotta Rich, Niki Lee, and Robert Ruvo. I would like to thank Nan Clarke for her careful and intelligent editing of early drafts of the manuscript. Heartfelt appreciation goes to Aerin Csigay for his tremendous help with the art program. I'd like to thank Amy McCormick for her conviction that *NorthStar* can help students achieve their goals when they are challenged and respected. And finally, for making significant direct contributions throughout every step of the project, I owe deep appreciation to Debbie Sistino, Editorial Manager.

Between the first and fourth editions, I've have had the fortunate experience of traveling worldwide, visiting lots of classrooms, and working with teachers and students who were using the *NorthStar* series. My observations and their feedback provided much of the impetus for this revision. I appreciate the willingness of teachers to engage students in material that challenges their assumptions and allows them to think critically about themselves and the world. I hope that students and teachers will find learning with this text as much fun as I had writing it.

Finally, I owe heartfelt thanks to my mom, Bernice, my mother-in-law, Rita, and my husband, Rich, for his patience and constant cheerleading. And thanks to my son, Alex, for his encouragement and advice along the way as he used *NorthStar* in his own teaching; and to my daughter, Elyse, thanks for simply saying, "Oh, you can do it, Mom!" whenever I needed to hear it. All of your support helped to propel me through the process.

Sherry Preiss

REVIEWERS

Chris Antonellis, Boston University – CELOP; Gail August, Hostos; Aegina Barnes, York College; Kim Bayer, Hunter College; Mine Bellikli, Atilim University; Allison Blechman, Embassy CES; Paul Blomquist, Kaplan; Helena Botros, FLS; James Branchick, FLS; Chris Bruffee, Embassy CES; Nese Cakli, Duzce University; María Cordani Tourinho Dantas, Colégio Rainha De Paz; Jason Davis, ASC English; Lindsay Donigan, Fullerton College; Bina Dugan, BCCC; Sibel Ece Izmir, Atilim University; Érica Ferrer, Universidad del Norte; María Irma Gallegos Peláez, Universidad del Valle de México; Jeff Gano, ASA College; María Genovev a Chávez Bazán, Universidad del Valle de México; Juan Garcia, FLS; Heidi Gramlich, The New England School of English; Phillip Grayson, Kaplan; Rebecca Gross, The New England School of English; Rick Guadiana, FLS; Sebnem Guzel, Tobb University; Esra Hatipoglu, Ufuk University; Brian Henry, FLS; Josephine Horna, BCCC; Arthur Hui, Fullerton College; Zoe Isaacson, Hunter College; Kathy Johnson, Fullerton College; Marcelo Juica, Urban College of Boston; Tom Justice, North Shore Community College; Lisa Karakas, Berkeley College; Eva Kopernacki, Embassy CES; Drew Larimore, Kaplan; Heidi Lieb, BCCC; Patricia Martins, Ibeu; Cecilia Mora Espejo, Universidad del Valle de México; Kate Nyhan, The New England School of English; Julie Oni, FLS; Willard Osman, The New England School of English; Olga Pagieva, ASA College; Manish Patel, FLS; Paige Poole, Universidad del Norte; Claudia Rebello, Ibeu; Lourdes Rey, Universidad del Norte; Michelle Reynolds, FLS International Boston Commons; Mary Ritter, NYU; Minerva Santos, Hostos; Sezer Sarioz, Saint Benoit PLS; Ebru Sinar, Tobb University; Beth Soll, NYU (Columbia); Christopher Stobart, Universidad del Norte; Guliz Uludag, Ufuk University; Debra Un, NYU; Hilal Unlusu, Saint Benoit PLS; María del Carmen Viruega Trejo, Universidad del Valle de México; Reda Vural, Atilim University; Douglas Waters, Universidad del Norte; Leyla Yucklik, Duzce University; Jorge Zepeda Porras, Universidad del Valle de México

THE FANTASTIC PLASTIC
Brain

1. For years, scientists thought that the brain's structure could not be changed—that the brain we were born with was the brain we were going to have forever. In recent years, a new science emerged, neuroplasticity, which confirmed that our brains are not fixed, or hard-wired; rather they are "plastic," meaning flexible. Look at the picture and the title of the unit. Why is this discovery important? How might it change our lives?

2. Look at the picture again. What is the artist trying to tell us about the way our brains work? How does the image reflect or not reflect the new science of neuroplasticity?

3. Working with a partner, decide if each statement is a fact (**F**) or a myth (**M**). Read the article on pages 4–5 to check your answers.

   a. _____ We only use 10% of our brain.

   b. _____ Brain damage is always permanent.

   c. _____ Our working memory can only store seven digits.

   d. _____ We get new brain wrinkles when we learn something.

   e. _____ It is possible for us to simply think ourselves into being positive, calmer, and more compassionate.

GO TO MyEnglishLab TO CHECK WHAT YOU KNOW.

3

VOCABULARY

🎧 Read and listen to the article published in a popular science magazine. Pay attention to the **bold-faced** words and phrases. Then read the list of definitions that follows. Work with a partner. Write the number of the bold-faced word or phrase next to its definition.

THE BRAIN: MYTH AND FACT

1. **We only use 10% of our brains.**

   This **(1) astounding** myth has been around for a long time. This myth has persisted because, at any given time, people may **(2) perceive** they are using 10% of their brains, especially when they are resting, thinking, or taking a walk. It turns out, however, that with the advent of brain imaging technology, neuroscientists have proven that most parts of our brains are continually active over a 24-hour period.

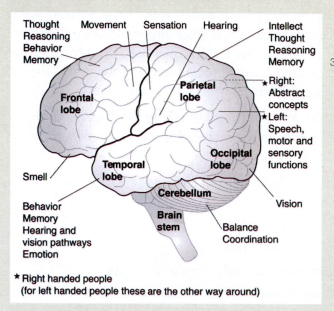

Thought Reasoning Behavior Memory — Movement — Sensation — Hearing — Intellect Thought Reasoning Memory

Parietal lobe

Frontal lobe

★Right: Abstract concepts
★Left: Speech, motor and sensory functions

Occipital lobe

Temporal lobe

Smell

Cerebellum

Behavior Memory Hearing and vision pathways Emotion

Brain stem

Vision

Balance Coordination

★ Right handed people
(for left handed people these are the other way around)

This fact has now been **(3) authenticated** in numerous studies.

2. **Brain damage is always permanent.**

   Not so, say neuroscientists. It is simply not true that a brain injury resulting in brain damage **(4) renders** the brain permanently damaged in every case. In some cases, the **(5) affected** brain cells, or neurons, may be permanently damaged. In other cases, these neurons connect to other neurons to form networks. The new connections, or networks, form new pathways. In this sense, the brain has the capacity to **(6) rewire**, and thus repair, itself.

3. **Our working memory can only store seven digits.**

   This is true, and it's why many telephone numbers don't go beyond seven digits. In 1956, Harvard psychologist George Miller did a **(7) rigorous** study to confirm that most people can only hold seven things in short-term memory. That said, there are rare memory champions, **(8) the best and the brightest**, who can outperform this "number seven" memory constraint.[1] Most of us, however, notice that a new thought, perception, or number **(9) does not register** immediately and is easily forgotten.

---

[1] **constraint:** something that limits freedom; restriction

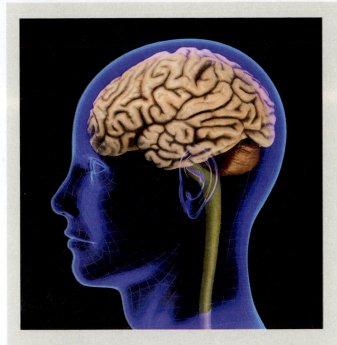

while ago, people thought that these **wrinkles** were **(10) animate**, but now it is widely known that they do not grow and change as other brain structures and functions do. Instead, their role is to help squeeze the human brain inside of our relatively small skull. During our long evolution, the brain grew **(11) incrementally** in order to manage the higher-order thinking functions, such as creativity, **(12) ingenuity**, and imagination. Without the wrinkles, the brain would be as big as a pillowcase!

5. **It is possible for us to simply think ourselves into being positive, calmer, and more compassionate.**

In fact, this is true. Tibetan Buddhists have long claimed that meditation changes them in positive ways. They call this "le-su-rung." **(13) Skeptics** have doubted them. Yet hundreds of Buddhist monks have **(14) gone through** careful testing. **(15) Meticulous** scientists have concluded from their studies that "le-su-rung" is another name for neuroplasticity. In other words, our brain can change with experience.

4. **We get new brain wrinkles when we learn something.**

This may be fun to imagine, but actually, it's been proven false. The brain does have wrinkles, called *gyri* and *sulci*, which actually appear on the human fetus at 40 weeks. A

_____ **a.** alive

_____ **b.** careful about details

_____ **c.** exact, precise

_____ **d.** causes to be

_____ **e.** cleverness

_____ **f.** doubters

_____ **g.** endured

_____ **h.** increasingly

_____ **i.** changed

_____ **j.** is not noticed

_____ **k.** most talented

_____ **l.** notice

_____ **m.** proven

_____ **n.** reconnect

_____ **o.** surprising

GO TO MyEnglish**Lab** *FOR MORE VOCABULARY PRACTICE.*

PREVIEW

Dr. Norman Doidge is a neuroscientist who studies the brain. He is the author of *The Brain That Changes Itself*. In the interview, he tells the story of a 90-year-old gentleman, Stanley Karanski, who had trouble performing certain activities due to aging. Karanski had trouble with several daily-life activities: remembering, focusing, driving.

🎧 Work with a partner. Predict the effects that a brain training program had on Karanski's performance of daily activities. Then listen to the excerpt to verify your predictions.

1. _____

2. _____

3. _____

MAIN IDEAS

🎧 Look at the chart. Listen to the whole interview and take notes on the main ideas. Use the key phrases in the left column to help you. Use a separate piece of paper if necessary. (You will note details later.) Work with a partner to compare and revise your notes.

MAIN IDEAS	DETAILS
Meaning of metaphor *brain = machine*	Reasons the metaphor is wrong
Reason for eye surgeon example	Problem/treatment/reasons behind 1st treatment choice
Assumption behind Taub's therapy	How Taub's therapy works
Taub's reputation in scientific community	Evidence for Taub's reputation
Michael Merzenich's contribution to brain research	Examples of brain plasticity applications with children and adults

DETAILS

🎧 Read the chart again. Fill in as many details as possible to support the main ideas. Then listen to the interview again to check your work. Work with a partner to compare and revise your notes.

GO TO MyEnglishLab FOR MORE LISTENING PRACTICE.

MAKE INFERENCES

RECOGNIZING DEGREES OF CERTAINTY

An **inference** is an **educated guess** about something that is **not directly stated**, but which you believe is true based on the intention, attitude, voice, pausing, and word choices of the speaker.

Dr. Norman Doidge, a neuroscientist speaking to laypeople on the radio, presents surprising and important information about our brains. He expresses varying degrees of certainty about the results of scientific practices.

🎧 Listen to and read the example. Then answer the question and read the explanation.

Example

DOIDGE: And it turns out that that metaphor was actually just spectacularly wrong.

Think about the way in which Dr. Doidge expresses certainty about this claim about the brain. What is Doidge's degree of certainty about his assertion? What are the clues that helped you decide?

a. not very certain

b. certain

c. absolutely certain

The answer is *c.* There are two clues which indicated his absolute certainty: **1)** use of the word "spectacularly" meaning "totally" and **2)** tone of voice. Doidge places emphasis and stress on the word "spectacularly" to convey he is completely convinced that the mechanistic view of the brain is wrong.

🎧   Listen to each excerpt. Decide how certain Doidge is about his assertions and note the clues that helped you decide.

Excerpt One

1. What is Doidge's degree of certainty? What are the clues?

   a. not very certain

   b. certain

   c. absolutely certain

Clues:

_____

_____

_____

(continued on next page)

2. What is Doidge's degree of certainty? What are the clues?

   a. not very certain

   b. certain

   c. absolutely certain

Clues:

_____

_____

Excerpt Three

3. What is Doidge's degree of certainty? What are the clues?

   a. not very certain

   b. certain

   c. absolutely certain

Clues:

_____

_____

_____

EXPRESS OPINIONS

1 Discuss the questions with the class. Give your opinions and give reasons for them.

1. After hearing about "the fantastic plastic brain" in this interview, what changes could you make in your life to strengthen the power of your brain? In other words, how would you exploit neuroplasticity for your own benefit? What implications might the research have for your parents, grandparents, and/or children?

2. Brain injuries, such as strokes or concussions, or learning disabilities, such as dyslexia, can create serious challenges. Have you or someone you know ever suffered a brain injury or had to cope with overcoming a learning disability? What was the recovery process like? How might you have applied this research to helping you or someone you know with this injury or disability?

3. Doidge believes that we can increase our mental fitness by doing "neurobic exercises," or activities to strengthen our brain functions.

2 Look at this list of activities. Prioritize which activities you would like to do in order to increase your brain power. Number **1** is your first choice and number **11** is your last choice. Share your list with a partner and explain your reasons. Discuss why these activities might be useful in improving brain function.

_____ learning and playing a musical instrument

_____ eating "superfoods": blueberries, wild salmon, nuts & seeds, avocados, whole grains

_____ exercising daily

_____ playing games such as crossword puzzles, chess, or complex video games

_____ memorizing long poems

_____ learning Braille

_____ doodling

_____ napping

_____ meditating

_____ learning to juggle

_____ (add your own)

▪▪▪▪▪▪▪▪▪▪▪▪▪▪▪▪▪▪▪ **GO TO** MyEnglishLab **TO GIVE YOUR OPINION ABOUT ANOTHER QUESTION.**

LISTENING TWO THE MERITS OF UNITASKING

VOCABULARY

1 Read the sentences. You will hear the **bold-faced** words and phrases in the next listening selection. Notice them as you listen.

- The switching of attention from one task to another, **task shifting**, occurs in the part of the brain behind our foreheads in the brain's prefrontal cortex.

- Multitasking, or doing several things at once, is a **competency** particular to humans. Animals cannot multitask.

- We have **fooled ourselves into thinking** that women are better at multitasking, but actually there is no scientific evidence supporting that view.

(continued on next page)

- In addition, many people have **bought into** the myth that members of the Net Generation are better at multitasking than members of older generations.

- Some researchers disagree with the idea that multitasking **degrades** innovation. They see multitasking as an efficient, dynamic process which leads to innovation.

2 Match the words and phrases on the left with the definitions or synonyms on the right. Write the corresponding letter in the blank.

_____ 1. task shifting   **a.** skill

_____ 2. competency   **b.** completely convinced about

_____ 3. fool oneself into thinking   **c.** diminish the importance of

_____ 4. bought into   **d.** trick oneself into believing

_____ 5. degrade   **e.** changing from one thing to another

GO TO MyEnglishLab *FOR MORE VOCABULARY PRACTICE.*

COMPREHENSION

Listen to the interview. M.I.T. Professor Sherry Turkle offers her opinions about multitasking. Check (✓) all statements that represent her point of view.

Turkle believes that multitasking

1. _____ is an unavoidable 21st century phenomenon.

2. _____ is an important learning skill.

3. _____ is an ability supported by research.

4. _____ worsens our performance on certain tasks.

5. _____ is a tragically bad habit.

6. _____ is a rewarding, positive experience which makes us feel good.

7. _____ is definitely useful in situations such as filing or checking email.

8. _____ should be valued as much as unitasking.

LISTENING SKILL

REVIEWING ASSUMPTIONS AND LISTENING FOR REVISIONS

In the second listening, Professor Sherry Turkle debunks the myth that multitasking—doing several things at once—is a skill that promotes effective performance. She believes that we need to value unitasking—the art of doing one thing at a time—over multitasking. She supports her thesis with statements that revise previously held beliefs and assumptions.

🎧 Read and listen to the example. Then answer the questions and read the explanation.

Example

TURKLE: We believed for so long that multitasking was a 21st century alchemy, that we could make more time by doing all of these things together. . . . And now we know—the research is clear—that we can multitask, but we degrade our performance for every task we multitask.

The earlier belief is that multitasking was efficient and effective.

1. What language does Turkle use to introduce the revised belief?_____

2. What is the revised belief?_____

Turkle introduced the revised belief by saying, "And now we know."

The revised belief is multitasking is not effective and in fact our performance worsens when we multitask.

🎧 Listen to Turkle's comments. Identify the language used to introduce the revised belief and then paraphrase the new belief in a single sentence.

Excerpt One

The earlier belief is that people can look like they are multitasking in certain situations.

Language used to introduce the revised belief: _____

Revised belief: _____

Excerpt Two

The earlier belief is that you can think you are multitasking and you think all is going well because the brain is producing chemicals that make you feel like you are doing better.

Language used to introduce the revised belief: _____ and _____ and _____

Revised belief: _____

(continued on next page)

Excerpt Three

The earlier belief is that it is OK to task shift when you are doing minor tasks.

Language used to introduce the revised belief: _____

Revised belief: _____

■ *GO TO* MyEnglishLab *FOR MORE SKILL PRACTICE.*

CONNECT THE LISTENINGS

STEP 1: Organize

Both speakers, Dr. Doidge and Dr. Turkle focus on brain functioning. Yet each addresses the topic from a slightly different perspective. Review your notes on page 6.

Imagine that you have interviewed both Doidge and Turkle for a variety of tips for effective brain functioning. Unfortunately, your notes are a mess and now you can't remember who said what. Kick your frontal lobe into action and use your best analytical and problem-solving skills to figure out who said what! Write the appropriate tip in the speech bubble above the appropriate photo on the next page.

TIPS for EFFECTIVE BRAIN FUNCTIONING

- Face a wall when working

- Turn off all social media links if you want to get something done while on your computer

- Take a different route to school or work at least twice a week

- Memorize phone numbers instead of putting them automatically in your mobile phone

- Take one very interesting photo each day

- Take a nap each day

- Stir your coffee or tea backwards after putting in sugar or milk

- Learn how to juggle

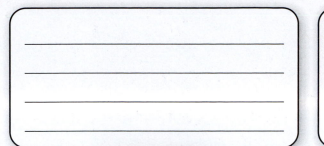

STEP 2: Synthesize

Work with a partner. Imagine you are either Dr. Doidge or Dr. Turkle. You are giving a talk together about effective brain functioning to 200 professionals between the ages of 65–85 years old.

Below are two slides both of you will use. Practice by telling each other what you intend to say about each of the slides. Use tips from Step 1 on the previous page. Ask each other questions to get further information. Use these expressions:

Student A: On this slide you see . . . the point I would like to make here is . . .

Student B: Could you be a bit more specific . . . I think you need to give an example . . . so what you are saying is . . .

GO TO MyEnglishLab *TO CHECK WHAT YOU LEARNED.*

3 FOCUS ON SPEAKING

VOCABULARY

REVIEW

Taxi drivers in London are known as the "Olympic athletes" of memory according to Joshua Foer, author of the bestselling book *Moonwalking with Einstein: The Art and Science of Remembering Everything*. Dr. Janet Alcalde, professor of neuroscience, recently spoke about the book to an audience at a community event for senior citizens. Alcalde discusses a well-known study detailed in Foer's book.

1 🎧 Read and listen to a transcript of the discussion. Notice the **bold-faced** words.

AUDIENCE MEMBER 1: Tell us . . . do London taxi drivers really grow bigger brains simply by navigating their routes? It's tough for me to **buy into** the idea that we can **rewire** our brains just by driving a taxi!

ALCALDE: Yes, I know. There are a lot of **skeptics** out there who don't buy into this conclusion. But listen. **Meticulous** research was conducted by a British neuroscientist named Ellen Maguire who wanted to find out what effect all the driving around the spaghetti-like, higgledy-piggledy London streets might have on the cabbies' brains. A few years later, this initial study was **authenticated**, and it **rendered** the same conclusion. The results are simply **astounding**.

Street Map of London

Audience Member 2: Professor Alcalde, I am not sure I understand. Are you saying that the drivers' brains were **affected** by the driving itself?

Alcalde: Not exactly. Let me back up a bit. In order to be certified as a cab driver in London, you have to **go through** a really challenging process, which involves memorizing the locations and traffic patterns of all 25,000 maze-like streets, 20,000 landmarks and 320 routes connecting all of it—an incredibly confusing landscape. Then the cabbies have to take a **rigorous** test called "the Knowledge" in which they have to produce by heart all of this information. The ones that pass the test are not necessarily **the best and the brightest** or the cabbies displaying creativity or **ingenuity** or anything like that. Rather, success depends on hours and hours of practice and the **competency** to mentally **register** and have memorized all the names and landmarks.

Audience Member 2: OK. Well, so why are these cabbies called the Olympic athletes of memory?

Alcalde: Well, the neuroscientist, Maguire, examined the cabbies' brains and found that the right posterior hippocampus, the part of the brain responsible for spatial navigation was 7% larger than normal. Now, don't **fool yourself into thinking** that that percentage is not a big deal. Trust me. It is small, but very significant. So, she concluded that the act of finding your way around London physically altered the structure of the brain. In addition, the effects grew **incrementally** each year the cabbies weaved their way through those London streets.

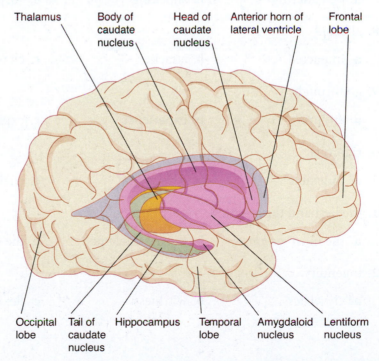

2 Look again at the **bold-faced** words and phrases in the transcript on pages 14–15. Work with a partner and guess the meaning from the context of the transcript. Then cross out the word in each group below that does not have a meaning similar to the word as it is used in the conversation.

1. buy into

   a. believe   b. accept   c. create

2. rewire

   a. reconnect   b. replace   c. change

3. skeptics

   a. believers   b. doubters   c. disbelievers

4. meticulous

   a. careful   b. detailed   c. cautious

5. authenticated

   a. proven   b. realized   c. documented

6. rendered

   a. came up with   b. drew   c. caused to become

7. astounding

   a. bewildering   b. shocking   c. surprising

8. affected

   a. impacted   b. attacked   c. changed

9. go through

   a. endure   b. experience   c. explain thoroughly

10. rigorous

    a. inflexible   b. demanding   c. challenging

11. the best and the brightest

    a. the most famous   b. the most talented c. the cream of the crop

12. ingenuity

    a. cleverness   b. wittiness   c. flexibility

13. competency

    a. skill   **b.** personality   **c.** ability

14. register

    a. enroll   **b.** notice   **c.** note

15. fool (into thinking)

    a. trick   **b.** force   **c.** deceive

16. incrementally

    a. increasingly   **b.** progressively   **c.** rapidly

EXPAND

1 Read the following statements, and then read about confusing pairs of words. Notice the **bold-faced** words.

- The stroke caused a loss of brain cells which, in turn, **affected** her ability to move her legs.

- After the stroke, the doctors encouraged her to do crossword puzzles saying that the "brain gymnastics" would **effect** a change in brain functioning.

- After 8 weeks of the "brain gymnastics," she and her doctors perceived the positive **effects** of the rigorous mental exercise.

"Affect" and "effect" are words that are often confused. "Affect" as a verb means to influence. "Effect" as a verb means to bring about. It is nearly always followed by the word "change," such as "effect a change." "Effect" is more commonly used as a noun meaning "result."

2 🎧 Listen to and repeat each set of confusing pairs. Some differ in pronunciation; others do not.

1. accept/except	**6.** council/counsel
2. access/excess	**7.** disinterested/uninterested
3. advise/advice	**8.** eminent/imminent
4. assure/ensure	**9.** imply/infer
5. affect/effect/effect	**10.** principal/principle

3 Read the sentences. Use the context to identify the meaning of each **bold-faced** word. Then write the letter of the appropriate sentence next to each definition.

1. **a.** The twin girls both wanted to compete in the World Memory Championships, but the judges allowed only one child per family. The parents allowed the teacher to choose which child could compete. They made every effort to remain **disinterested**.

   b. The twins had always been **uninterested** in memorizing boring facts for school exams, but they were very motivated to compete in memory challenges.

   _____ impartial

   _____ not curious about

2. **a.** The **principal** reason the journalist Joshua Foer entered the USA Memory Championship was to master the powerful techniques used by world class "mental Olympians."

   b. These mental Olympians use **principles** of remembering and learning once employed by the ancient Greeks and Romans, who memorized long speeches and books.

   c. The **principal**, a two-time World Memory Champion herself, insisted each child in the school memorize a poem a week.

   _____ beliefs

   _____ main

   _____ director of a school

3. **a.** Last year, the **eminent** Grand Master Simon Reinhard, broke the World Record in the Abstract Images category. He recalled 396 images after 15 minutes of memorization.

   b. However, most fans of the World Memory Championships predict that the loss of Reinhard's championship title is **imminent** this year.

   _____ about to happen

   _____ outstanding

4. **a.** In training for the USA Memory Championship, Foer's coach **advised** him to push himself to remember more and more until he felt uncomfortable.

   b. The coach's **advice** was to fail often and learn from mistakes.

   _____ an opinion about what someone should or shouldn't do

   _____ gave an opinion about what someone should or shouldn't do

5. a. Foer's memory coach had a responsibility to **ensure** Foer understood the "art of remembering"—the ability to create imagery in one's mind that is so unusual and colorful that it is likely to be remembered.

    b. The other World Memory Championship competitors **assured** Foer that he would not be eliminated in the first round.

      _____ make sure or certain that something happens

      _____ tell someone something to lessen their worries

6. a. Years ago, we had no **access** to external tools which could store our memories.

    b. Clearly there is no **excess** of digital devices that can hold our memories for us. Foer believes we have "forgotten how to remember" because of external devices.

      _____ surplus

      _____ way to enter

7. a. Sadly, Foer **implied** that memory training was a lost art.

    b. From the interview, we can **infer** that "mental athletes" are not naturally talented: They have simply learned and mastered a long lost tradition.

      _____ conclude; derive meaning

      _____ suggest; hint at

8. a. In training for the memory competition, Foer **accepted** the widely held belief that memorization was a creative process, not boring or rote.

    b. As soon as he **accepted** his prize for winning the USA Memory Championship, Foer tried to forget the details of the competition.

    c. Foer says his memory techniques help him remember lots of things, **except** maybe where he left his car keys.

      _____ apart from

      _____ receive

      _____ agree to

(continued on next page)

9. **a.** The World Memory Sports Council is the independent governing body of the mind sport of memory and regulates competitions worldwide. Tony Buzan is president of the **council**.

   b. The leading mentalists **counsel** new competitors to start practicing by memorizing phone numbers and dates.

   c. One of the competitors accused another competitor of cheating. The judges had to call in legal **counsel** to settle the dispute

     _____ advise

     _____ an attorney

     _____ official group

10. **a.** How did the hours and hours of "shuffled deck" memorization **affect** Foer's life?

   b. Foer admitted that the memorization techniques he mastered had no **effect** on his long-term memory skill.

   c. His experience in the Memory Championships **effected** a huge change in his views on learning.

     _____ have an influence on

     _____ cause to happen

     _____ consequence

CREATE

Work with a partner. Look at the graphs. Take turns discussing the graphs with your partner. Use the sentence starters to help.

1.

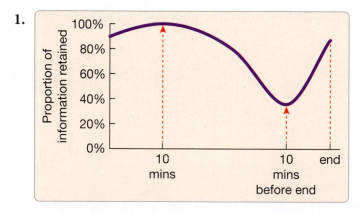

   a. It is **astounding** that . . . *we forget information so quickly.*

   b. The amount of information declines **incrementally** probably because . . .

   c. Probably a basic learning **principle** is . . .

   d. I am assuming that if the person is **uninterested** in the information . . .

2.

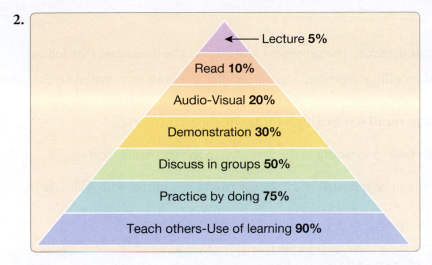

- Lecture **5%**
- Read **10%**
- Audio-Visual **20%**
- Demonstration **30%**
- Discuss in groups **50%**
- Practice by doing **75%**
- Teach others-Use of learning **90%**

a. From the chart, it seems we build **competency** by . . .

b. If I were a teacher I would definitely **advise** the students to . . .

c. It is interesting to see that information is **registered** best when . . .

d. The information presented here **assures me** that if . . .

3.

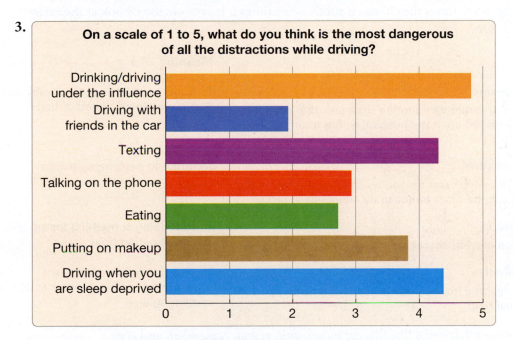

On a scale of 1 to 5, what do you think is the most dangerous of all the distractions while driving?

- Drinking/driving under the influence
- Driving with friends in the car
- Texting
- Talking on the phone
- Eating
- Putting on makeup
- Driving when you are sleep deprived

a. From this graph, we can **infer** that . . .

b. The information given seems to **imply that** . . .

c. It is obvious that we only **fool ourselves into thinking** that . . .

d. I know people who would refuse to **buy into** . . .

GO TO MyEnglishLab FOR MORE VOCABULARY PRACTICE.

GRAMMAR

1 Work with a partner. Examine the sentences and discuss the questions that follow.

- He **stopped recalling** important memories after a serious concussion on the soccer field.

- He **stopped to recall** some of his favorite childhood memories.

1. What is the difference in meaning of the verb *stop* in the two sentences?

2. What other verbs can be followed by either a gerund or infinitive with a change in meaning?

VERBS FOLLOWED BY GERUNDS OR INFINITIVES WITH A CHANGE IN MEANING

Some verbs must always be followed by a **gerund** (base form of verb + *ing*). Other verbs must be followed by an **infinitive** (*to* + base form of verb). Others can be followed by either a gerund or an infinitive with no change in meaning.

However, certain verbs that can be followed by either a gerund or an infinitive do have a change in meaning. Sometimes the change is subtle; sometimes it is very obvious. Look at the verbs *forget* and *stop*.

Verb	Meaning
***Forget* + gerund** He will never **forget winning** the championship even though he ended up in the hospital with a traumatic brain injury (TBI).	To forget an experience—usually one that is particularly good or bad
***Forget* + infinitive** After his TBI, which was caused by heading the ball in the soccer match, he often **forgot to do** simple daily tasks.	To forget to perform an action
***Stop* + gerund** He **stopped playing soccer** after the injury.	To stop doing something for an extended period time
***Stop* + infinitive** When he realized how much his head hurt, he **stopped to get** medical help.	To stop doing something for a short period of time in order to do something else

NOTE: Some other verbs like this are *mean, quit, regret, remember,* and *try.*

2 Read the sentences. From the context, choose the best meaning of the **bold-faced** verb. Write the letter of the appropriate sentence next to the correct definition.

1. **a.** His parents **tried** to convince him not to play American football since the game was too dangerous and his father had gone through a long recovery from a serious football injury.

   b. Knowing how dangerous football was, he **tried** playing gentler sports such as ping pong, but the game just wasn't the same.

   _____ experimented with

   _____ attempted

2. **a.** He can't **forget** making the decision to play American football even though he knew the very real and serious risks to his health.

   b. He **forgot** to tell the doctor that in addition to the severe headaches, he had problems concentrating, remembering simple things, and speaking clearly.

   _____ not remember something unpleasant

   _____ did not remember to do a task or duty

3. **a.** He told the doctor he **remembered** feeling the blood all over his hand after the ball smacked into his head.

   b. The doctor wondered if he had **remembered** to wear the new helmets designed to provide more protection.

   _____ kept something in mind

   _____ recalled

4. **a.** After he received the depressing diagnosis of traumatic brain injury, the soccer star, one of the best and brightest players on the team, **regretted** ever learning to play soccer.

   b. His coach **regretted** to inform him that heading the ball thousands of times during the year could cause memory loss.

   _____ felt sad about telling someone something or to do something

   _____ felt sad about something that happened in the past

5. **a.** Knowing the danger, the coach **stopped** asking the kids to head the balls during practice.

   b. The young player **stopped** to check on his fellow teammate who had collapsed right after making the winning goal.

   _____ finished doing something in order to do something else

   _____ quit

(continued on next page)

6. a. The boxer finally **quit** competing. The latest jolt to his brain felt like a 15 pound bowling ball traveling at 20 miles per hour.

   b. He **quit** to teach young people about the dangers of certain sports like football, soccer, boxing, cycling, and horseback riding, and to teach them how to protect themselves from injury.

   _____ stopped

   _____ stopped doing something in order to do something else

7. a. The professional football player knew that playing the game **meant** risking long-term mental health, so he refused to let his son play.

   b. The coach **meant** to remind the young player to wear his helmet, but forgot. The child suffered a traumatic brain injury and his parents are now suing the coach for millions of dollars.

   _____ intended; planned

   _____ signified; involved

GO TO MyEnglishLab *FOR MORE GRAMMAR PRACTICE.*

PRONUNCIATION

STRESSING IMPORTANT WORDS

In a sentence, one or two words usually express the most important information. These are words that the speaker wants the listener to notice.

🎧 Listen to how the capitalized words are stressed in these sentences.

Example One

I've GOT to get some more sleep.

I REALLY need to check my email again.

We stress the most important words by saying them on a high pitch, or with strong stress: the stressed vowel is long and loud. When you speak, make sure your voice is high enough when you stress an important word.

In English, we emphasize new information (usually the last important word of the sentence), and we emphasize information that contrasts or corrects.

Example Two

Today we're going to talk about MULTItasking.

The kids are doing email instead of HOMEwork.

1 🎧 Listen to the sentences. Underline the words that are stressed. Some sentences may have more than one stressed word. Then practice saying the sentences with a partner.

Mohammed

1. Mohammed was listening to hours and hours of lectures on brain plasticity.

2. He was eating lots of "brain food" every day.

3. Wild salmon was his absolute favorite.

4. He was desperate to change his brain.

Patricia

5. Multitasking was making her crazy.

6. She couldn't concentrate on a single thing for more than five minutes.

7. Something was totally destroying her brain cells.

8. She couldn't get rid of her smart phone fast enough.

2 🎧 Read the conversation. Work with a partner and underline the words you think will be stressed. Then listen to the conversation to check your answers. Correct any errors. Practice reading the conversation with your partner, emphasizing the stressed words.

A: Multitasking isn't so bad. Some people are really good at it.

B: Others think they are, but they're just fooling themselves.

A: Agreed, but success at any cost may not be such a good thing.

B: Yeah, that makes me think of my father. He was so hooked on work. When he drove, he was on his cell phone; at red lights, he checked his email.

A: You must be joking. That's multitasking at its best!

B: Well, not exactly. He lost his driver's license after his third accident, which was also his fifth ticket.

SPEAKING SKILL

DEBUNKING MYTHS AND REVISING MISCONCEPTIONS

When research actually creates new knowledge, we have to change our ideas. We often call this process "debunking myths" or "revising misconceptions." It can take a long time for people to learn about and accept the new science. Doidge and Turkle are involved in spreading the new research and debunking myths.

🎧 **Read and listen to the conversation. Notice how the underlined expressions are used (in conversation) to correct a myth or misconception.**

Example

A: Our brains shut down when we sleep.

B: <u>Actually, that's not true.</u> <u>For the longest time, we thought</u> our brains shut down when we slept, but <u>it turns out</u> our brains never shut down.

A: Our brains stop developing after we are about 7 or 8 years old.

B: <u>Sorry, but that's no longer an accepted fact.</u> We <u>used to believe</u> that brain development stopped during childhood, but <u>now we know</u> our brains continue to grow and change throughout our life span.

A: We only use 10% of our brains.

B: <u>Actually, that's been proven false.</u> <u>A while ago, people thought</u> we used only 10% of our brains, but <u>now it's widely known that</u> all parts of our brains are continually active.

Useful Expressions for Debunking Myths and Revising Misconceptions

- Actually, that's not true . . . For the longest time, we thought . . . but it turns out . . .

- Sorry, but that's no longer an accepted fact. We used to believe . . . but now we know . . .

- Actually, that's been proven false. A while ago, people thought . . . , but now it's widely known that . . .

- That's a myth. For centuries people believed . . . but now we have clear proof that . . .

Work with a partner.

Student A: Read each of the three myths on the next page aloud.

Student B: Cover the left column. Correct each myth using one of the expressions listed above and the information provided. Switch roles after item 3.

Example

A: (Myth) Genes determine the fate of our brains.

B: (Correcting the myth) <u>That's a myth.</u> <u>For centuries people believed that</u>, but <u>we now have clear proof that</u> our experiences can shape our brains' capabilities.

STUDENT A	STUDENT B
Myth	**Correcting the myth**
1. People are either "right brained" or "left brained."	1. People use both sides of their brains to perform everyday tasks.
2. Male and female brains are very different.	2. There may be small differences, but basically males and females learn in the same way.
3. Most of our learning occurs between the ages 0–3.	3. Many connections between brain cells are formed during this time, but learning occurs throughout our lives.

Now switch roles.

4. There is only one way to train your brain.	4. You can improve brain function through a number of ways such as physical and mental exercise, meditation, brain games, etc.
5. Our brain functions automatically degrade as we age.	5. There is nothing fixed or determined in the way our brains function as we age.
6. Children exposed to two languages from birth become confused or will fall behind in school.	6. Bilingualism is a form of mental exercise. It provides brain training and physically remodels parts of the brain.

■■■■■■■■■■■■■■■■ *GO TO* MyEnglishLab *FOR MORE SKILL PRACTICE AND TO CHECK WHAT YOU LEARNED.*

FINAL SPEAKING TASK

In this task, you will use "Rich Pictures" to discuss case studies. During the Middle Ages, people seemed to know that words accompanied by imagery are much more memorable. Nowadays, brain scientists have proven that associating images and pictures with words enhances memory and learning. One technique used by students and professionals in all disciplines is the "rich picture technique." A Rich Picture is a picture that uses symbols, sketches, or "doodles" to present a problem or situation. Rich Pictures are an illustrative and creative way of conveying an understanding of a particular situation. Try to use the vocabulary, grammar, pronunciation, and listening and speaking skills that you learned in this unit.*

Example

Case Study: Michael's Story

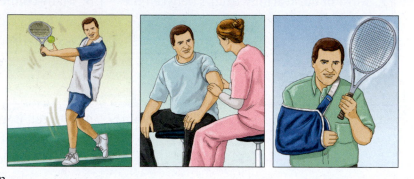

Michael Bernstein was an eye surgeon, classical pianist, and tennis player. One day while playing tennis, half of his body was rendered completely immovable. He was given 6 weeks of rehabilitation and then sent home, but he was still not able to move half of his body. Another doctor had the ingenuity to try something different. He put the good limb in a sling or cast so Michael couldn't use it and then incrementally trained the affected limb. It worked. Dr. Bernstein is now practicing medicine and playing tennis.

Work in groups of 3. Imagine that you are in a science class studying the brain. Read Case A, B, or C on pages 29–31. Follow the steps to create a brief oral presentation using the Rich Picture technique. In your presentation, be sure to include 1) the problem; 2) the solution; 3) the science behind the solution. Use the vocabulary, grammar, and speaking skills you have learned in the unit.

STEP 1: Study the case.

- Read and discuss the case with your group.
- Discuss the problem, the solution, and the science behind the solution.

STEP 2: Draw

- Draw a Rich Picture that depicts the problem.
- Use any symbols, sketches, or doodles that you think will clearly illustrate the problem.

---

* For Alternative Speaking Topics, see page 32.

STEP 3: Present

- Deliver your oral presentation to the class.

- Remember to include the problem, the solution, and the science behind the solution. Be sure to use your Rich Picture as a prop to visually support your presentation.

STEP 4: Reflect

After all case studies have been presented, discuss these questions with the class:

- How effective were the Rich Pictures for conveying the complexity of the case?

- Which case interests you the most? Why?

Case Studies

A.

Jill's Story

In 1996, Jill Bolte Taylor, a Harvard trained neuroanatomist who had studied the brain for years, had an opportunity few brain scientists could ever imagine. One morning, she realized that she herself was having a massive stroke. For several days, she felt her brain functions slip away one by one, speech, movement, understanding, and memory. While her brain functions continued to degrade, she was able to apply her scientific training and study and remember every moment.

Her mother led her rehabilitation process which included strategies such as 1) ensuring she slept as often and how much as she wanted; 2) forcing her to finish sentences she started in order to find the "brain network" on her own; 3) breaking large challenges into small steps to keep her motivated towards recovery; and 4) typing on a computer in the early days when she could not read or write.

It took Jill 8 years to recover, a recovery period which she documented in her book, *A Stroke of Insight*, published in 2008. In addition, Jill gave a TED talk describing her experience. This talk has become one of the 10 most popular TED talks ever given. In her book, Taylor chronicles her eight-year full recovery, which proves the plasticity and strength of the human brain.

(continued on next page)

B.

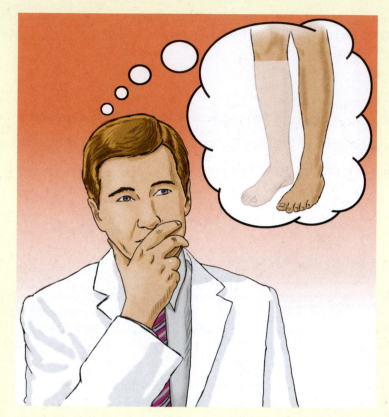

Debbie Smith was vacationing on the island of Bali in Indonesia when she had a severe bicycle accident. With just minutes to spare before dying, Debbie arrived at the hospital and fought for her life for the next few weeks. After two weeks, severe gangrene set in and the doctors amputated her leg.

She returned home to the UK soon after, only to begin experiencing excruciating pain and shock-like feelings in the same area where her leg used to be. Doctors diagnose this condition as "phantom limb syndrome." Most medical experts believe that phantom limb pain is caused by the brain having to adjust the feedback it gives to the body as the territory of the body changes. Different areas of the body are controlled by different parts of the brain. In other words, the areas of the brain responsible for the limb that is no longer there are receiving information from other areas after the limb has been amputated.

Debbie was treated with a famous technique using a "mirror box." For thirty minutes a day, Debbie reflected her remaining leg in a mirror so that the other leg appeared to be still present. Surprisingly enough, this treatment reduced her pain. The visual pathway to the brain was strong enough to convince it that the "territory" of the leg was still there. After three weeks of treatment, Debbie experienced almost no pain and could even move her "phantom toes."

C.

Ben's Story

At the age of two, Ben was diagnosed with cancer of the retina. He had his eyes removed at the age of 3. When he turned 5, he discovered that he was able to identify the location of objects simply by making clicking noises with his tongue and then listening for the returning echo. Using this technique Ben was able to play basketball, cycle, rollerblade, skateboard, and play football.

Other blind individuals have mastered this technique now known as echolocation. Echolocation is a way of locating sounds that reflect off surrounding objects in order to identify their location. Dolphins, whales, and bats are expert echolocators.

Remarkably though, researchers have discovered that these blind human echolocation experts do not use the "auditory" part of the brain to register the echos. Rather they use the "visual" parts of the brain, those areas that normally process visual information in sighted individuals. The brain areas used to process auditory information are not activated. The brain seems to be able to perceive information from a variety of sources of which we are not aware.

UNIT PROJECT

Topic 1

STEP 1: Choose one of these topics:

1. Hyperthymesia—total recall disease

2. Hoarding and the brain

3. Asperger's Syndrome

4. The teenage brain

STEP 2: Research the topic using the Internet or the library. Organize your research into three parts:

1. Definition and explanation of the topic

2. A story or example of the topic

3. Information about the brain as it relates to the topic

STEP 3: Present your research to the class.

(continued on next page)

Topic 2

STEP 1: There are many brain fitness games or activities to improve brain fitness on the Internet. Research these games and select one that you think would be effective. Prepare to teach it to a small group in your class.

STEP 2: In a small group, try out your game with your classmates. Observe and record their reactions.

STEP 3: After all group members have introduced their games, discuss these questions:

1. Which game did you like best? Why?

2. Which one was most or least effective? Why?

3. Why do you think these "brain fitness" games have become so popular?

ALTERNATIVE SPEAKING TOPICS

Discuss one of the topics. Use the vocabulary and grammar from the unit.

Topic 1

For several years, Jeremy Gleick, a sophomore majoring in neuroscience at the University of California, Los Angeles, devoted an hour a day to learning something new. He had one rule: It could not be related to his university work; nor could it be simply reading a book. Wherever he was, Jeremy simply said, "I am sorry, but I need to have my 'learning hour.'" He recently passed his 1,400th hour of "learning hours." Over the years, he has learned about the Aztecs (3 hours), Punic Carthaginian military commander Hannibal Barca (14 hours), the Korean War (4 hours), Confucianism (1 hour), the 700-verse Dharmic scripture Bhagavad Gita (14 hours), voodoo (4 hours), juggling (39 hours), piano (65 hours), astronautics (4 hours), volcanology (1 hour), robotics (2 hours), knife-throwing (1 hour), American sign language (9 hours), guitar (102 hours), card tricks (17 hours), the American Revolutionary War (27 hours), Parkour or urban acrobatics (8 hours), and wushu (28 hours).

What would you like to learn if you challenged yourself the way Mr. Gleick has? Create a list of your top 5. Work in groups of 3 and share your list. With passion and enthusiasm, explain why you have chosen what you have chosen.

Topic 2

Jose Luis Borges, the world renowned Argentinian writer, wrote a short story called "Funes the Memorious." In the story, Borges describes a man who is unable to forget anything. His memory is too good, and he cannot tell the difference between things that are important and things that are not. Borges concludes the story by saying that "forgetting, not remembering, is the essence of what makes us human. To think is to forget." Do you agree with Borges' view that in order to understand the world we must be able to prioritize, to order, to filter? Why? What message is Borges trying to convey? How do our memories shape who we are?

Topic 3

Work with a partner. What do you think should be done to minimize the potential for serious brain injuries in certain sports such as football, soccer, cycling, etc.? Football and boxing in particular, are two of the most dangerous of these sports. Should they be banned? Should people watch them even though they know that players can suffer serious brain injuries? Why or why not?

■■■■■■■■■■■■■■■■■■ *GO TO* MyEnglishLab *TO DISCUSS ONE OF THE ALTERNATIVE TOPICS, WATCH A VIDEO ABOUT TRAINING YOUR BRAIN, AND TAKE THE UNIT 1 ACHIEVEMENT TEST.* ■■■■■■■■■■■■■■■■■■

IS HONESTY THE Best Policy?

1 FOCUS ON THE TOPIC

1. Look at the title of the unit and the photo. Why do people tell lies? Work with a partner. List your ideas on a piece of paper.

2. Are all lies equal? Some people think there is a range from little "white lies" to very harmful lies. Read situations 1–3 and with your partner, write the number of the lie on the continuum where you think it belongs.

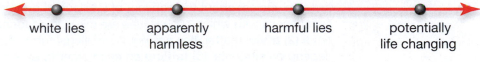

white lies   apparently harmless   harmful lies   potentially life changing

1. A person gives someone else an unopened gift that they themselves didn't want.

2. A doctor withholds information from a dying patient to keep her from worrying.

3. A company sells a harmful pesticide even though it knows it will soon be banned.

GO TO MyEnglishLab *TO CHECK WHAT YOU KNOW.*

35

LISTENING ONE | INTERVIEW WITH A PSYCHIATRIST

VOCABULARY

Plagiarism, or presenting another's work or ideas as your own, is a kind of lying. It affects many people, especially because other people's work and ideas are now so available on the Internet. This kind of dishonesty is a common topic of discussion at educational institutions. What can or should be done about it? The administration at a large university has decided to purchase access to anti-plagiarism software. A dean, a professor, and a student express their thoughts in the online editorials below.

1 🎧 Read and listen to the editorials. Pay attention to the **bold-faced** words and phrases. Then read the list of definitions that follows. Work with a partner. Write the number of the bold-faced word or phrase next to its definition.

Midlake University

CURRENT ISSUE   PAST ISSUES   ADVERTISE WITH US

Home > News > Letters to the Editor

LETTERS TO THE EDITOR

Home

News

Around Campus

Employment

Publications

Media Relations

Contact Us

Plagiarism: An Important Message from the Administration

To the Editor:

As many know, the university has decided to subscribe to a service that provides software designed to detect plagiarism.

With the rise of the Internet, plagiarism has become more **(1) pervasive** and problematic on campuses worldwide, including our own. A recent survey found that 54 percent of U.S. students admitted to plagiarizing from the Internet. In many cases, students do not intend to deceive. Rather, they are unclear about the concept of intellectual property[1] and about the seriousness with which such issues are taken in academia. Plagiarism is not a **(2) trivial** matter. It is a serious and illegal form of stealing. We cannot depend on students' **(3) tattling on** each other to expose cheaters; nor can we rely only on professors' intuition and experience to identify plagiarized work. Therefore, this administration feels we have no choice but to use a tool specifically targeted to detect and battle plagiarism.

–Janet Miller, Dean of Academic Studies, Midlake University

[1] **intellectual property:** creation of the mind, such as literary and artistic works, or inventions and designs

Plagiarism: A Professor Speaks Out

To the Editor:

I would offer a different perspective in response to Dean Miller's editorial regarding the administration's decision to invest in anti-plagiarism software.

First, I feel it is important to acknowledge that plagiarism is not limited to the university campus. For example, writers **(4) mislead** their readers by plagiarizing someone else's work. We can recall the embarrassing case of Jayson Blair, the *New York Times* reporter found guilty of copying his work directly from other newspapers. Blair maintained the **(5) veneer** of a respected journalist for years before his crime was eventually uncovered.

When it comes to plagiarism in academia, why are administrators engaged in such a **(6) relentless** pursuit of cheaters? Is that really their job? I suggest that the administration give professors the main responsibility for dealing with this problem.

Most professors who take the time to know students and to give them regular writing assignments have a **(7) finely honed** sense of each student's writing style or ability, making it difficult for the student to **(8) conceal** unoriginal material.

It is our job to help students stay honest. The administration's total **(9) preoccupation** with plagiarism and with this software is a costly waste of time and resources.

–Jerome Anderson, Professor, Department of Political Science,
Midlake University

Plagiarism: A Student Speaks Out

To the Editor,

Now we know the truth: The administration doesn't trust us. Really, the **(10) rule of thumb** most students follow is simple, "Don't cheat!" Administrators may try to sugarcoat the issue, but the fact remains that this is an unreliable and overly **(11) intrusive** method that leads to the **(12) erosion** of trust between students and teachers at our university. The promoters of this software have an **(13) inflated** opinion of its value. This software won't catch all plagiarists, but it *will* succeed in fueling mistrust between students and professors.

Most students are not interested in getting through college by deception, by lying. Only the most overconfident narcissists[2] think they can really **(14) put one over on** their professors and get away with cheating. The rest of us know that cheaters lose in the long run. At the end of the day, it is up to us as students to be honest with ourselves and follow our own internal, moral compass.

–Margarita Hernandez, Junior, Biochemistry, Midlake University

---

[2] **narcissists:** people who admire themselves

_____ **a.** telling something bad that another person has done

_____ **b.** exaggerated; overly important

_____ **c.** a cover that hides the way someone or something really is

_____ **d.** affecting someone's private life in an annoying way

_____ **e.** general guideline

_____ **f.** hide something carefully

_____ **g.** unimportant; of little value

_____ **h.** existing or spreading everywhere

_____ **i.** condition of thinking about only one thing

_____ **j.** make someone believe something that is not true

_____ **k.** continuing without stopping or losing strength

_____ **l.** the gradual reduction or wearing down of something

_____ **m.** sharpened; perfected

_____ **n.** trick; deceive

2 Work with a partner. Take another look at the editorials. Do you agree with the dean, the professor, or the student? Explain.

GO TO MyEnglishLab FOR MORE VOCABULARY PRACTICE.

PREVIEW

Lying is a topic of public discussion in the media. On a radio program called *The Infinite Mind*, Dr. Fred Goodwin interviews a psychiatrist, Dr. Paul Ekman, on the subject. In the interview, Dr. Ekman defines lies as meeting two criteria.

Predict Ekman's two criteria. Then listen to the excerpt and verify your predictions.

1. _____

2. _____

MAIN IDEAS

Listen to the entire interview. First, Dr. Goodwin presents the topic of the show, lying (Parts 1–2), then he interviews Dr. Ekman (Parts 3–5). Stop after each part and write the main idea about the topic. Work with a partner. Compare your main idea statements. Revise them and write them in the Details chart on page 39.

Part One

Main idea: _Liars are narcissistic._ _____

Part Two

Main idea: _____

Part Three

Main idea: _____

Part Four

Main idea: _____

Part Five

Main idea: _____

DETAILS

Listen to the interview again. Add details that support the main idea. Some have been done for you.

MAIN IDEA	DETAILS
PART ONE *Liars are narcissistic.*	• *Exaggerated sense of themselves* • • • *Focus on the moment and not the future; lack sense of self*
PART TWO	• • *Most people avoid lying because of consequences; loss of trust* •
PART THREE	Two criteria: • • *Not giving advance notification of lying* Ways to lie: • *Conceal information* • •

(continued on next page)

MAIN IDEA	DETAILS
PART FOUR	1. *avoid . . .* 2. 3. *protect . . .* 4. 5. 6. 7. 8. *maintain . . .* 9.
PART FIVE	• • *Difficult to repair trust*

GO TO MyEnglishLab *FOR MORE LISTENING PRACTICE.*

MAKE INFERENCES

NOTICING AND UNDERSTANDING WHY SPEAKERS "HEDGE"

An **inference** is an **educated guess** about something that is **not directly stated**, but which you believe is true based on the intention, attitude, voice, pausing, and word choices of the speaker.

In order to be more truthful, modest, and cautious, speakers often use tentative language. The speaker purposefully uses vague language showing hesitation or uncertainty. Speakers (and writers) hedge in order to weaken or diminish their stance for a variety of reasons such as to:

1. appear polite or humble
2. avoid personal accountability
3. express the speaker's understanding of the facts as he or she knows them

🎧 Listen to and read the example. Then answer the questions and read the explanations.

Example

DR. GOODWIN: As you'll hear during this show, lying can be approached from a variety of perspectives: moral, legal, interpersonal. Let me offer the perspective of one psychiatrist.

In this excerpt, Dr. Goodwin uses some hedging language in order to be polite and cautious. He knows the subject is complex, and he'll just talk about one part of it. What phrases does he use to hedge?

1. a variety of perspectives

2. _____

3. _____

Dr. Goodwin hedges by using the phrases *a variety of perspectives, let me offer*, and *one psychiatrist*.

Why does Dr. Goodwin use the introductory phrase *let me offer*?

a. to be polite

b. to avoid personal accountability

c. to express his understanding of the facts

Goodwin is saying that there are a number of perspectives, including those of a psychiatrist, which offer insights into lying. In using the phrase, *let me offer*, he seems to be carefully and tentatively saying that none of these perspectives is supported by absolute scientific evidence. Since Goodwin is not an expert himself, he hedges in order to appear humble or more polite.

Listen to each excerpt. Identify the reason the speaker has used "hedging" or cautious language.

Excerpt One

1. Goodwin hedges using the word "most" in order to:

   a. be polite

   b. avoid personal accountability

   c. express his understanding of the facts

Excerpt Two

2. Ekman uses a series of the modal verb "can" as a way to hedge in order to:

   a. be polite

   b. avoid personal accountability

   c. express his understanding of the facts

Excerpt Three

3. Ekman hedges using qualifying adverbs such as "pretty" and "a little less" in order to:

   a. be polite

   b. avoid personal accountability

   c. express his understanding of the facts

EXPRESS OPINIONS

Working in small groups, discuss your ideas about these questions.

1. Goodwin claims that the basis of lying is narcissism. In other words, people lie in order to feel better about themselves. Does that idea make sense to you? Why or why not?

2. What kinds of "white lies" or half-truths have you told? Referring to the chart on pages 39–40, use Dr. Eckman's taxonomy of lies to describe dishonesty. Describe a situation in which you didn't tell the whole truth. Do you regret it or not? Explain.

3. "Lying has long been a part of everyday life. We couldn't get through the day without being deceptive." (Professor Leonard Saxe of Brandeis University, Boston, Massachusetts) Do you agree or disagree with Professor Saxe? Explain.

■■■■■■■■■■■■■■■■■■■■■■■ *GO TO* MyEnglishLab *TO GIVE YOUR OPINION ABOUT ANOTHER QUESTION.*

LISTENING TWO   FAMILY SECRETS

VOCABULARY

1 Read the sentences. You will hear the **bold-faced** words and phrases in the next listening selection. Notice them as you listen.

*We started to **put the pieces together**.*

*It was as though I were seeing my father **reincarnated** standing there.*

*It's really **uncanny**.*

*The feeling of trespassing was actually very **elating**.*

*I used to kind of **mull over** these things alone.*

2 Match the words or phrases on the left with the definitions or synonyms on the right. Write the corresponding letter in the blank.

_____ **1.** put the pieces together   **a.** think about

_____ **2.** reincarnated   **b.** exciting

_____ **3.** uncanny   **c.** figure out something puzzling

_____ **4.** elating   **d.** strange and difficult to explain

_____ **5.** mull over   **e.** born again in another body

COMPREHENSION

Concealing the truth is a kind of lying. In this excerpt, you will hear a filmmaker, Pola Rapaport, discuss a time when she uncovered a family secret. She made a documentary film about this important part of her life.

🎧 Listen to the interview. Circle the correct answer.

Part One

1. In a desk, Pola Rapaport found a photo of _____.

   a. her father

   b. someone who resembled her father

2. Later, Pola's mother received a letter written by _____.

   a. her father

   b. Pierre

3. Still later, Pola went to Romania to _____.

   a. meet Pierre

   b. make a film

Part Two

4. Pola says that her father was very secretive because he _____.

   a. had to run from persecution

   b. was ashamed

Part Three

5. When she found the photo, Pola had a feeling of trespassing, which _____.

   a. made her uneasy and ashamed

   b. made her feel happier and freer

6. Pola believes that, especially for children, _____.

   a. the truth is always better

   b. the truth can leave a hole

GO TO MyEnglishLab FOR MORE VOCABULARY PRACTICE.

LISTENING SKILL

IDENTIFYING SPEAKER ATTITUDES

Unlike the first listening, which is more academic and factual, "Family Secrets" is a very personal interview. The goal of the interviewer is to pose questions that prompt the interviewee, Pola Rapaport to reveal her attitudes towards the events in the story she narrates. Through her skillful interviewing, the interviewer uncovers Pola's real feelings. In the interactions between these interlocutors, there is an unusual level of trust. Pola has agreed to reveal information and feelings that few people ever talk about publicly.

🎧 Read and listen to this example. Then answer the question and read the explanation.

Example

INTERVIEWER: So that the photograph that you found in the drawer was, in fact, your long lost half brother.

POLA: That's who it was, I mean, the suspicion was right that he was, our long lost brother or half brother, living in Bucharest all that time.

The interviewer directly states the mystery behind the photo in order to elicit Pola's reaction. How does Pola feel about the interviewer's statement?

a. relieved

b. embarrassed

c. validated or supported

The answer is *c*. Go through your thinking process step-by-step. What are the linguistic clues that lead you to the answer? The interviewer used the words "so" and "in fact" to acknowledge Pola's story. By making the connection, the interviewer validated the event.

🎧 Listen to the short exchanges between the interviewer and Pola. Identify Pola's attitude or feelings that have been prompted by the interviewer's question. Then imagine that you are Pola and think about how you would have felt if you had been asked the question.

Excerpt One

1. The interviewer directly states that Pierre bears a close resemblance to Pola's father. How does Pola feel at this moment?

   a. uncomfortable

   b. relieved

   c. thoughtful

Excerpt Two

2. The interviewer asks a series of short, direct questions to get Pola to share her feelings about uncovering the secret. At this moment, how does Pola feel about the discovery?

    a. relieved

    b. guilty

    c. thrilled

Excerpt Three

3. The interviewer suggests that Pola's father may have lied to her by not telling her about Pierre. At this moment, how does Pola feel towards her father for keeping this family secret?

    a. accepting

    b. angry

    c. confused

GO TO MyEnglishLab *FOR MORE SKILL PRACTICE.*

CONNECT THE LISTENINGS

STEP 1: Organize

In the interview Pola Rapaport shares several family secrets as she tells her story. Fill in the chart with the concealments and lies. Then write which of Ekman's nine reasons for lying (in the chart on pages 39–40) might apply in each case. You may find more than one reason.

CONCEALMENTS AND LIES FROM POLA'S STORY	POSSIBLE REASONS FOR THE CONCEALMENT OR LIE
Pierre didn't tell his father's family who or where he was.	

STEP 2: Synthesize

Work with a partner. Use the vocabulary from the interview and from the chart on page 45 to role-play a conversation between Pola and Dr. Ekman.

If you are taking the part of Pola, tell the story of how you uncovered the family secret and why you want to know what motivated your father to keep the secret. Try to use some of the "feeling words" such as "accepting," "elated," "thrilled," and so on.

If you are taking the part of Dr. Ekman, explain to Pola what may have motivated her father to conceal the family secret. You could begin your role play like this:

> **POLA:** After hearing an interview with you on the radio, I was thrilled, because . . .
>
> **DR. EKMAN:** Oh, you may be surprised to hear that that kind of deception isn't uncommon. . . .

Now continue the conversation or originate your own.

GO TO MyEnglishLab *TO CHECK WHAT YOU LEARNED.*

3 FOCUS ON SPEAKING

VOCABULARY

REVIEW

English is rich in the vocabulary of honesty, dishonesty, and half-truths. As a class, review the list of words and phrases on pages 36, 37, and 42 from Listenings One and Two. Then use the words or phrases to complete the short paragraphs on page 47.

conceal	mislead	preoccupation	relentless
finely honed	mull over	put one over	tattling
inflated	pervasive	put the pieces together	

Take Notes!
The Art of Liar Spotting

Most people care deeply about the truth and do not like it when authors **(1)** _____ them with false information. Therefore, editors and publishers must be **(2)** _____ in determining whether a nonfiction work is true. They need to check many sources and verify all their facts. Recently, an editor with a(n) **(3)** _____ sense of telling fact from fiction came across some suspicious details in a memoir manuscript. After closely examining the author's story, she **(4)** _____ and realized he had lied about certain facts from his life. The publisher canceled publication immediately, and the editor remarked that "saving readers from this writer's con was an elating experience."

Are liars easy to spot? Many people think it's a snap. They actually have a(n) **(5)** _____ sense of their ability to catch a liar by noticing physical signs of deception: covering the mouth, looking around, fidgeting nervously with hands, and so on. However, studies show that catching a liar is tough for two reasons. First, lying is **(6)** _____. Everyone lies. And second, there are so many ways to hide or **(7)** _____ the truth. In fact, recent research has revealed that probably less than 5 percent of the population has the ability to detect a liar. Scientists continue to study precise visible signs of deception—the body's own way of **(8)** _____ on a person who is lying.

An international study of lying shows that while children from nearly all cultures deceive each other, most cultures have different attitudes about lying and their ability to trick or **(9)** _____ on others. One group of researchers found that honesty was not a huge **(10)** _____ for some people in the United States. They felt confident that they could get away with lying 56 percent of the time. Another group of researchers found that Chileans and Argentineans think they will be caught about 60 percent of the time while those living in Moldova and Botswana believe they will only be detected fibbing less than 25 percent of the time. Scientists must now **(11)** _____ the results, since some of the data are inconclusive.

EXPAND

Part One: A Scientist Blows the Whistle on a Colleague

Beatriz, a young food science researcher, suspects that her friend and colleague, Martin, has lied about the results of his experiment using a new artificial sweetener on laboratory animals. She decides to tattle on Martin to the lab director, Dr. Sanborn.

🎧 Work with a partner. Read each line of the conversation between Beatriz and Dr. Sanborn. Write the letter of each of Dr. Sanborn's responses next to Beatriz's lines. The **bold-faced** words provide a clue. Then listen to the conversation and check your answers. Read the conversation aloud with your partner. Be sure to use good eye contact and a natural, expressive voice.

Beatriz

_____ 1. Dr. Sanborn, I hate to have to tell you this, but I am concerned that Martin has **fudged** the results of his study.

_____ 2. Yes, I am pretty sure that he is **bluffing** about the safety of his sweetener.

_____ 3. Well, apparently his ambition is blinding him. I'm telling you, he's going down a **slippery slope** with this project.

_____ 4. I know, but he's too afraid to **fess up** to the fact that his sweetener might pose a health risk.

_____ 5. Well, trust me, Dr. Sanborn, Martin's project is definitely a **recipe for disaster**. His results will not be duplicated, I'm sure.

Dr. Sanborn

a. Oh, come on, Beatriz. It's really hard to believe that Martin would **lie** about his work. He has always been an accurate, honest researcher.

b. I can't bear to hear that such a bright, intelligent researcher would be **headed toward disaster**.

c. Thanks, Beatriz. I understand. If his project is a **failure**, our lab will lose funding. I'll speak to Martin tomorrow.

d. You mean he has **manipulated** the data in order to get the result he wanted?

e. Beatriz, I've known Martin for years. I can't believe he wouldn't **tell** me if his experiments were failing.

Part Two: The Colleague Defends Himself

The next day, Martin confronts Beatriz about her conversation with Dr. Sanborn. He defends himself against her accusations.

Work with a new partner. Read each line of the conversation between Martin and Beatriz. Write the letter of each of Beatriz's responses next to Martin's lines. The **bold-faced** words provide a clue. Then listen to the conversation and check your answers. Read the conversation aloud with your partner.

Martin

_____ **1.** Wow, Beatriz. I absolutely cannot believe the **whopper** you told Dr. Sanborn about my experiment. You're just jealous that I'm finally getting the results that will make me famous.

_____ **2.** I thought I did, Bea, but you are **twofaced**. I can't trust you now.

_____ **3.** That's not true. The chubby mice have lost weight, and my sweetener is safe. I am being totally **up front** with you and everyone else about my results.

_____ **4.** My reputation does depend on this project, but I would never risk my career to **pull the wool over everyone's eyes**.

Beatriz

a. Martin, I'm not being **deceptive**. Whatever I told Dr. Sanborn, I would tell you directly. Look, I don't trust the results of your study. You are falsifying the data.

b. You can't really believe that! You're so preoccupied with success, you're not being **honest**.

c. I'm sorry, Martin, but the facts show you _are_ trying to **trick** us, despite our lab policy to "relentlessly pursue knowledge and truth."

d. Are you kidding? I didn't tell him a **lie**, and I am not envious of you. You should know me better than that.

CREATE

Work with a partner.

Student A: Read statements 1 through 4 on page 50 to Student B. Complete each one according to your own opinions or experiences.

Student B: Respond to Student A using the words listed. You may agree, disagree, ask a question, or share information of your own. Then switch roles after item 4.

Example

STUDENT A: In a family relationship, it is important to be up front about . . . things that happened in your past.

STUDENT B: Maybe, but I think all people have some experience, some skeleton in their closet, that they would rather **conceal** forever, even from a family member.

(continued on next page)

Student A	Student B
1. In a family relationship, it is important to be up front about . . .	conceal
2. My culture/family/best friend has a preoccupation with . . .	rule of thumb
3. The best/biggest whopper I ever told was . . .	fess up
4. I remember putting one over on my parents when I . . .	tattle on

Now switch roles.

Student A	Student B
5. Athletes who conceal the fact they have taken drugs to improve their performance should . . .	mull over
6. In my opinion, bluffing about _____ is never OK.	recipe for disaster
7. One time, I fudged the truth by . . .	deceive
8. The news media misleads the public when . . .	inflated

■■ **GO TO** MyEnglishLab **FOR MORE VOCABULARY PRACTICE.**

GRAMMAR

1 Work with a partner. Examine the statements, and discuss the questions that follow.

- Some studies have concluded that most people lie, fib, or sugarcoat the truth once or twice a day. In order to identify a liar, you **could** pay attention to a change in voice or you **could** watch for unusual body language.

- You **should** be able to spot a liar by noticing a contradiction between his or her words and facial expressions.

1. Which statement is more certain?

2. Which modal verbs could you substitute for the bold-faced words and keep the same meaning?

MODALS—DEGREES OF CERTAINTY

Use **modal verbs** to express different **degrees of certainty** about the present, the past, and the future. The modal you use shows how strongly you believe something is true or not true.

Almost Certain

Present	*Must*	The students' papers are identical, although they insist they didn't cheat. Clearly, one of them **must** be lying.
Past	*Must* + *have* + past participle *(must've)**	He claimed to have received a music award in high school, but there is no official record of it. He **must have (must've)** lied on his application.

Almost Certain, Negative (Impossible)

Present / Future	*Can't / couldn't*	His excuse for missing the exam due to illness **can't** possibly be true. I just know he is telling a big, fat whopper!
Past	*Can't / couldn't* + *have* + past participle *(couldn't've)**	I'm shocked. The university's president **couldn't have (couldn't've)** committed plagiarism in his speech. He is known for his impeccable integrity.

Quite Sure

Future	*Should / ought to*	Due to improvements in technology, brain scans **should** soon be able to help us detect liars and cheaters more accurately.
Past	*Should* + *have* + past participle *(should've)**	He **should've** read the university's Honor Code by now. All first-year students do.

Less Certain

Present / Future	*Could / may / might*	The final grades in the professor's class look a bit inflated. He **might** be fudging them to make himself look like a better teacher.
Past	*Could / may / might* + *have* + past participle *(might've)**	Walt has always been so honest, but he **might have (might've)** cheated on the exam because of the intense competition and the pressure from his parents.

---

* In speaking, the auxiliary *have* (modal + *have* + past participle) is pronounced /əv/ and is joined to the preceding word. This form is used only in speech.

2 Work with a partner.

Student A: Cover the right column. Ask a question or make a comment.

Student B: Cover the left column. Respond using the cues and a present, past, or future modal verb of certainty. Refer to the chart on page 51. Be sure to pronounce the reduced modal forms (*must've, couldn't've, should've, might've*) correctly. Then switch roles after question 4. Use expressive intonation.

Example

STUDENT A: Will Tomás be punished for lying to his boss about his work hours?

STUDENT B: (*less certain*) Maybe. There's a chance he **might** even lose his job.

Student A

1. Do you think I'll be able to tell if she is lying by just looking at her?

2. Will she be able to conceal the fact she copied her paper from the Internet?

3. Do you know why some doctors lie to their dying patients?

4. Why does Stella send exam answers to her friends over her cell phone?

Now switch roles.

5. Is Mohammed feeling better now that he finally fessed up to fudging the results of the experiment?

6. The baseball player's drug tests came back positive. He has to leave the team.

7. Bad news. The results of Gordon's experiment cannot be duplicated.

8. Why didn't Marco ever tell anyone about his name change?

Student B

1. (*quite sure*) Probably. You (able / tell) by watching for small changes in her facial expressions.

2. (*impossible*) No way. She (get away with) plagiarizing. Her professor uses anti-plagiarism software.

3. (*almost certain*) I think so. They (want) to protect the patients and their family from hearing bad news.

4. (*less certain*) I'm not really sure. Her friends (pay) her for the answers.

5. (*quite sure*) He (be / relieve). It usually feels better to be up front about things.

6. (*impossible*) Unbelievable! He just (deceived) his fans like that. They adored and trusted him.

7. (*almost certain*) Hmmm . . . he (cut corners) on the research.

8. (*less certain*) Well, I'm not sure, but he (conceal) his identity to protect himself.

 **3** Work with a partner.

Student A: Cover the right column. Ask the question. Check Student B's answer against the words in parentheses.

Student B: Cover the left column. Answer the question using an appropriate past modal of certainty. Use short-answer forms. Be sure to pronounce the modal perfect forms correctly. Then switch roles after question 4.

Example

STUDENT A: Did Maria know that her boyfriend lied to her about his whereabouts last Saturday night? (must've)

STUDENT B: (*almost certain*) Well, she <u>must've</u>. She told me she was pretty sure she saw his car in front of Sarah's apartment.

Student A	Student B
1. Did she tattle on her brother when she found out he had been driving without a license? (must've)	1. (*almost certain*) Yes, she _____. She looked happy. He looked miserable, and their parents looked furious.
2. Did that young Harvard student really write that book that just won a major award? (couldn't've)	2. (*impossible*) No, she _____. The book was too good. In fact, they think she plagiarized 50 percent of the novel.
3. She refused to look in my eyes when she answered my question. Do you think she was lying? (could've been / might've been / may've been)	3. (*less certain*) Hmmm . . . she _____. Not making eye contact is one sign of lying.
4. Did he really have to spend a year in jail for cheating on his taxes? (must've had to)	4. (*almost certain*) Yes, he _____. I heard he hadn't paid any taxes for six years!

(continued on next page)

Now switch roles.

5. Do you think she lied about her plans so she wouldn't have to go to the party? (could've / might've / may've)

6. Have all the airports installed the special tracking device to spot people lying about their identities? (should've)

7. Were the lab directors pleased with the doctoral students' results? (couldn't've been)

8. Do you think Ms. Rapaport could tell immediately that Pierre was her half-brother? (must've known)

5. (*less certain*) I'm not sure, but she _____. She is sort of two-faced, so it's hard to know her real feelings.

6. (*quite sure*) Yes, they _____. The government has required these since 9/11.

7. (*impossible*) Unfortunately, they _____. The results were misleading.

8. (*almost certain*) Of course, she _____. He looked exactly like her father.

■■■■■■■■■■■■■■■■■■■■■■■■■■■ *GO TO* MyEnglishLab *FOR MORE GRAMMAR PRACTICE.*

PRONUNCIATION

REDUCTION OF THE AUXILIARY *HAVE*

🎧 Listen to the statements. Then read the explanation.

- I know I **should've told** the truth, but I was afraid I'd get in trouble.
- If you had made an excuse for missing the appointment, your client **wouldn't've fired** you. It's not acceptable to say you just didn't feel like working that day.

In spoken English, the auxiliary ***have*** is reduced when used with ***could, might, must, should***, and ***would*** in the unreal conditional tense as well as in modal perfect forms. It is pronounced /əv/, and joins to the preceding word. The main verb is stressed.

1 🎧 Listen to these modal perfects and repeat them.

1. could have done	5. must have done	9. might not have done
2. would have done	6. couldn't have done	10. must not have done
3. should have done	7. wouldn't have done	
4. might have done	8. shouldn't have done	

2 🎧 In this conversation, Anton has just heard Molly compliment their friend, José, on his new haircut. Listen to the conversation and fill in the blanks with modal perfects. Draw a line through the **ha** of **have** and use an underline to link the modal and **have**. Then practice the conversation with a partner.

ANTON: I think José's hair looks awful. I ___could h̶a̶ve given___ him a better haircut with

my eyes closed. Do you really think he looks good?

MOLLY: No, I agree he looks terrible. He _____ his hair long. But I

couldn't tell him that.

ANTON: No, but he didn't ask you what you thought. You volunteered the compliment.

You _____ anything at all.

MOLLY: But he saw me staring at him. If I hadn't said anything, he _____

I didn't like his haircut. He knew I'd noticed, so I told a white lie. What's the

harm?

ANTON: Well, first, you told a lie when you _____ nothing. But what's

worse, now José thinks he looks good when he really doesn't.

MOLLY: But if I hadn't said anything, it _____ awkward. Anyway, when

his hair grows, I'll tell him he looks even better.

_____

Note: After *might* and *must*, the full negative *not* is more common than the contraction *n't*.

3 Work with a partner.

Student A: Cover the right column. Read your statements to Student B.

Student B: Cover the left column. Respond to your partner using *would've, should've, could've, might've,* or *must've,* or their negative forms. Then switch roles after item 5.

Student A	Student B
1. My university just expelled a student when a professor caught him plagiarizing.	1. Uh-huh. I heard about that. The university should / not / expel him. *Uh-huh. The university shouldn't have expelled him.*
2. But he was caught. He was cheating.	2. Yeah, but it was his first time. They should / give / him another chance.
3. How do you know it was his first time? Maybe it was just the first time he got caught.	3. That's true. He might / plagiarize before.
4. I think the policy is right, but it has caused a lot of distrust between the students and the administration.	4. I know. I think the university could / handle it better.
5. I wonder if the students really understand plagiarism.	5. Well, they must / hear about it in the news.

Now switch roles.

6. Yesterday, I decided to do a little experiment. I decided to go for a whole day without telling a lie, not even the smallest deception.	6. Well, that should / not / be hard for you. You're one of the most honest people I know. What happened?
7. Well, I was late for my first appointment with a new client. When I told her I'd forgotten about the appointment, she fired me.	7. This sounds like an expensive experiment. Could / not / you / say that you were in another meeting and unable to leave?
8. Yes, but remember the experiment. Then Joe asked me to go to lunch, and I said no. When he asked me why, I said I didn't feel like listening to his problems.	8. He must / be furious. I know how I'd feel if someone said that to me. So, you lost a client and a friend. What happened next?
9. Well, then I decided I'd better go home and not talk to anyone else. But I passed the test—I didn't tell a single lie for the whole day.	9. Maybe you should / start the experiment with a different definition of a lie, one that doesn't lead to lost clients and friends.

SPEAKING SKILL

SEEING MULTIPLE SIDES TO AN ISSUE

Lying, cheating, and secrecy, as well as honesty, truth-telling, and openness, require people to reflect on their ethics and values. Ethical dilemmas are rarely clear-cut. Generally, when we make ethical or moral decisions, we need to consider several perspectives of an issue. The following is a list of expressions to use when reflecting on an ethical dilemma.

INTRODUCTORY EXPRESSION	ADDITIONAL CONSIDERATION OR RESPONSE
One way to look at _____ is . . .	And another way could be . . .
Of course, it depends on . . .	It could also depend on . . .
On the one hand, you could say . . .	On the other hand, . . .
One thing to take into consideration could be . . .	Another thing might be . . .
There are several things to consider. One . . .	Two . . . Three . . . etc.
One way to think about _____ is . . .	But the flip side would be . . .
If you look at it from the perspective of . . .	But seen from another perspective . . .

With a partner, discuss the ethics of the common dilemmas listed in the box below and on the next page.

Student A: Flip a coin. If it lands on "heads," you must defend the action listed, using an introductory expression above.

Student B: Respond using the expression for additional information or opposing response from the right column in the chart above. It should correspond to the expression used by Student A.

Switch roles after each item.

Daily Ethical Dilemmas

Is it honest or ethical to take office supplies from your company for personal use?

Example

STUDENT A: On the one hand, you could say that it's ethical because sometimes I bring things from home to the office.

STUDENT B: On the other hand, the things you bring from home, such as decorations, are not really "supplies" that you need to do your job, so it's not ethical.

- Download music from the Internet without paying?
- Buy a new sweater and then return it after wearing it?

(continued on next page)

- Turn in a paper you had actually written for another class two years ago?

- Not tell your professor when he or she inadvertently marks an answer "correct" when, in fact, you find out it is incorrect?

- Claim that computer problems caused you to turn in a project late, when really you just didn't have time to finish it?

■■■■■■■■■■■■■■■■■■■■■ GO TO MyEnglishLab FOR MORE SKILL PRACTICE AND TO CHECK WHAT YOU LEARNED.

FINAL SPEAKING TASK

In this task, you will plan a group discussion about dilemmas and lying. Use the vocabulary, grammar, pronunciation, and listening and speaking skills that you learned in the unit to discuss multiple sides of an issue.*

Work in groups of four. Each student will read key information in Student Activities on page 248 about one actual ethical dilemma and then summarize it for the group. As each dilemma is presented, the other group members will take notes on a separate piece of paper. Then, as a group, brainstorm possible solutions or answers to the questions in the chart below. Take brief notes below each question. Use the modals of certainty on page 51 and the expressions for seeing multiple sides to an issue on page 57. Choose one dilemma to present to the class.

DILEMMA A: TRADING A LEMON	DILEMMA B: VIDEO PIRACY	DILEMMA C: A DOCTOR'S DEBATE	DILEMMA D: TURTLE TROUBLE
• What should he do?	• What should the woman tell her child?	• Should the doctor tell the patient his diagnosis?	• Was the woman's lie justified?
• What should he tell a potential buyer?	• Should she discuss the issue with the neighbor?	• Should the doctor respect the family's wishes not to tell the patient how serious his illness is?	• What other options did she have?

* For Alternative Speaking Topics, see page 60.

UNIT PROJECT

Choose a topic and research it. Follow the steps:

Topic 1: Lying in Movies

There are a number of movies in which the theme is truth, deception, or concealment. Some examples of these are *Goodfellas, Shattered Glass, The Man Who Never Was, The Good Shepherd, Catch Me If You Can, The Hoax,* and *Liar, Liar.*

STEP 1: Watch one of these movies. Summarize the plot and the theme to the class.

STEP 2: Analyze the movie using concepts and language that you have learned in this unit.

Topic 2: Stories about Lying

A "whopper" is an informal word meaning "a really big lie."

STEP 1: Interview several friends, neighbors, or family members. Ask them to tell you the biggest whopper they have ever told in their life.

STEP 2: Present their stories to your class.

ALTERNATIVE SPEAKING TOPICS

Choose a research study to respond to. Use ideas, vocabulary, grammar, pronunciation, and the language you learned in the unit to discuss multiple sides of an issue.

Look at the following statistics. Working with a partner, discuss why you think the statistics are true. What accounts for the numbers? What is surprising or not surprising to you?

Research Study 1

According to an online résumé writing business, of 1,000 résumés vetted over six months, 43 percent contained one or more "significant inaccuracies."

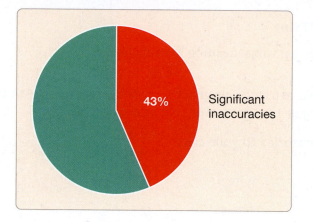

Research Study 2

One study found that most people lie once or twice a day. Both men and women lie in 20 percent of their social exchanges lasting more than 10 minutes. In one week, they will lie in 30% of their one-to-one contacts.

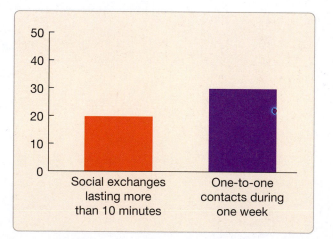

Research Study 3

When students communicate, they often tell lies. In fact, fibs occur in 15 percent of email messages, 33 percent of phone calls, 25 percent of face-to-face conversations, and about 20 percent of instant message chats.

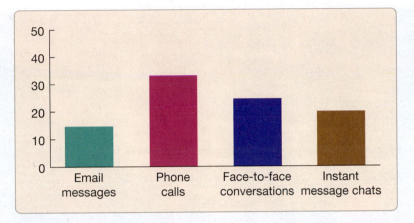

GO TO MyEnglishLab *TO DISCUSS ONE OF THE ALTERNATIVE TOPICS, WATCH A VIDEO ABOUT WHY KIDS LIE, AND TAKE THE UNIT 2 ACHIEVEMENT TEST.*

REVOLUTION
OF THE
50%

1. Look at the photo and the title of the unit. How do you think the young woman in the corner is feeling? Describe a time when you might have felt this way. What do you think the 50% in the title means?

2. Are you an introvert or an extrovert? One-third to one-half of people are introverts. Introversion is a natural personality trait marked by a constellation, or collection, of characteristics. Some think introversion is the same as shyness, but shyness is anxiety about social situations. Most people fall somewhere on a continuum between introversion and extroversion. Put an X on the continuum marking where you might fall on this personality spectrum. Discuss your decision with a partner. Then look at page 249 in Student Activities. Take the informal quiz and find out how accurate you were on the personality spectrum.

Introvert	Ambivert	Extrovert
quiet/reserved/introspective		talkative/outgoing/gregarious

3. In your opinion, is introversion a positive or negative quality? Explain.

GO TO MyEnglishLab **TO CHECK WHAT YOU KNOW.**

VOCABULARY

New research on personality by Susan Cain is part of a long tradition that can be traced back to Carl Jung, the Swiss psychologist. In the early 1900s, Jung first proposed the theory of personality temperaments or types. In his view, introversion and extroversion represent not only two different personality temperaments, but also two differing attitudes toward life—two different ways of reacting to circumstances. No one lives completely as one type or the other.

1 🎧 Read and listen to the sentences. Then try to determine the meaning of the **bold-faced** words or phrases from the context of the sentences. Write a definition or similar expression under the sentence.

1. "Thoughtful," "focused," and "independent" are positive **attributes** that often describe introverts.

   _____

2. According to Jung, the overall life **orientation** of the introvert is toward the "inner world" of thoughts, ideas, reflections, and memories.

   _____

3. Some introverts are seen as dull, quiet, and boring, **whereas** extroverts are perceived as superficial and insincere.

   _____

4. Most introverts regard superficial small talk as a **colossal waste** of time.

   _____

5. As the new CEO and a classic introvert, she was **mindful of** the strategies she would have to implement to perform successfully in an extroverted role.

   _____

6. The award-winning novelist, known to be a "classic" introvert, **craved** hours of uninterrupted solitude and avoided book readings and interviews.

   _____

7. All of her business school colleagues **discounted** her opinions during the seminar because she voiced them in a quiet, soft-spoken tone.

   _____

8. He was **on the verge of** going to the party, but ultimately turned down the invitation. He dreaded making endless small talk and meaningless chit-chat.

   _____

9. Some economists say that we are undergoing a **sea change** in education. In the future, introverts will be valued for their superior powers of concentration.

   _____

10. Gregarious, outspoken, and charismatic, she had been **groomed for** the CEO spot since joining the company 10 years ago.

    _____

11. Many psychologists advise introverts to explore their own **psyche** in order to figure out how to make the most of their temperament.

    _____

12. In a famous study, management researcher Jim Collins reported that leaders of the best-performing companies of the 20th century were known not for their charisma, but rather for their **profound** humility and intelligent, quiet temperament.

    _____

13. A reserved and thoughtful child, his natural talent and intelligence **came to light** when he won the national junior chess championship.

    _____

14. Never the center of attention in law school or at the law firm, the young attorney won heaps of praise for **putting his stamp on** important environmental legislation.

    _____

15. In his latest study, the psychologist concluded that most introverts think through a task carefully instead of quickly **running with** it without careful thought.

    _____

2 Match the words or phrases on the left with the definitions or synonyms on the right. Write the corresponding letter in the blank. Then work with a partner and compare answers.

_____ 1. colossal waste

_____ 2. attributes

_____ 3. groomed for

_____ 4. mindful of

_____ 5. came to light

_____ 6. crave

_____ 7. discounted

_____ 8. on the verge of

_____ 9. orientation

_____ 10. profound

_____ 11. psyche

_____ 12. put one's stamp on something

_____ 13. run with

_____ 14. sea change

_____ 15. whereas

a. be aware of

b. be prepared for

c. deep

d. dismissed; thought less of

e. on the other hand

f. a very ineffective use

g. adapt; make a contribution

h. execute

i. was revealed

j. desire intensely

k. major break with the past

l. innermost self

m. tendency

n. characteristics

o. nearly; almost

GO TO MyEnglishLab **FOR MORE VOCABULARY PRACTICE.**

PREVIEW

Susan Cain, the researcher interviewed in Listening One, has just published a book called *Quiet: The Power of Introverts in a World that Can't Stop Talking*. In this book, she claims that many cultures throughout the world, particularly western cultures, are biased against certain personality traits and that the bias is harmful.

🎧 Work with a partner. Predict the personality traits that Cain might mention and the reason that the bias towards these traits might be harmful. Write them on the lines. Discuss your ideas with your partner. Then listen to this excerpt of the interview to check your predictions.

1. *shyness*

2. _____

3. _____

4. _____

MAIN IDEAS

🎧 Listen to each part of the interview and write a statement summarizing the main idea behind each of Susan Cain's points.

Part One

1. cultural bias towards introverts

_____

2. difference between introverts and extroverts

_____

Part Two

3. similarities between gender orientation and personality orientation

_____

4. parallel between introversion and the condition of women in the 1950s and 1960s

_____

(continued on next page)

Part Three

    5. difference between extroverts and introverts as leaders

    _____

    6. changes that Susan Cain would like to see

    _____

DETAILS

🎧   Listen to the interview again. Read the sentences, and write **T** (true) or **F** (false). Correct the false statements. Then discuss your answers with a partner.

Part One

_____   **1.** One of the attributes introverts possess is power.

_____   **2.** Introverts are encouraged to pretend to be extroverts.

_____   **3.** Most people think that introverts are anti-social and different from other people.

Part Two

_____   **4.** Half the population is biased against introverts.

_____   **5.** The bias against introverts is similar to the bias against women in the 1950s and 1960s.

_____   **6.** It will take a sea change for us to really understand the personality type of introversion.

Part Three

_____   **7.** Cain thinks that good leaders are extroverts with charisma and loud voices.

_____   **8.** Proactive and engaged employees seem to perform better with introverted leaders because introverted leaders give them more freedom.

_____   **9.** Cain thinks introverts should stop hiding their introversion.

_____   **10.** Cain thinks that introverts should help schools and workplaces change to meet their needs better.

MAKE INFERENCES

PRESENTING A BALANCED POINT OF VIEW

Remember that an **inference** is an **educated guess** about something that is **not directly stated**, but which you believe is true based on the intention, attitude, voice, pausing, and word choices of the speaker.

Author Susan Cain believes that her research shows that introverts have been highly misunderstood and undervalued. She passionately urges thinking people everywhere to become aware of this issue and to change their behavior. Still, she argues her case carefully. Her goal is to gain equal recognition for the value of both personality types, not overlook one at the expense of the other.

🎧 Listen to and read the excerpt. Then answer the question and read the explanation.

Example

SUSAN CAIN: So introverts are people who like more quiet, less stimulating environments, <u>whereas</u> extroverts crave more stimulation <u>to feel at their best.</u>

In this balanced comparison of the two personality types using "whereas," what does Cain intend to say?

a. Both introverts and extroverts need some kind of stimulation in order to feel good.

b. Extroverts have greater needs than introverts.

c. Introverts are dull compared to extroverts.

The answer is *a*. Cain softens the differences between the two to create a more balanced position by adding "to feel at their best." We can infer that she is saying that BOTH introverts and extroverts react to their environments, and they BOTH want to feel good. The point is that one group simply needs a less stimulating environment than the other. Through this technique, Cain is stepping back as an academic presenting a balanced point of view.

🎧 Listen to each excerpt. Notice how Cain implies a balanced point of view. Then choose the meaning that she implies.

Excerpt One

1. In this balanced definition of introversion, Cain corrects a common mistake with the sentence: "... it's really not that at all." She intends to say:

a. People make many assumptions about introverts.

b. Introverts are as social as extroverts but in another way.

c. Introverts are not as social as extroverts.

(continued on next page)

Excerpt Two

2. In this analogy, Cain compares the place of introverts today to the place of women in the 50s and 60s. With this comparison, she intends to:

    a. help women who are introverts feel more comfortable with this orientation

    b. communicate the magnitude of the change in attitude towards introverts which needs to take place

    c. encourage more women to speak out against bias against introverts

Excerpt Three

3. Cain's research shows that employees work very well under both introverted and extroverted leaders. She draws the comparison with qualifying phrases such as "often do better" and "almost without realizing it." With these phrases, she intends to:

    a. express uncertainty about the comparison she is making

    b. indicate that the research is not 100% clear

    c. present a fair picture of the differences between the two kinds of leaders

EXPRESS OPINIONS

1 Discuss the questions in a small group. Give your opinions. Then share your answers with the class.

    1. Do you agree with Cain that we need "a quiet movement"—that is, a new appreciation of the value of quieter people—in the workplace and in society? Why or why not? What things would you like to change in the workplace, daily interactions, or in cultures that are familiar to you? How do you think the change can happen?

    2. Cain says that introverts possess all kinds of "surprising powers." What might these powers be? For what kinds of roles, situations, or places would these powers be useful?

2 Work with a partner. Look at the cartoon on the next page and discuss the answers to the questions.

    1. With which sections of the cartoon do you most agree? Disagree? Why?

    2. How would you change the cartoon using information about yourself (if you are an introvert) or introverts you know?

GO TO MyEnglishLab *TO GIVE YOUR OPINION ABOUT ANOTHER QUESTION.*

VOCABULARY

Are you more of an optimist or a pessimist? Have you ever run into a person with an overly optimistic outlook? In this on-air essay, Julie Danis gives her opinion about people with the Pollyanna syndrome—people who refuse to accept that anything bad can happen. The name comes from the heroine of a 1913 novel, Pollyanna, who had a consistently optimistic outlook on life, which many people today see as unrealistic.

1 You will hear the phrases below in the next listening selection. Notice them as you listen.

carried away	make lemonade out of lemons
diagnosis for blurred vision	no time to be cranky
fill the void	wallow in one's misery

2 Match the words or phrases on the left with the definitions or synonyms on the right. Write the corresponding letter in the blank.

_____ **1.** wallow in one's misery   **a.** make the best out of a bad situation

_____ **2.** diagnosis   **b.** overcome loneliness

_____ **3.** cranky   **c.** make oneself unhappy

_____ **4.** make lemonade out of lemons **d.** analysis

_____ **5.** fill the void   **e.** in a bad mood

_____ **6.** carried away   **f.** overly excited

COMPREHENSION

Read the items on the left. Then listen to Julie Danis's commentary. Listen again, and match Danis's unlucky event with Pollyanna's "bright side" view on the right.

Danis's thinking about her problems

_____ **1.** went to the eye doctor but did not get a diagnosis for the problem of blurred vision

_____ **2.** stop-and-go commute

_____ **3.** computer crashes and 1-800-HELP line is very busy

_____ **4.** snowed in with no hope of flying

_____ **5.** toothache and no dental insurance for the root canal

The Pollyanna's solutions to Danis

a. time to purge, or clean out, the computer files

b. time to catch up on movies

c. a chance to skip the mascara and rest eyes every two hours

d. (no solution)

e. a chance to listen to language tapes while doing relaxation exercises

■■■■■■■■■■■■■■■■■■■■■■■■■■■■■ **GO TO** MyEnglishLab **FOR MORE VOCABULARY PRACTICE.**

LISTENING SKILL

IDENTIFYING CREATIVE AND EFFECTIVE EXAMPLES

In this commentary, the speaker, Julie Danis cleverly and creatively uses examples in order to create the persona of a Pollyanna, an overly optimistic and sometimes annoying personality type. She creates this annoying personality type with a string of examples that she delivers in a particular way. She also concedes that, occasionally, the Pollyanna can be helpful. To make this contrast, she also uses certain techniques. Here are some of the techniques Danis uses:

Pitch:	high-pitched, squeaky voice	usual speaking voice
Pace:	fast-paced speech	usual pace of speech
Suggestions:	off-topic, annoying suggestions	on-topic, helpful suggestions
Kind of speech:	direct (quoted) speech	indirect speech

Read and listen to the example. Then answer the question and read the explanation.

DANIS: Arriving at the office after a visit to the eye doctor with no diagnosis for my blurred vision, I was in a grouchy mood.

"No time to be cranky," a coworker said. "We have a project due."

Of the options above, what technique does Danis use to help form the Pollyanna persona?

Technique: _____

The answer is _pitch_. Danis uses a high-pitched, squeaky voice to communicate the Pollyanna's cheerfulness and "get to it" attitude.

1 🎧 Listen to the excerpts that illustrate the way Danis is giving examples and creating a Pollyanna character. Identify the technique(s) used from the box above.

Excerpt One

1. Problem: Blurred vision

   Technique(s): _____

Excerpt Two

2. Problem: Stop-and-go commute

   Technique(s): _____

Excerpt Three

3. Problem: Long hold time on computer HELP line

   Technique(s): _____

Excerpt Four

4. Problem: Snowed in, 24 hours

   Technique(s): _____

2 Notice the contrasting example in the last excerpt. Why does Danis change her technique here?

GO TO MyEnglishLab *FOR MORE SKILL PRACTICE.*

STEP 1: Organize

Use the information in Listenings One and Two to complete the chart. Use information that is directly stated and information that is implied.

PERSONALITY TYPES	POSITIVE ATTRIBUTES	NEGATIVE ATTRIBUTES	WAYS TO COPE
INTROVERT	• *reserved* • •	• •	•
EXTROVERT	• *proactive* • •	• *dominant* •	•
OPTIMIST	• *outgoing* • •	• •	
PESSIMIST	•	• •	• •

STEP 2: Synthesize

Work with a partner. Read the situations and use the words and phrases from Step 1 to improvise a short conversation between a Pollyanna and an introvert. Then present the conversation to your class.

Situation 1

STUDENT A: You are an employee with an introverted orientation. Your manager has just told you that you have to give a presentation to 75 salespeople about a new product your company has just launched. Following the presentation, you will have to host the reception, making sure everyone feels comfortable. You are petrified. Explain your concerns about meeting your manager's expectations.

STUDENT B: You are the Pollyanna coworker. Give advice to Ms. Introvert to help her succeed in her task. Help her make lemonade out of lemons.

(continued on next page)

Situation 2

STUDENT B: You have just been chosen as the president of the campus environmental club because of your intelligence, knowledge of the subject matter, and ability to get things done. However, you are very introverted. In this role, you have to be a leader, organize events, give speeches, and convince your members to follow your agenda. You are not sure you can manage. Discuss all of your reservations.

STUDENT A: You are a Pollyanna, and you are Mr. Introvert's club adviser. Convince him that he should be "comfortable in his own skin" and that he can do the job. Give him tips for doing it. Help him find the silver lining.

GO TO MyEnglishLab *TO CHECK WHAT YOU LEARNED.*

3 FOCUS ON SPEAKING

VOCABULARY

REVIEW

How does birth order affect personality? Some researchers believe that being the firstborn, the only child, or the "baby" in a family has a significant impact.

Read the letters to a newspaper on the next page. Fill in the blanks with the correct form of the appropriate expression from the box. Use the clues under the blanks to help you. Then work with a partner and compare answers.

attributes	crave	mindful of
came to light	diagnose	orientation
carried away	fill the void	put one's stamp on something
colossal waste	groomed for	run with
cranky	make lemonade out of lemons	wallow in one's misery

STAR DAILY.com

Each week the *Star Daily* posts our favorite responses to questions posed to our readers. Here are our favorites:

BIRTH ORDER: DOES IT MATTER?

Dear *Star Daily*:

Like most later-born children, as the youngest of 5, I am _____ my need for
1. (aware of)
solitude. Unlike my oldest brother who was destined to be a president of something, I simply was not _____ anything.
2. (prepared for)
Rarely _____, I have a positive
3. (in a bad mood)
outlook on life and find ways to

_____. Always
4. (make the best out of a bad situation)
upbeat, I just never _____ in my

own _____.
5. (make myself unhappy)

NANCY KAKOWSKI
Springfield, Missouri

Dear *Star Daily*:

Effect of birth order on personality? Seriously?! I don't buy it! Thinking about this is a

_____ of time. I dismissed these
6. (very ineffective use)
ideas since they _____ about 5
7. (appeared)
years ago. Everyone gets so

_____ with these ideas and
8. (overly excited)
explains every kind of behavior with birth order! Honestly, I think personality traits are determined by genetics. You can't change the order of your birth. People should just accept

their personality _____, and make
9. (tendency)
the most of the character they were born with.

MARTHA JOHNSON
New York City, New York

Dear *Star Daily*:

Being the first born in the family does have its

positive _____. Decisive,
10. (qualities)
dominant, and competitive, I get an idea and I

just _____ it. Like many first
11. (execute)
born children, I am a successful politician and

often praised for my ability to

_____ and treat complex urban
12. (analyze)
problems. I am most well known for

_____ environmental policy
13. (making a contribution)
in my very wet, but "green" state of Oregon.

MARK BALDINO
Portland, Oregon

Dear *Star Daily*:

I'm an independent, only child. So I

spent a great deal of time alone. To

_____, I had to learn many new
14. (overcome loneliness)
skills. For example, I learned how to lose my

awkwardness and self-consciousness. When I

was younger I, _____ all
15. (desired intensely)
attention from my parents. Now, I am lucky to

have developed many attributes common to

both introverts and extroverts. I am a true

ambivert!

JANE BENNER
Pensacola, Florida

EXPAND

1 English has a wealth of vocabulary to talk about personality and temperament. Work with a partner. Write each word in the most appropriate category on the chart that follows. Some words may fit in more than one category. For help, use information from the unit and a dictionary.

anti-social	grouchy	Pollyanna	social butterfly
assertive	inhibited	positive	standoffish
bold	killjoy	proactive	talk a blue streak
charismatic	life of the party	reserved	timid
dominant	methodical	reticent	upbeat
engaged	negative	self-conscious	wallflower
gloomy	outgoing	shrinking violet	whiny
gregarious	petrified	sociable	

BEHAVIOR		ATTITUDE	
INTROVERT	EXTROVERT	PESSIMIST	OPTIMIST

2 You are thinking about using an online video dating service to find a suitable partner. The video dating site requires that you send in a 2–3 minute video introduction in which you describe your personality. Work with a partner to practice your introduction, using the vocabulary from the unit and plenty of examples. Your partner should take notes and jot down each time she or he hears you say one of the unit vocabulary words. Have fun!

CREATE

Work in small groups. Read the questions on the next page. Discuss the answers and defend your opinions. Use words from the box above to help you express yourself. Play devil's advocate if possible. (If you "play devil's advocate," you support a less popular opinion in order to encourage debate.) Add your own examples.

Who Would You Rather Have?

1. Who would you rather have for your doctor?

 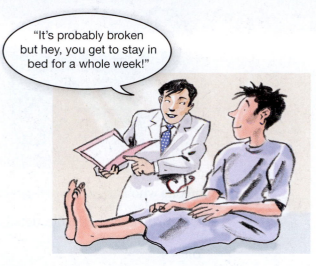

Someone who is _____.

a. highly experienced, but also reticent and a bit reserved

   OR

b. a recent medical school graduate, who is also outgoing . . . always makes lemonade out of lemons.

2. Who would you rather have for your teacher?

Someone who is _____.

a. gregarious, can talk a blue streak, but also is gloomy at times

   OR

b. confident, but also is a bit self-conscious or anti-social at times

3. Who would you rather have as your spouse?

Someone who is _____.

a. sensitive, kind, but also methodical and introverted

   OR

b. the life of the party, gregarious, but is a bit standoffish and sometimes grouchy

(continued on next page)

4. Who would you rather have as your tour guide on vacation?

Someone who is _____.

a. extremely knowledgeable, detail-oriented, but a killjoy

OR

b. charismatic, assertive, but inexperienced and a bit scattered and disorganized

GO TO MyEnglishLab *FOR MORE VOCABULARY PRACTICE.*

GRAMMAR

1 Work with a partner. Examine the sentences and discuss the questions that follow.

- Cain's research, <u>which she started in 2005</u>, focused on many introverts <u>who had a secret sense of shame about who they were</u>.

- In the late 1960s, American women were a part of the population <u>that was on the verge of feeling its own power</u>.

- Many extroverts think of themselves as leaders <u>whose role it is to put their own stamp on things</u>.

- A constellation of personality traits, <u>most of which are exaggerated</u>, is often applied to introverts.

1. What is the purpose of the underlined clauses?

2. Compare the five underlined clauses. How are they similar? How are they different?

ADJECTIVE CLAUSES—IDENTIFYING AND NON-IDENTIFYING

Adjective clauses are used to add variety, sophistication, and interest to sentences. They are useful in combining sentences to provide more detail and information. There are two kinds of adjective clauses: identifying and non-identifying.

Identifying Adjective Clauses	Examples
An **identifying adjective clause**: • has a subject and a verb • modifies specific nouns and pronouns • can be introduced by *who, whom, which, that, whose, where*, and *when* • is not set off by commas • is essential to the meaning of the sentence	• A Pollyanna is a person **who has an overly optimistic outlook.** • Consider the division between those **who always see the bright side** and those **who'd rather wallow in their misery.**

Non-identifying Adjective Clauses	Examples
A **non-identifying adjective clause**: • has a subject and a verb • is used with the relative pronouns *who, whom, which*, and *whose*. It is also used with *where* and *when* and cannot be used with *that* • must describe a specific person or thing • is set off by commas • is not essential to the meaning of the sentence and may be omitted	• Adam Grant, **who is a professor of Management at the Wharton School of Business**, concluded that proactive and engaged employees do better with introverted leaders. • Introversion, **which can be mistaken for timidity**, can be an effective trait for leaders.

Quantifying Expressions	Examples
Non-identifying adjective clauses often contain **expressions of quantity** such as *many of, most of, some of, none of, two of, several of, half of, all of, each of, both of*, and *a number of*. Use the structure: quantifier + preposition + relative pronoun (only *who, whom, where, when*, or *which*).	• Negative attributes, **most of which are false**, are often applied to introverts. • Cain's interviewees, **all of whom were introverts**, felt that they were starting to be accepted by society.

2 Read the paragraph. Underline all the adjective clauses. Circle the relative pronouns. Draw an arrow from each clause to the noun it modifies. Label the clause **I** (identifying) or **N** (non-identifying).

A study, which he called "Reversing the Extroverted Leadership Advantage," was conducted by Professor Adam Grant, who is a management professor at the Wharton Business School in Philadelphia, Pennsylvania. Most people believe leaders are men and women who speak out boldly, assert themselves, and generally dominate a group. The study, which was published in the *Academy of Management Journal*, explored this issue by examining a business that could track team effectiveness easily—the pizza delivery business. The data that the researchers received led to the conclusion that pairing an introverted leader with a proactive team can limit an organization's effectiveness. Professor Grant, who has since replicated his study with other businesses, concludes that introverted leaders, most of whom listen more and talk less, encourage their employees to be proactive, take charge, and allow their own ideas to come to light.

3 Work with a partner.

Student A: Ask Student B questions 1 through 4.

Student B: Cover the left column. Answer the questions. Use a variety of adjective clauses in your answers. Then switch roles after question 4.

Student A	**Student B**
1. Who is Dr. Adam Grant?	**1.** Oh, he's the one who led the study on leadership.
2. What was the conclusion of Grant's study?	**2.** Hmm. I think (that) . . .
3. What's an extrovert?	**3.** As far as I can remember . . .
4. What kind of leaders are most effective?	**4.** I'm not sure I remember, but I think . . .
Now switch roles.	
5. What's an introvert?	**5.** Well . . .
6. What's a Pollyanna?	**6.** Oh . . .
7. What's a shrinking violet?	**7.** I guess it's . . .

GO TO MyEnglishLab *FOR MORE GRAMMAR PRACTICE.*

PRONUNCIATION

GROUPING WORDS TOGETHER

When you speak, group your words into shorter phrases, or thought groups. Like punctuation in writing, thought groups help the listener understand speech. Pronounce the words in a thought group together.

- I'm the firstborn from a large family.

Join thought groups together smoothly. Hold (or lengthen) the end of one thought group briefly before you start the next group. There is often a small change in the pitch of your voice between thought groups.

- I'm the firstborn from a large family.

There are no fixed rules for the length of thought groups. Many thought groups are also grammatical groupings, for example, non-identifying clauses.

As you become more fluent, you will be able to use longer thought groups.

1 🎧 Listen to the sentences. Underline the thought groups. Then work with a partner to compare your groupings, and practice reading the sentences. If you and your partner have different groupings, discuss these differences.

1. We discovered that about 40 percent of all Americans label themselves as currently shy.

2. Over the past 10 years, that figure has increased to about 48 percent.

3. Do you find these days that it's more difficult meeting people?

4. Two out of every five people you meet think of themselves as shy.

5. There are just many things in a culture, our culture, which lead lots of people to be introverted.

6. Children don't see . . . don't have the opportunity to see their parents and relatives relating in a natural, easy, friendly way.

7. When you're at a party, or just in a conversation with someone anywhere, and you recognize that the person is shy, what do you do to draw that person out or try to make him or her more comfortable?

8. Admitting your shyness is really an important first step because if you don't, people make misattributions.

2 🎧 Listen to the sentences, and circle the letter of the one you hear. Then, working with a partner, choose sentence **a** or **b** to read to your partner. Your partner will tell you which one you have chosen. Then switch roles.

1. **a.** "Philip," said the doctor, "doesn't suffer from shyness."

   b. Philip said the doctor doesn't suffer from shyness.

2. **a.** My sister, who lives in California, is a Pollyanna.

   b. My sister who lives in California is a Pollyanna.

3. **a.** Suzanne's manager told me she's gotten over her shyness.

   b. Suzanne's manager told me, "She's gotten over her shyness."

4. **a.** The researcher interviewed the students, who said they were introverted.

   b. The researcher interviewed the students who said they were introverted.

5. **a.** Everything he said was based on research.

   b. "Everything," he said, "was based on research."

6. **a.** The therapy, which the clinic provides, gets people to be more outgoing.

   b. The therapy which the clinic provides gets people to be more outgoing.

SPEAKING SKILL

BREAKING THE ICE AND MAINTAINING A CONVERSATION

Introversion is a natural and healthy personality trait. In certain situations—perhaps when speaking another language—many of us may share some traits of introverts. That said, sometimes introverts need to "act like" extroverts in certain situations. In other words, some introverts need to move along the personality continuum towards ambivert and behave like someone who enjoys social interaction as well as solitude.

One skill that introverts can learn and master is how to break the ice and maintain a conversation.

Breaking the Ice	Examples
Introduce yourself.	"Hi, how are you?" "Hello, I'm Susan Cain."
Comment on something shared:	
• weather	"Nice weather, don't you think?"
• shared situation	"How do you know the host?"
• uncontroversial news	"What a game last night, huh?"

Maintaining a Conversation	Examples
Ask open-ended and follow-up questions.	"What brings you to _____?" "What kind of work do you do?"
Volunteer information.	"I am a writer who studies personality temperament."
Listen actively and look interested. (Use eye contact.) (Smile or nod your head occasionally.)	"Really?" "You're kidding!"
Change the topic if the conversation is dying, or excuse yourself.	"On another topic, did you see . . . ?" "Excuse me. I'd like to get a drink."

Work with a partner. Role-play a situation from the list. Student A starts the conversation. Both students keep it going for at least three minutes, throwing it back and forth like a ball. Use the chart above as a guide. Then change roles and role-play a second situation.

Situations

a. You are in a long checkout line at the supermarket. Start a conversation with the person behind you.

b. You are stranded at an airport gate waiting for a delayed flight. Start a conversation with the person next to you.

c. You are on a bus. Start a conversation with the person in the next seat.

d. You are at a party and feel very self-conscious. Start a conversation with a person who also looks a bit uncomfortable or awkward. Admit your uneasiness, but inside feel comfortable about who you are. Remember the statistic that 50 percent of the people in the room share your feeling.

■■■■■■■■■■■■■■■■ *GO TO* MyEnglishLab *FOR MORE SKILL PRACTICE AND TO CHECK WHAT YOU LEARNED.*

FINAL SPEAKING TASK

In this task, you will play the role of consultants who advise companies on how to build effective teams to achieve better results. Use the vocabulary, grammar, pronunciation, and speaking skills that you learned in this unit.*

Background

What's the perfect personality mix to accomplish a given task? The choice can make the difference between success and frustration, or even failure.

You are consultants working in a company called Personality Profiles, Inc. Personality Profiles is a highly specialized company which advises other companies on how to create "project teams" to execute large, very important projects. Specifically, Personality Profiles

- defines the specific personalities of the people best suited for each "project team."

- interviews final candidates who will serve on the "project teams."

This month, Personality Profiles has been hired by three clients, each with a unique project.

Work in groups of three or four to complete items 1 through 3 for each project:

1. Read the descriptions of the special project from each client.

2. In groups, discuss what kinds of individuals would be best suited to perform the task. Use adjective clauses to characterize people: *We need people who are . . . Demanding people, who are . . . People who would not be suitable are . . .* Use expressions for maintaining the conversation when it begins to die.

    As you discuss, complete the chart on page 89 with descriptions of the type of team members needed and interview questions to evaluate potential candidates.

3. Present your choices. Imagine the class is one of the clients. Explain the reasons for your recommendations.

---

* For Alternative Speaking Topics, see page 91.

Descriptions of Projects

Client One: Global Space Project International (GSPI)

GSPI, an international consortium of space travel professionals, has asked Personality Profiles, Inc. to assist in the process of selecting a three-person crew for a mission to Mars. The mission will last approximately 2.5 years.

Some of the specific challenges of this mission include:

- Long periods of confinement and isolation
- Possibility of emergencies
- Low physical activity
- Intense, rigorous scientific experiments
- Repetitive and monotonous tasks

Client Two: *Canadian Post* Newspaper

Canadian Post newspaper has asked Personality Profiles, Inc. to assist in the process of selecting a three-person team of young university students to accompany a well-respected, famous investigative reporter on a ten-city tour of Africa. The trip will last approximately three months. The reporter and his three-student team will report on health, economic, and educational conditions in the ten poorest areas of the African continent.

Some of the specific challenges of this mission include:

- Rough, unsophisticated living conditions
- Unpredictable and risky travel
- Lack of cell phone or electronic communication at times
- Exposure to illness, disease, and death
- Daily reporting and writing deadlines

(continued on next page)

Client Three: Cactus Production Studio

Cactus Production is a leading Mexican movie studio and has asked Personality Profiles, Inc. to assist in the process of selecting a three-person team to develop, create, and execute a creative and competitive marketing campaign for a new, highly anticipated movie by a prominent Mexican director and starring a popular Mexican movie star. The team will have only three weeks to develop the campaign, which will include television advertising, billboards, movie previews, newspaper and magazine advertising, a website, actor tours, and interviews.

Some of the specific challenges of this task include:

- Tight, unreasonable deadlines
- Conflicting needs, interests, and demands from actors, producers, directors
- Insufficient advertising budget
- High expectations for the movie to make an extraordinary amount of money
- Complex campaign that includes several media (television, Web, billboards, print, etc.)

Example

Client: ___Canadian Post___

TEAM MEMBERS (student names)	PERSONALITY	DETAILED PERSONALITY REQUIREMENTS	PROBING QUESTIONS FOR INTERVIEW
1.	Classic introvert	Good listener, excellent observer, doesn't have to be the center of attention	1. How will you feel meeting new people every day? 2.
2.			
3.			

UNIT PROJECT

Follow the steps to research the topic and present findings to the class.

STEP 1: There are many things that people can fear. A phobia is an excessive or irrational fear of a situation, creature, place, or thing. Shy people, for example, have a phobia labeled "social anxiety." They are afraid of social situations. Choose one or two phobias from the box below. You may also choose to present another phobia you come across in your research.

---

acrophobia: fear of heights

agoraphobia: fear of leaving the house

ailurophobia: fear of cats

arachnophobia: fear of spiders

aviophobia: fear of flying

claustrophobia: fear of closed spaces

glossophobia: fear of public speaking

nomophobia: fear of being without a mobile phone

testophobia: fear of taking tests

technophobia: fear of technical devices— computers, etc.

triskadekaphobia: fear of the number 13

STEP 2: Research one or two of these phobias on the Internet or in the library. Organize your research into three parts:

1. Definition and statistics, particularly from different countries

2. Examples from research and personal experience

3. Treatment options

STEP 3: Present your research to the class.

ALTERNATIVE SPEAKING TOPICS

Choose a topic. Use ideas, vocabulary, grammar, pronunciation, and expressions from the unit to discuss each topic.

Topic 1

Gail Vennittie, a principal with PricewaterhouseCoopers, said, "I grew up as the middle child of seven kids. Depending on the situation, I had to try and figure out how to interact. Every scenario is slightly different."

Being the middle child, Gail has had to be sensitive to other points of views as well as learn to be an independent thinker. Do you agree with Gail? Think about your own birth order. How has this birth order affected your personality or your skills?

Topic 2

1. Look at these quotes from Susan Cain. Paraphrase each one and give your opinion.
   a. "The charisma of ideas matters more than a leader's gregarious charms."
   b. "Solitude is a catalyst for innovation."
   c. "Sometimes it helps to be a pretend-extrovert. There's always time to be quiet later."

2. Have you ever witnessed the bias against introverts? Describe the experience. Have you ever been a victim of the bias yourself? Explain.

3. Gandhi was known to be an introvert. He said, "In a gentle way you can shake the world." What does he mean? Do you agree with him? Why or why not?

GO TO MyEnglishLab TO DISCUSS ONE OF THE ALTERNATIVE TOPICS, WATCH A VIDEO ABOUT HOW TO BECOME SUCCESSFUL, AND TAKE THE UNIT 3 ACHIEVEMENT TEST.

ANCIENT WISDOM TRAVELS
West

1 FOCUS ON THE TOPIC

1. *Feng shui* (pronounced *fung schway*) is an ancient Chinese practice that aims to create harmony in the placement of things in space. Look at the photo of the home built by American architect Frank Lloyd Wright. What elements in the photo might illustrate *feng shui* principles?

2. Think about each item below. Does it create favorable or unfavorable *feng shui*? Write **F** (favorable) or **U** (unfavorable) on the line. Share your answers with a partner. Which ones seem like common sense? Which ones seem superstitious? Check your answers in Student Activities on page 250.

_____ 1. aquarium
_____ 2. colors red and purple
_____ 3. desk facing a view
_____ 4. living near a cemetery
_____ 5. living on a dead-end street
_____ 6. mirrors
_____ 7. flowing water
_____ 8. odd number of dining room chairs

_____ 9. pictures of bats on the walls
_____ 10. plants and flowers
_____ 11. room full of windows
_____ 12. tiger statue outside an office door
_____ 13. staircase in the middle of the house
_____ 14. natural materials, such as stone or wood

GO TO MyEnglishLab TO CHECK WHAT YOU KNOW.

VOCABULARY

Read and listen to the magazine article. Pay attention to the **bold-faced** words and phrases. Then read the list of definitions that follows. Work with a partner. Write the number of the bold-faced word or phrase next to its definition.

THE PRINCIPLES OF *FENG SHUI*

INTRODUCTION

More and more Western architects, real estate developers, and interior designers are using the principles of the Chinese practice of *feng shui* in their life and work. Previously, Westerners **(1) frowned upon** *feng shui* as mere superstition. **(2) Hard-bitten** designers and architects, scientifically trained, refused to acknowledge any possible **(3) transcendent** explanation for successes brought on by the application of *feng shui* principles. Originally, they dismissed interest in *feng shui* as a **(4) digression** from established technical and artistic practices. Nowadays, however, *feng shui* is becoming more accepted in places outside of Asia, such as the United States, Canada, Europe, and Latin America.

THE MEANING OF *FENG SHUI*

Feng shui, meaning "wind" and "water" in Chinese, is an ancient form of geomancy, or the art of **(5) aligning** things in the environment to create harmony and good luck. An art and a science, *feng shui* aims to create both physical and psychological comfort. Practitioners believe that the arrangement of the elements in our environment can affect many aspects of our lives such as health, happiness, and fortune. *Feng shui* experts generally recommend simple changes; for example, they instruct people not to sit with their backs to the door because they can be **(6) caught off guard** and startled unnecessarily. Or they encourage business owners to put an aquarium in the entrance of their building since an aquarium symbolizes **(7) abundance**, as in the saying, "there are always more fish in the sea."

In classical *feng shui*, water always symbolizes wealth and abundance. Very simply, where there was water, crops could grow. In ancient agrarian society, water was the source of wealth. Aquariums represent the water element.

THE THEORY OF *FENG SHUI*

The theory behind *feng shui* is that there is an invisible life force or energy, called *ch'i* ("chee"), that **(8) circulates** through all things—rooms, buildings, people, hills, rivers, power lines. If ch'i flows smoothly and freely, then things go well for people. If ch'i is blocked, then the people in that space may feel discomfort or unhappiness. Sharp corners, narrow openings, poor lighting, and clutter are some of the many factors that can create blocked or unfavorable ch'i. Relying on tools and knowledge that are centuries old, trained *feng shui* experts can **(9) sense** immediately if the ch'i is circulating properly. They consider the shape, size, and location of objects as well as materials, colors, and numbers.

THE ORIGIN OF *FENG SHUI*

Feng shui grew out of the practical experience of farmers in southern China over 3,000 years ago. Those who built their huts facing north were battered by the wind and dust from the Gobi Desert in Mongolia. In contrast, those who built their huts facing south enjoyed the warmth of the sun and protection from the wind. As a result, south became the favored direction. Over the years, south came to be associated with fame, fortune, summer, the number nine, and the color red. In fact, to **(10) quote** world-renowned *feng shui* expert Lillian Too, red, the color of the south, "could well bring you good fortune." Ms. Too encourages red wallpaper, curtains, carpets, and all red in the southern part of a room, office, or building.

THE SPREAD OF *FENG SHUI*

Today the work of *feng shui* masters is in great demand among Chinese populations in China, Taiwan, Singapore, Hong Kong, Malaysia, and the Philippines. It is estimated that nearly 85 percent of Hong Kong residents apply *feng shui* principles when choosing an apartment or business. Now the ancient art of *feng shui* has migrated to the West. Well-known architects, designers, and businesspeople no longer view the practice **(11) skeptically**. In fact, there are many popular books filled with **(12) anecdotes** about people whose lives have been dramatically changed by *feng shui*.

_____ **a.** properly positioning

_____ **b.** disapproved of

_____ **c.** personal stories

_____ **d.** tough, experienced

_____ **e.** surprised

_____ **f.** beyond the limits of ordinary experience

_____ **g.** moves, flows

_____ **h.** a large quantity of something

_____ **i.** with doubt

_____ **j.** feel and know

_____ **k.** idea that is unrelated to the topic

_____ **l.** repeat what someone else has said or written

GO TO MyEnglishLab FOR MORE VOCABULARY PRACTICE.

PREVIEW

Sedge Thomson, the radio host of *West Coast Live* from San Francisco, interviews Kirsten Lagatree, author of the book *Feng Shui: Arranging Your Home to Change Your Life*. At the end of the interview, Thomson asks Lagatree about the impact of favorable *feng shui* on how one feels.

Work with a partner. Favorable *feng shui* has both physical and psychological benefits. Think of a house or an office where the energy flows freely because it is arranged according to *feng shui* principles.

🎧 Predict how favorable *feng shui* might make a person feel. Write your predictions on the lines. Then listen to an excerpt from the interview to check your answers.

1. _____

2. _____

3. _____

4. _____

5. _____

MAIN IDEAS

🎧 Listen to the interview and complete the chart by writing the main idea of the topic discussed. Then share your answers with a partner.

TOPIC	MAIN IDEA
PART ONE	
1. definition of *feng shui*	*a system of arranging things around you to create harmony and balance, and to make you feel better*
2. popularity of *feng shui* in other countries	
3. Donald Trump's attitude toward *feng shui*	
4. basic design of Lagatree's home office	
TOPIC	**MAIN IDEA**
PART TWO	
5. role of mirrors	
6. Lagatree's overall attitude toward *feng shui*	
7. who can sense good *feng shui*	

DETATILS

🎧 Read the questions. Then listen to the interview again and write short answers. Compare your answers with those of a partner. Complete the questions with as much detail as possible.

Part One

1. Lagatree doesn't think *feng shui* is a way to keep out evil spirits. Why not?

   _____

2. Thomson says that *feng shui* is very important in Asia. What three examples does he give to support this statement?

   _____

3. What two countries make up part of Lagatree's background? What influence have they had?

   _____

4. Why do some Chinese people living in San Francisco ask to have one-way street signs removed?

   _____

5. Why didn't Lagatree place her desk facing the window?

   _____

6. How does she feel about the impact of *feng shui* on the design of her home office?

   _____

Part Two

7. What two reasons does Lagatree give for not putting mirrors in the bedroom?

   _____

8. What three reasons does she give for putting mirrors in other rooms?

   _____

9. As a journalist, how did Lagatree feel about *feng shui* at first?

   _____

(continued on next page)

10. When Lagatree's skeptical friends asked her if she believed in *feng shui*, how did she respond?

_____

11. You don't have to be a *feng shui* expert to know if a place has good *feng shui*. Why not?

_____

GO TO MyEnglishLab **FOR MORE LISTENING PRACTICE.**

MAKE INFERENCES

LISTENING FOR INTENTION

Inferential listening involves the ability to recognize or infer speakers' intention or purpose for saying something. In other words, speakers choose certain words, expressions, or a tone of voice for specific reasons.

To understand the interaction between Sedge Thomson and Kirsten Lagatree on a deeper level, you need to be able to make inferences about their intentions. In other words, why did they say what they did in a particular way?

🎧 Read and listen to this excerpt. Then answer the question and read the explanation.

Example

THOMSON: So *feng shui* is exactly, what, a way of ordering buildings, rooms, corridors in your life to keep out evil spirits?

Why does Thomson use the words to "keep out evil spirits" to define *feng shui*?

He intends to:

  a. embarrass Kirsten

  b. establish his skeptical point of view right away

  c. create humor in his radio piece

The answer is *b*. Sedge is using exaggeration in order to convey his skeptical attitude. Instead of saying "keep out evil spirits," he could have said something more neutral, such as "in order to keep your house free from harm." However, he uses exaggeration as a way of subtly conveying his skepticism.

🎧 Listen to each excerpt. Listen for the intention or motivation behind the speaker's comment or question and circle the correct answer.

Excerpt One

1. Lagatree's comments that *feng shui* is not superstitious in order to _____.

    a. show that the host, Thomson, is a bit silly and uninformed

    b. defend herself as a *feng shui* authority

    c. appear as a polite radio guest

Excerpt Two

2. Lagatree mentions Donald Trump in order to _____.

    a. show how well connected she is to famous people, like the well-known business person, Donald Trump

    b. give an example of how *feng shui* has successfully traveled to the United States

    c. provide evidence for the scientific validity of *feng shui*

Excerpt Three

3. Thomson quickly responds to Lagatree's comment about Trump in order to _____.

    a. show how well connected he also is to famous people like Trump

    b. show he agrees with Lagatree about Trump's authority and knowledge about *feng shui*

    c. devalue Lagatree's example of Trump by using sarcasm

Excerpt Four

4. Lagatree told this story to Thomson and the radio audience in order to _____.

    a. convey the fact that she did not always believe in *feng shui* 100 percent and, at one time, was even quite skeptical

    b. let Thomson know that she is still as skeptical as he is

    c. amuse the audience with an anecdote

EXPRESS OPINIONS

Work in a small group and discuss the answers to the questions.

1. What was the most interesting thing you have found out so far about *feng shui*? At this point, are you a believer, like Lagatree, or a skeptic, like the interviewer, Sedge Thomson?

2. Would you be interested in applying *feng shui* principles to make changes in your home or office? If so, what changes would you like to make? If not, why are you skeptical?

3. Lagatree says that *feng shui* might be practiced in Scandinavia, but she isn't sure. Does *feng shui* remind you of any practices from other cultures? Which ones? Think, for example, of ideas in architecture or design that stress simplicity as an aesthetic principle.

■■■■■■■■■■■■■■■■■■■■■■■ *GO TO* MyEnglishLab *TO GIVE YOUR OPINION ABOUT ANOTHER QUESTION.*

LISTENING TWO   *FENG SHUI* IN THE NEWSROOM

VOCABULARY

1 🎧 The **bold-faced** words and phrases will appear in the next listening selection. Notice them as you read and listen to this brief entry in Master Lin's popular *feng shui* blog.

MASTER LIN: *Feng Shui*

HOME

CONTACT

ABOUT US

Hi. I am back to share with you the latest *feng shui* tip which I learned at the 10,000 Blossoms *Feng Shui* Institute last weekend. It is called The *Feng Shui* Salt Water Cure. If your home or office lacks **vitality** and energy and if you are open, optimistic, and **young at heart**, I highly recommend that you try this promising cure. All you need is salt, water, a container, and six brass Chinese coins. Salt, an ancient mineral, **governs** the energy in our body and the space around us. The water, brass, and salt combination **enhances** the precious properties of all three substances. To get the full benefit of the cure—an overall **abundance** of positive *ch'i* and mental **acuteness**—I recommend changing the water at least twice a year. Also, be sure that you or your pets don't drink the water, no matter how thirsty you or they may be!

2 Match the words or phrases on the left with the definitions or synonyms on the right. Write the corresponding letter in the blank.

_____ **1.** abundance   **a.** intensifies

_____ **2.** acuteness   **b.** directs

_____ **3.** enhances   **c.** sharpness

_____ **4.** governs   **d.** youthful outlook

_____ **5.** vitality   **e.** large quantity

_____ **6.** young at heart   **f.** energy, liveliness

In Listening Two, Lagatree visits a radio newsroom to record an interview. Her host, Steve Scher, asks her to suggest changes in the newsroom based on *feng shui* principles. She does so while making notes on a *bagua*.

In *feng shui*, the bagua (pronounced *BAHG-wah*) is an octagonal chart (see page 102) used to determine how parts of the house or a room relate to various areas of one's life. The *feng shui* master places the bagua over the floor plan of the room or house to see how to arrange the areas in order to promote the flow of good *ch'i*.

The bagua is used like a compass. Unlike Western compasses, in this compass, south, the most important direction, is placed at the top. The components of the bagua include: five basic elements (fire, earth, water, metal, and wood), colors of nature, numbers, animals, and areas of life (health, wealth, relationships, wisdom, business, etc.).

Feng shui **and the bagua can also be used to design gardens.**

COMPREHENSION

First, look at the bagua chart below. Then listen to the interview between Kirsten Lagatree and Steve Scher and fill in the missing information on the bagua chart. Also, draw arrows from the desks (both Steve Scher's and the news writers') and the aquarium to where Lagatree suggests placing them.

Bagua Chart

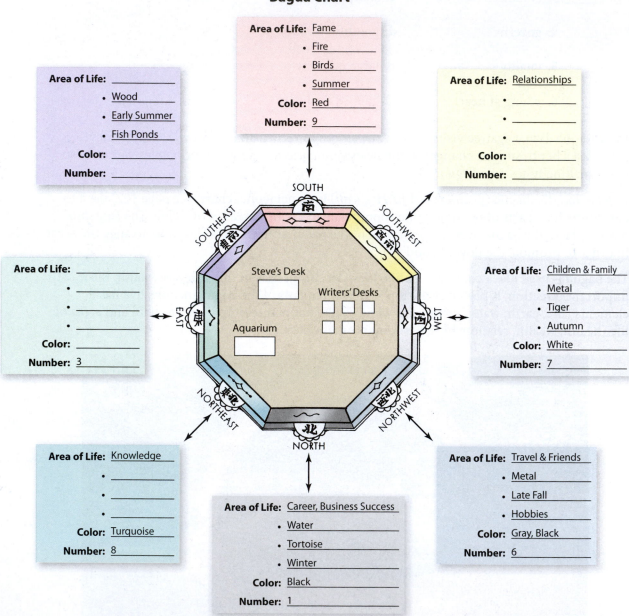

Area of Life: Fame
- Fire
- Birds
- Summer

Color: Red

Number: 9

Area of Life: _____
- Wood
- Early Summer
- Fish Ponds

Color: _____

Number: _____

Area of Life: Relationships
- _____
- _____
- _____

Color: _____

Number: _____

Area of Life: _____
- _____
- _____
- _____

Color: _____

Number: 3

Area of Life: Children & Family
- Metal
- Tiger
- Autumn

Color: White

Number: 7

Area of Life: Knowledge
- _____
- _____
- _____

Color: Turquoise

Number: 8

Area of Life: Career, Business Success
- Water
- Tortoise
- Winter

Color: Black

Number: 1

Area of Life: Travel & Friends
- Metal
- Late Fall
- Hobbies

Color: Gray, Black

Number: 6

SOUTH

SOUTHEAST

SOUTHWEST

EAST

WEST

NORTHEAST

NORTHWEST

NORTH

Steve's Desk

Writers' Desks

Aquarium

LISTENING SKILL

IDENTIFYING SUBTLE WAYS TO ASK FOR AND GIVE ADVICE

Often, people ask for and give advice in indirect or subtle ways, and frequently the requests are statements rather than questions. In the second listening, Kirsten Lagatree visits the newsroom of another radio host, Steve Scher. To understand the interaction, notice the subtle and sophisticated language that Scher uses to ask for her advice about *feng shui* principles in the newsroom. Notice too, the language that Lagatree uses to offer Scher advice.

Read and listen to the examples. Then answer the questions and read the explanations.

Example

SCHER: OK, so, I would like to walk into our newsroom, if we can, and have you just quickly kind of look at it and figure out what we can do for some of the people in here who need a little help in their careers or their happiness. Any initial thoughts you have looking at this room?

1. What two phrases does Scher use to ask for advice?

   1. _____

   2. _____

2. Are these requests statements or questions?

   Request 1 _____

   Request 2 _____

The phrases are *have you just quickly look at it and figure out* and *any initial thoughts you have . . . ?* Notice that the first request for advice is in the form of a statement and the second is a question. Notice also that Scher uses qualifiers such as *kind of look at it* and the words *any initial thoughts* as a way of asking for advice in a very hesitant and indirect way.

Example

LAGATREE: So maybe that's what makes you so peppy, Steve, and so young at heart. I'd like to say something about this southeast wall right here. That is your money corner.

What phrase does Lagatree use to offer unsolicited advice? _____

The phrase *I'd like to say something* indicates that Lagatree is about to offer advice that Scher didn't ask for. Previous to that, they were talking about a different topic—how the direction his desk faces affects his energy level.

🎧 Listen to the excerpts and identify the language of requesting or giving advice.

Excerpt One

1. To ask for advice Scher says, _____

Excerpt Two

2. To offer advice Lagatree says, _____

Excerpt Three

3. To offer advice Lagatree says, _____

GO TO MyEnglishLab *FOR MORE SKILL PRACTICE.*

CONNECT THE LISTENINGS

STEP 1: Organize

Work in pairs. Follow the directions to apply the *feng shui* principles you studied in Listenings One and Two.

1. With a partner, choose a work or living space that is familiar to both of you. It could be a place in your school, a store, etc. Brainstorm problems with the space.

2. Review the principles of *feng shui* as well as the bagua chart on page 102. Brainstorm the changes you would like to make according to these principles.

STEP 2: Synthesize

Draw the space on a separate sheet of paper, including as many details as possible. Present the results to another pair or the whole class. Describe the space before and after. Describe the changes you would make based on the new design. Finally, describe how favorable *feng shui* could help people who live and/or work in this space.

GO TO MyEnglishLab *TO CHECK WHAT YOU LEARNED.*

VOCABULARY

Work with a partner. Fill in the other forms of the words in the chart. A colored space indicates that there is no related form or that the form is not commonly used.

NOUN	VERB	ADJECTIVE
abundance	abound	
• acuteness • acuity		
		aligned
		digressive
	frown upon	
• • governance		
• • quote (informal)		
enhancement		
• sense •	• •	• •
• •		skeptical
	transcend	
		vital
anecdote	tell an _____	

EXPAND

1 Complete the imaginary interview between Kirsten Lagatree (the author) and Donald Trump (the famous New York City real estate developer) with the appropriate forms of the words from the box. Use the phrases under the blanks to help you.

at heart	get into	keep out	scare the heck out of
can't hurt	hard-bitten	make a move	sharp
catch off guard	huge	peppy	talk (someone) into
clean	in the midst of	rise or fall	work around

LAGATREE: Mr. Trump, ever since I heard you _____ *feng shui*, I've been
1. (became interested in)

dying to meet you. Referring to you as not only an astute businessman but

also as an artistic designer _____, I often quote you when I
2. (essentially)

do interviews or speak on book tours.

TRUMP: Kirsten, the pleasure is mine. I've read your handbook on *feng shui* and have

always thought you were a _____, intelligent writer.
3. (quick, smart)

LAGATREE: Why, thank you, Mr. Trump. Now, I understand that you absolutely do not

_____ in business without consulting your *feng shui* master,
4. (take action)

Mr. Tin Sun. Is that true?

TRUMP: Absolutely. I am currently _____ complicated negotiations
5. (involved in)

involving some highly valued property on the Hudson River in New

York City. However, Master Sun has informed me that the windows and

doors are not aligned properly and the views are not that great. I thought

about selling the property, but Master Sun _____ me
6. (convinced)

_____ keeping it. He said it is very valuable and, by applying

feng shui principles, we can easily _____ the problems.
7. (compensate for)

Fortunately, the overall design of the building is _____.
8. (simple)

LAGATREE: How did such a _____ businessman like yourself get into
9. (tough, experienced)

feng shui?

TRUMP: I've been doing business in Asia for years and am well aware of the fact that

feng shui is _____ there. In Hong Kong, you know, business
          10. (very popular)

deals _____ on *feng shui*.
     11. (succeed or fail)

LAGATREE: Have you used *feng shui* in your home as well?

TRUMP: Yes, Kirsten, I have. Master Sun started working on my house five years

ago. I must admit that when he first came over, he _____
                                     12. (frightened)

me. He connected many of my personal and physical problems to the poor

circulation of *ch'i* in my house. After many adjustments and a great deal of

money, I was finally able to _____ the unfavorable *ch'i*.
             13. (prevent from entering)

LAGATREE: I'm sure. I know there are many skeptics out there. However, I

do believe that if you live in a house with good *feng shui*, you feel

_____ and more energetic. In addition, you'll be able to live
     14. (livelier)

comfortably day in and day out without getting _____ in
                                          15. (startled)

your own home.

TRUMP: Of course. Anyway, I always tell those hard-bitten businessmen who tease

me, "Try *feng shui*. It _____."
             16. (can do no harm)

2 Work with a partner. Take the role of Lagatree or Trump and read the interview aloud with drama, interest, and expression.

CREATE

Work with a partner. Conduct a sophisticated conversation about *feng shui*. Practice using new expressions in answers consisting of several connected sentences.

Student A: Cover the right column. Ask questions 1 through 5.

Student B: Cover the left column. Answer each question, using the key word or expression in parentheses. Add additional information to clarify and explain. Then switch roles after question 5.

Student A	Student B
1. After learning about *feng shui*, how would you talk a skeptic into using it?	**1.** I guess . . . (couldn't hurt) I guess I'd say that it's been around for thousands of years, so it must work. At the very least, it couldn't hurt. In other words, . . .
2. Do you really believe that *feng shui* can affect people's moods and feelings?	**2.** Hmmm . . . (sharp, peppy) So, what I mean is . . .
3. What other Eastern practices would you be interested in getting into?	**3.** Perhaps . . . (get into) To put it another way . . .
4. What is your favorite way of keeping out unfavorable *ch'i*?	**4.** Let me see . . . I think . . . (keep out) What I mean is . . .
5. Why do you think *feng shui* has become so popular recently?	**5.** I imagine it . . . (huge) . . . Actually, what I am trying to say is . . .

Now switch roles.

6. Do you prefer simple, clean designs or more complicated, cluttered arrangements?	**6.** Actually, I think . . . (clean) So, in other words . . .
7. What kind of *ch'i* did you sense when you first walked into your current home?	**7.** I'm not sure I remember, but . . . (sense) You see, what I mean is . . .
8. Can you describe a place you know with good *feng shui*?	**8.** Sure, I felt like I was . . . (in the midst of) good *feng shui* when I . . . I think you could also say . . .
9. If your classroom had poor lighting and immovable desks that faced the wall, what would you do to create better *feng shui*?	**9.** Wow. That's a tough one. I guess . . . (work around) . . . To put it another way . . .

■■■■■■■■■■■■■■■■■■■■■■■■■■■■■■■■■■■■ **GO TO** MyEnglishLab **FOR MORE VOCABULARY PRACTICE.**

GRAMMAR

1 Work with a partner. Examine the excerpt related to Listening One and discuss the questions that follow.

Before radio host Sedge Thomson invited author Kirsten Lagatree to be interviewed on *West Coast Live*, he asked his researcher, Robin Tennenbaum, about Lagatree's qualifications.

THOMSON: Is Kirsten Lagatree a *feng shui* master?

TENNENBAUM: Well, Sedge, she doesn't claim to be a *feng shui* master. I mean, she hasn't studied in China or anything. **But** she has done a great deal of research, especially on the spread of *feng shui* in the United States. **On top of that**, she's written a well-respected book on the subject, which has led to a number of positive book reviews and successful radio interviews. **As a result**, she's become known as somewhat of an expert on *feng shui*.

1. What purpose does each of the **bold-faced** phrases serve? Identify each of the three purposes.

2. What other words could be substituted for each phrase?

DISCOURSE CONNECTORS

Discourse connectors are words and expressions that can connect ideas in speaking and writing. They join ideas both within sentences and between sentences. When you express yourself at length or in detail on a topic, you need to use these words to help the reader or listener follow your ideas. In written English, we use formal connectors to express the meaning of contrast, addition, and result—*in contrast, unlike (contrast); moreover, furthermore (addition); consequently, therefore (result)*. In spoken English, we often use more informal connectors to express the same meaning.

Contrast	Addition	Result
yet (unexpected result)		
but	plus	so
however	in addition	as a result
on the other hand	on top of that	

2 Working with a partner, fill in the blanks in the story with the appropriate informal discourse connectors from the chart. There may be more than one correct answer. Then read the story aloud to each other with drama, interest, and expression. Be sure to look up as often as possible when you read.

A *feng shui* master told this story:

One client told me that her business was doing very poorly and she needed to take some

action. _____, she was eager to revive her social life as well. When we first talked,
       (1)

she expressed her skepticism about *feng shui*, _____, she hired me, and I spent
                  (2)

several hours assessing her home. At first glance, I sensed that the *ch'i* was flowing smoothly

throughout the house. _____, a few minutes later, I did notice an old armchair in
          (3)

her living room blocking the front door. I asked her where she had bought it. She told me it was

from the set of a movie about a dangerous killer. _____ she mentioned that she
                        (4)

had only had the chair for about four months, and that this was the time when her business and

social life began to fail. It was clear to me that the chair had negative energy, which was related to

her bad luck. _____, we moved the chair outside immediately. As soon as we did,
        (5)

the telephone rang. It was a friend asking her on a date. _____, one month later,
                        (6)

her business took off. _____, she now understands the importance of bringing
       (7)

objects with only positive *ch'i* into the house.

3 Work with a partner. Practice using discourse connectors to help the listener.

Student A: Read the statement aloud, select a discourse connector for the meaning given, and then continue with additional information.

Student B: Read the next sentence, following the same directions.

1. *Feng shui* is an Eastern practice. [contrast]

   Example

   But it's becoming very popular in the West. In particular, Western corporations are using *feng shui* in their business locations.

2. Some people say *feng shui* is just a superstition. [addition]

3. Placing a plant in a corner can help positive *ch'i* (energy) circulate. [result]

4. Many real estate developers in Western countries are consulting *feng shui* experts. [result]

5. In China, *feng shui* is taken quite seriously. [contrast]

6. To create positive *ch'i*, you can put an aquarium in the southeast corner of the room. [addition]

GO TO MyEnglishLab **FOR MORE GRAMMAR PRACTICE.**

PRONUNCIATION

PAUSES AND INTONATION WITH DISCOURSE CONNECTORS

Speakers often use very informal discourse connectors such as **Well**, **First**, **In addition**, and **On the other hand**. They show how a sentence relates to other sentences in a conversation or longer message. They may also show the speaker's perspective on the information.

When speaking, these informal discourse connectors are often separated from the following sentence, especially when the connector consists of several words. Short connectors like *Well* or *But* may either be separated from the following sentence or pronounced with it.

🎧 Read and listen to the bold-faced informal discourse connectors.

A: **You know**, I don't like this paint color. It's too bright. **Plus**, it's too green. What should we do?

B: **Well**, we might get used to it.

A: Maybe. **Anyway**, I don't want to repaint.

These connectors are separated from the sentence by a pause or, in writing, by a comma. They have:

- their own intonation pattern
- intonation which often falls at the end of the introducer and then may rise a little

You know, I don't like this paint color.

1 🎧 Listen to the story about Bruce Lee and fill in the blanks with the informal discourse connector you hear. Add a comma after the connector if it is separated from the following sentence.

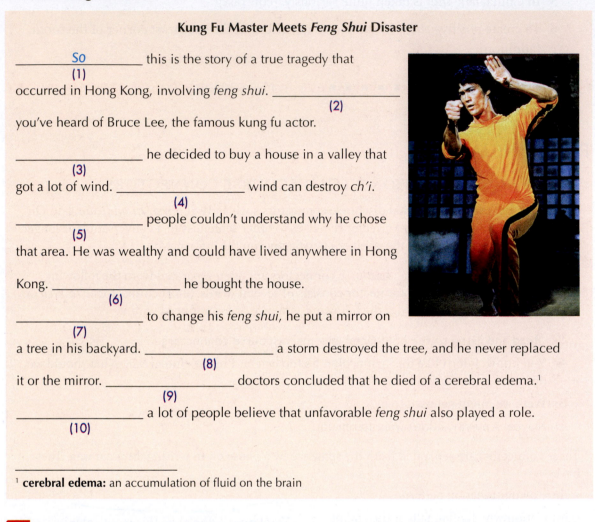

Kung Fu Master Meets *Feng Shui* Disaster

_____So_____ this is the story of a true tragedy that
(1)
occurred in Hong Kong, involving *feng shui*. _____
(2)
you've heard of Bruce Lee, the famous kung fu actor.

_____ he decided to buy a house in a valley that
(3)
got a lot of wind. _____ wind can destroy *ch'i*.
(4)
_____ people couldn't understand why he chose
(5)
that area. He was wealthy and could have lived anywhere in Hong

Kong. _____ he bought the house.
(6)
_____ to change his *feng shui*, he put a mirror on
(7)
a tree in his backyard. _____ a storm destroyed the tree, and he never replaced
(8)
it or the mirror. _____ doctors concluded that he died of a cerebral edema.[1]
(9)
_____ a lot of people believe that unfavorable *feng shui* also played a role.
(10)

_____

[1] **cerebral edema:** an accumulation of fluid on the brain

2 Read the conversation and fill in the blanks with one of the informal discourse connectors in the box. In some blanks, more than one connector is possible. Work with a partner and compare answers. Then read the conversation aloud.

Actually	Plus	So	Well

A: How can you live in this mess?

B: _____, it doesn't bother me at all.

A: _____, it looks awful. _____ it smells like dirty shoes.

B: _____ I guess you're saying I should do some cleaning.

3 Work with a partner.

Student A: Ask your partner questions about his or her surroundings.

Student B: Use an introducer to begin your answer. Then switch roles after question 4. Practice creating multi-sentence answers with informal discourse connectors and natural intonation.

Example

STUDENT A: How important is it for you to have a view in your living space?

STUDENT B: <u>Actually, it's really important. I'm living in a dorm room now, and my view is the brick wall of another building. So it really bothers me.</u>

1. How do you feel in a messy room?

2. How well can you concentrate in a noisy room?

3. How do you feel in a windowless room?

4. Can you sleep if it's noisy? Explain.

Now switch roles.

5. Can you concentrate if you're working at a messy desk? Explain.

6. How important is it for you to have an attractive living space? Workspace?

7. How important is it for you to have sunlight in your living space?

8. Do paint or furniture colors affect your mood? How?

SPEAKING SKILL

EMPHASIZING A POINT

When communicating informally with a skeptical listener, English speakers may use an emphatic speaking style. In Listening One, for example, Kirsten Lagatree knows that Sedge Thomson and many listeners may be skeptical of *feng shui*. As a result, she emphasizes her point by using emphatic expressions such as *boy* and *would no more do [this] than [that]*, and by using emphatic intonation.

🎧 Read and listen to the examples.

Examples

- "Well, **I wouldn't say** to keep out evil spirits. **But I would say** it's a system of arranging all the objects around you at home or at work."

- "He **would no more** start working on a building project without a *feng shui* master **than he would** without, you know, if it was L.A., build without a seismologist."

- "The new Regency Hotel in Singapore just opened with two beautiful fountains in the lobby. **Talk about** great *feng shui*! The hotel is booked solid for the next two months!"

- "Now, based on just simple things I've done, and also lots and lots of people I talked to for the book, **I'd have to say** it works . . . and at the very least it couldn't hurt."

- "We can't see it but, **boy**, is it there doing things!"

1 Look at the examples and explanation in the chart.

EMPHASIZING A POINT		
EXPRESSION	**EXPLANATION**	**EXAMPLE**
Boy . . .	used as an exclamation followed by an inversion, auxiliary then main verb	**Boy**, did Bruce Lee have bad luck!
I wouldn't say . . . , but I would say . . .	used to clarify the meaning	**I wouldn't say** *feng shui* is huge in the United States, **but I would say** it's becoming popular.
. . . would no more . . . than . . .	followed by something obviously unreasonable	**I would no more** hire a *feng shui* expert to design my house **than** I would hire a palm reader to predict my future.
Talk about . . .	followed by an explanation	**Talk about** a perfect location! The house was surrounded by lovely streams and beautiful gardens.
I'd have to say . . .	used to emphasize a strong point	Well, since I moved my desk to the northeast corner, **I'd have to say** my writing has improved.

2 Work with a partner.

Student A: Ask the question or make the comment.

Student B: Cover the left column. Respond emphatically or skeptically. Use an expression from the chart and appropriate intonation. Add further comments. Then switch roles after question 5. Practice choosing expressions and using intonation to emphasize your point.

Student A	**Student B**
1. You really hired a *feng shui* expert to boost profits? Did it work?	1. Boy, _____ did it _____! Profits are up 100 percent.
2. How about hiring a professional "clutter consultant" to clean the clutter out of your house? A trained professional will clear the "stuck energy" in your house and bring you instant luck.	2. Are you kidding! I would no more hire a professional "clutter consultant" than I would _____ (add something unreasonable).
3. Listen to this! You won't believe it! A Chinese American millionaire paid a *feng shui* expert $50,000 to advise him on the alignment of his building.	3. Talk about _____ (add an explanation)!
4. I think *feng shui* practitioners are nothing more than superstitious fortune tellers with a compass.	4. Well, I wouldn't say _____, but I would say _____.
5. Don't you think that *feng shui* is really more than just putting up mirrors or hanging wind chimes?	5. Absolutely! I'd have to say _____.

Now switch roles.

Student A	**Student B**
6. My friend Michael had had two robberies in his apartment. Then he used a *feng shui* expert, who advised him to set up an aquarium. He's had no robberies since.	6. That's amazing! Talk about (add an explanation)! But I don't think *feng shui* had anything to do with it.
7. Another friend added flowers, wind chimes, crystals, and mirrors in his house. Two days later, he got the biggest promotion of his life.	7. Boy, _____ (use an inversion).
8. Would you buy a house near a cemetery?	8. No, I would no more _____ than _____.

(continued on next page)

9. What do you think of other Eastern practices like *tai chi*, macrobiotic diets, and so on?

10. *Feng shui* is trendy in the West now. It'll fade in a few years.

9. Well, I'd have to say _____.

10. I wouldn't say _____, but I would say _____.

■ ■ ■ ■ ■ ■ ■ ■ ■ ■ ■ ■ ■ ■ ■ ■ ■ ■ **GO TO** MyEnglishLab **FOR MORE SKILL PRACTICE AND TO CHECK WHAT YOU LEARNED.**

FINAL SPEAKING TASK

In this activity, you will form an opinion and present an argument based on an article. Use the vocabulary, grammar, pronunciation, and listening and speaking skills that you learned in the unit.*

For years, people all over the world have believed that good *feng shui* fosters positive benefits such as health, happiness, harmony, wealth, prosperity, creativity, and respect. Individuals and families have redesigned their homes in order to create positive and auspicious energy. Corporations have rebuilt their company buildings and workspaces to create greater prosperity and magnify success.

Even educational institutions, such as schools and universities, have tried to tackle and solve major challenges by implementing *feng shui* on campus. However, *feng shui* is a controversial practice and many people are highly skeptical of its potential to create significant change.

1 Read this article, which combines elements of real cases.

New University President Plans to Implement *Feng Shui* on Campus
Government, Faculty Outraged!!

This public university, esteemed for decades for its beautiful campus and strong academic programs, appears to be in shambles: dying trees, brown lawns and withered flower beds, crumbling staircases, cracked walls, water-stained ceilings, windowless classrooms, neglected computer labs, and buildings never repaired properly following several devastating earthquakes in the 1990s. On the inside, one finds demoralized professors fleeing to teach in private universities, and unhappy students with plummeting exam scores, low job placement rates, and few acceptances to graduate programs. Enrollment is still declining, and there have been four campus-wide student strikes so far this year.

Can this picture get any worse?

As one of the oldest public universities in Latin America—once world-renowned and prestigious—this beloved university is desperate for total and complete change.

---

* For Alternative Speaking Topics, see page 119.

Can Luis Miguel Sánchez make good on his promise of change?

Hired just three months ago, Luis Miguel Sánchez, grandson of Chinese immigrants, pledged that he would succeed in transforming the university from a devastated educational institution to one the entire country could once again be proud of.

How would he do this?

He will start with 15 million dollars! Yes, it is true. The university suddenly announced that the development office had received an anonymous 15 million dollar donation from a wealthy donor of Chinese descent to renovate the university. Inspired by his 3-week trip to Shanghai and wanting to be respectful of the donor's heritage as well as the large number of students of Chinese descent at the university, the president has recommended that planners, architects, designers, and builders plan the renovation according to *feng shui* principles. What inspired him? After visiting many buildings in Shanghai, the president became convinced that *feng shui* could be the key to creating peace and harmony at home and throughout the nation. His idea was to redesign both the public display and private living areas of the university.

President Sánchez is 100 percent confident that implementing *feng shui* on campus will establish

harmony among the students, the government, and the faculty; raise academic standards; and return the university to its glory days. The student body is supportive of his innovative plans.

In stark contrast, the faculty and the government are adamantly opposed to his strategy. Skeptical of *feng shui*, they aim to renovate according to the country's history, tradition, and culture. They advocate rebuilding according to colonial architectural tradition, famous for richness and creativity. Moreover, they see *feng shui* as superstitious nonsense and doubt that adding ponds and lakes will solve the university's serious problems. Restoring the traditional décor, they believe, will bring pride, honor, and self-esteem to the entire university population and the country as a whole.

---

2 Follow the steps.

STEP 1: Divide into two groups and take these roles:

- the president and the students
- the government and the faculty

STEP 2: Using the information in the news article, each group outlines the arguments for its side.

STEP 3: Work in pairs (one from each group) to practice the arguments. Use discourse connectors, informal discourse connectors, and expressions for emphasizing a point.

(continued on next page)

STEP 4: Conduct the meeting in which both groups present their opinions. Use discourse connectors, informal discourse connectors, and expressions for emphasizing a point.

STEP 5: As a class, vote on how the president should handle the donation.

UNIT PROJECT

Choose a topic and follow the steps for researching it.

Topic 1: Exploring Other Ancient Traditions That Have Traveled West

Besides *feng shui*, other traditional Eastern practices have become popular in the West. Examples are *tai chi, yoga, reiki, shiatsu* massage, *karate*, and *tae kwon do*.

STEP 1: Conduct an interview. Try to find someone who practices one of these arts. Look for either a professional or an amateur. Ask friends or neighbors, or look online, in the telephone book, or a local business directory.

STEP 2: Work with a partner. Brainstorm a list of questions that you would like to ask the practitioner. For example:

- How did you get into this practice?

- How and why did this art become popular in the West?

- How is it practiced differently here? Why do you suppose it is practiced differently in the West?

STEP 3: Interview the person and take notes.

STEP 4: Report your findings to the class.

Topic 2: Internet Research

In the past few years, the popularity of *feng shui* has skyrocketed all over the world. Many people are studying *feng shui* and applying its principles in order to improve their lives. However, some people think these principles are being exploited for commercial reasons. For example, a cosmetics company recently launched a new line of makeup called "*feng shui* makeup." Company representatives claim that this new makeup contains the right *feng shui* "balance" of colors and texture to guide the user through a smooth or rocky passage as her face ages.

STEP 1: You can find many of these kinds of products on the Internet. Do research to find the most unusual applications of *feng shui*. What is your opinion of them? Take notes.

STEP 2: Prepare a short research summary and report your findings and opinions to the class.

ALTERNATIVE SPEAKING TOPICS

Talk about one of the topics. Use grammar and vocabulary from the unit.

Topic 1

Work with a small group. Read the following quotes that discuss the relationship between people and place (our homes, communities, environment). Paraphrase each quote. What does it mean, in other words? Comment on each quote. How do you feel about it?

Discuss this general question: How does the environment in which you live, study, or work affect you? In your discussion, use ideas, vocabulary, grammar, pronunciation, and expressions for emphasizing a point.

"As places around us change—both the communities that shelter us and the larger regions that support them—we all undergo changes inside. This means that whatever we experience in a place is both a serious environmental issue and a deeply personal one."

—Tony Hiss, *The Experience of Place*

"The basic principle that links our places and states is simple: A good or bad environment promotes good or bad memories, which inspire a good or bad mood, which inclines us toward good or bad behavior. The mere presence of sunlight increases our willingness to help strangers and tip waiters, and people working in a room slowly permeated by the odor of burnt dust lose their appetites, even though they don't notice the smell. On some level, states and places are internal and external versions of each other."

—Winifred Gallagher, *The Power of Place*

Topic 2

Discuss the questions in small groups.

What do you suppose leads Westerners to adopt Eastern practices, such as yoga, *feng shui*, meditation, and so on? In what ways does a traditional Eastern practice tend to change when it becomes Westernized? What might be positive and negative aspects?

GO TO MyEnglishLab TO DISCUSS ONE OF THE ALTERNATIVE TOPICS, WATCH A VIDEO ABOUT THE TRADITIONS OF JAPANESE GARDENS, AND TAKE THE UNIT 4 ACHIEVEMENT TEST.

BUSINESS NOT AS Usual

1 FOCUS ON THE TOPIC

1. Look at the photo and the title of the unit. What might it be like to work at this company? Why? What do you think the title of the unit means?

2. Think about a company whose products or services you use often, or a company where you have worked. How would you describe the experience either from an employee's or a customer's perspective? What are some positive things you experienced? Some negative? What would it be like to work there? How would you describe the values of this company?

3. Professor Peter Jackson, author of *Maps of Meaning: An Introduction to Cultural Geography*, said, "Cultures are maps of meaning through which the world is intelligible." The CEO of the company in the photo has created a unique "map of meaning" or special "corporate culture." What do you think "corporate culture" means? How can a company have a "culture"?

GO TO MyEnglishLab *TO CHECK WHAT YOU KNOW.*

VOCABULARY

🎧 Read and listen to this introduction to a popular best-selling business book on corporate culture in business today. Pay attention to the **bold-faced** words and phrases. Then read the list of definitions that follow. Work with a partner. Write the number of the bold-faced word or phrase next to its definition.

Corporate Culture: Going Above and Beyond

In order to improve **(1) productivity**, increase **(2) revenues**, and boost profits, some companies have created workplaces that communicate a certain set of values.

The term "corporate culture" refers to this set of values, customs, or traditions that make a company unique. The founders or leaders of the company create a corporate culture that represents their **(3) enduring** vision or long-lasting mission of the company. These leaders are convinced that in order to protect the **(4) bottom line**, it is critical to **(5) get** the culture, the values that contribute to the culture, exactly **right**.

Research suggests that a strong corporate culture may offer benefits such as:

- Competitive advantage from improved customer service
- A strong team atmosphere
- High employee morale with strong commitment to goals
- Top employee performance
- Creativity and innovation

With a lot of **(6) first-hand** knowledge and experience, many **(7) management gurus** offer unique **(8) insights** into the importance of building a strong corporate culture. **(9) By virtue of** the fact that there is a strong correlation between culture and organizational performance, these gurus recommend ongoing assessment of the corporate culture.

One manager reported receiving an email from an employee who clearly demonstrated the positive impact she felt from working in a place compatible with her own values and priorities:

"Our culture is home. It is where I want to be. It's not anything big, but you know the saying, 'it's the little things.' For example, I am not afraid of openly **(10) chit-chatting** with colleagues near our **(11) cubicles**. My manager knows we don't simply clock in and clock out. We **(12) do favors for** each other, enjoy an occasional after work **(13) happy hour**, and support each others' goals **(14) day in and day out**. We stay positive and optimistic, avoiding imagining **(15) worst-case scenarios**, such as a sudden drop in profits or some kind of financial scandal.

"What makes this company different? It is simple. We want to go above and beyond."

_____ **a.** all the time

_____ **b.** because of

_____ **c.** business experts

_____ **d.** casually talking

_____ **e.** directly experienced

_____ **f.** help

_____ **g.** income

_____ **h.** long lasting

_____ **i.** make accurate

_____ **j.** (the) most undesirable possible outcomes

_____ **k.** net or final income or loss

_____ **l.** outputs

_____ **m.** small offices without doors

_____ **n.** (a) time to have a cocktail around 5 P.M.

_____ **o.** understanding the true nature of something

■ ■■■■■■■■ GO TO MyEnglishLab FOR MORE VOCABULARY PRACTICE.

PREVIEW

You are going to listen to an interview with Tony Hsieh, the CEO of Zappos, an online shoe company. Hsieh talks about how other companies have applied some of Zappos's ideas in order to improve business.

Listen to this excerpt from the interview. Work with a partner to predict how Atlantic Refrigeration Company's business improved when it focused on building a strong corporate culture. Think about the impact on customers, employees, profits, etc.

1. customers: _customer service improved_ _____

2. employees: _____

3. profits: _____

4. _____

5. _____

MAIN IDEAS

1 Listen to the interview. Look again at your predictions from the Preview section. How did your predictions help you understand the interview?

2 Complete the following "sentence starters" to capture the main idea of each part of the interview.

Part One

The Zappos office call center differs from most other generic call centers in that

_____

Part Two

Hsieh believes that it is important to build an effective corporate culture because

_____

Part Three

When asked how the Zappos culture affects productivity, Hsieh responded

_____

Part Four

Zappos consists of two business operations: one _____

and the other _____.

DETAILS

 Read the statements. Then listen to each part of the interview and circle the letter of the correct answer. Compare your answers with those of another student.

Part One

1. At the main Zappos office in Las Vegas, employees spend time doing a variety of activities EXCEPT _____.

   a. handling merchandise returns

   b. playing games during work hours

   c. trying shoes on customers

2. The interviewer describes various motifs in which Zappos's employees decorate their cubicles. These include all EXCEPT _____.

   a. space aliens

   b. life in the 1960s

   c. surfing culture

Part Two

3. Zappos helps people understand their culture by offering _____.

   a. 60 tours of their offices each week

   b. 16 tours of Las Vegas and the offices each week

   c. 16 tours of their offices each week

4. Hsieh encourages employees to take a 20-minute nap each day because they will be _____.

   a. more awake at work

   b. more productive at work

   c. healthier at work

5. Tony Hsieh, the CEO, works in _____.

   a. a private office away from the workers' cubicles

   b. a cubicle called "Tony Hsieh's office"

   c. a cubicle decorated with jungle vines

Part Three

6. The interviewer is curious about how productive Zappos workers are because he observes employees who _____.

   a. are chatting with customers on the phone

   b. pretend to be selling buy may not be

   c. are attending a party down the hallway

7. New managers at Zappos are encouraged to spend 10-20 percent of their time _____.

   a. observing experienced managers

   b. out of the office socializing with their employees

   c. bowling with other new managers

(continued on next page)

8. Managers say that the Zappos culture does make workers more productive. When asked the question, "How much more productive?" these managers say _____.

    a. between 20 and 100 percent more productive

    b. a little more than 20 percent

    c. nearly 100 percent

9. The unique culture created at Zappos makes it a great place to work. In addition, it _____.

    a. has a negative impact on profits

    b. has a positive impact on profits

    c. has neither a positive nor negative impact on profits

Part Four

10. Tony Hsieh has written a book to help other people and companies learn how to _____.

    a. make work more fun and enjoyable

    b. build a corporate culture

    c. make employees happy

11. According to Tony, a strong culture can best be built in companies that are _____.

    a. new, innovative, and young

    b. led by a strong leader like Hsieh

    c. both Internet and non-Internet based

GO TO MyEnglishLab *FOR MORE LISTENING PRACTICE.*

MAKE INFERENCES

EXPRESSIVE INTONATION

Kai Ryssdal, the radio journalist who speaks with Tony Hsieh, demonstrates a lively and enthusiastic style. When commenting or questioning, Ryssdal conveys an underlying point of view through his expressive tone of voice. Rather than speaking in a monotone in which all words sound nearly alike, Ryssdal uses expressive voice techniques emphasizing certain words. He makes them longer and louder.

🎧 Read and listen to this example. Pay attention to the expressive quality of Ryssdal's questions or comments in order to infer his message. Then answer the question and read the explanation.

Example

RYSSDAL: That is just the way CEO Tony Hsieh wants it.

His underlying message is that Tony Hsieh would like to work in an environment which is

a. well-designed.

b. theme-based.

c. fun and different.

The answer is *c*. Ryssdal emphasizes the word "that" in referring to the unusual office environment in which Hsieh works.

🎧 Listen to each excerpt. Notice Ryssdal's expressive tone of voice and infer his underlying message from the words he emphasizes.

Excerpt One

1. On the tour, the different shoe departments greet Ryssdal with different kinds of noises. Ryssdal's reaction to the noisy greetings and his emphasis on the word "are" implies he is _____.

   a. confident the noise makers get their work done

   b. somewhat confident the noise makers eventually get their work done

   c. doubtful the noise makers get their work done

Excerpt Two

2. Ryssdal's last sentence emphasizing "all this" and "day in and day out" selling shoes implies that Ryssdal believes that productivity is _____.

   a. enhanced by the Zappos office atmosphere

   b. not affected by the Zappos office atmosphere

   c. reduced by the Zappos office atmosphere

(continued on next page)

3. Ryssdal emphasizes the "you" at the end of his sentence to imply Zappos's success is due primarily to Tony's _____.

    a. business and leadership skills

    b. public image as a management guru, or expert

    c. personality and charm

EXPRESS OPINIONS

First, work individually. Read the statements and write **A** (agree) or **D** (disagree) next to each one. Then, work in small groups to discuss your opinion about each statement.

_____ **1.** Building the culture of a company should be the number one priority for any chief executive officer (CEO).

_____ **2.** Working in a party-like, fun atmosphere such as the one that exists at Zappos would work in cultures and countries that are familiar to me.

_____ **3.** Productivity doesn't decrease in a fun, lively, wildly decorated office such as the one described in Zappos.

_____ **4.** Cultivating close friendships and socializing outside the office help improve the bottom line.

_____ **5.** Office architecture affects collaboration and the bottom line. Instead of offices with closed doors, it is better for business to work in open cubicles.

_____ **6.** More CEOs should follow Tony's example and sit in a cubicle next to employees rather than have their own private corner office with a closed door.

GO TO MyEnglishLab **TO GIVE YOUR OPINION ABOUT ANOTHER QUESTION.**

VOCABULARY

In Listening Two, Harvard University business professor and author Teresa Amabile presents a short commentary on her view of what factors motivate employees to perform at their best. With co-author, Steven Kramer, Amabile wrote a book, *The Progress Principle: Using Small Wins to Ignite Joy, Engagement, and Creativity at Work*. To research the book, the authors collected diary reports from hundreds of employees. They asked employees to respond to questions about their "inner work life" or the thoughts, feelings, and motivations of employees as they react to what happens to them during their work day.

1 🎧 The **bold-faced** words will appear in the next listening selection. Notice them as you read and listen to Daniel Lee's "work diary" response to the question, "Briefly describe one event from today that stands out in your mind."

Today, our whole team met to talk about the latest **setback** in the development of the new vocabulary learning app. With progress **stalled** on the technical side, the new team leader conveyed his disappointment in the **incremental** progress we have made. (He was harsh and unsympathetic!) My colleagues and I are fed up with the lack of **autonomy** he gives us to drive the development process. We blame him for the technical problems. In spite of the perks I enjoy here—like the free lunch, and discounted day care, and the **intangibles** such as a relaxed environment and nice colleagues—this new guy is really not motivating me.

2 Match the words on the left with the definitions or synonyms on the right. Write the corresponding letter in the blank.

_____ **1.** autonomy   **a.** paused

_____ **2.** incremental   **b.** independence

_____ **3.** intangibles   **c.** a reversal in progress

_____ **4.** setback   **d.** benefits not easily defined or measured

_____ **5.** stalled   **e.** gradual

COMPREHENSION

Harvard business professor, Teresa Amabile, and her research team analyzed nearly 12,000 work diaries from professionals in seven different companies. Put a check (✓) next to the research findings Amabile mentions in her commentary.

_____ **1.** The best places to work are ones that offer lots of perks and intangible rewards.

_____ **2.** If employees are successful at work, they will be more engaged and motivated.

_____ **3.** Managers need to move forward on work they care about to engage employees.

_____ **4.** Incremental "small wins" don't have much of an impact on motivation.

_____ **5.** The negative effect of setbacks is just as strong as the positive effect of progress.

_____ **6.** Good managers help their employees make progress every day.

_____ **7.** Goals and autonomy promote creativity and productivity.

_____ **8.** Perks, such as gourmet food and game time, help employees meet their productivity goals.

_____ **9.** Making progress towards goals is what keeps employees motivated.

GO TO MyEnglishLab FOR MORE VOCABULARY PRACTICE.

LISTENING SKILL

CONCEDING AND PRESENTING A COUNTERARGUMENT

In the second listening selection, Teresa Amabile presents her view on what drives employees to perform their best. As a commentator, she uses an effective technique.

- First, she **concedes**, or acknowledges, what the listener might think.
- Then she immediately **presents a counterargument** from her research.

By setting up this contrast, she shows that her research findings may be counterintuitive. In other words, the results are important because they may not be what the listener would typically think.

🎧 Read and listen to the example. Then answer the questions and read the explanation.

Example

AMABILE: The list might make you conclude that the best workplaces have fantastic perks and lots of fun every day. Sure, the techies at Google love the free gourmet food, and Zappos employees get a kick out of playing Nerf Dart war. But all of that misses the most important element of employee engagement: helping them succeed at work that matters.

1. First, Amabile **concedes** that perks are fantastic. However, her research has shown something else.

   What is Amabile's **counterargument**? _____

2. What specific language does she use to **set up the contrast and introduce her**

   counterargument? _____

Amabile first **concedes** that the best workplaces have fantastic perks and lots of fun every day. Then she **sets up the contrast and introduces her counterargument** by saying, "**But** all of that misses the most important element . . ." Notice that her use of *but* sets up the contrast between the concession and the counterargument: that helping employees succeed at work is what really matters.

🎧 Read the questions and then listen to the excerpts. Then, summarize the counterargument in a single sentence. Finally, identify the language used to set up the contrast and introduce the counterargument.

Excerpt One

1. First, Amabile concedes that "the progress principle" may sound like just another business term. However, her research has shown something else.

   counterargument:

   _____

   language that sets up the contrast and introduces the counterargument:

   _____

Excerpt Two

2. First, Amabile concedes that perks, like gourmet food and game time, are great. However, her research has shown something else.

counterargument:

_____

language that sets up the contrast and introduces the counterargument:

_____

■ **GO TO** MyEnglishLab **FOR MORE SKILL PRACTICE.**

CONNECT THE LISTENINGS

STEP 1: Organize

Using the information in Listenings One and Two, complete the chart. Use information that is directly stated and information that is implied.

	HSIEH'S POINT OF VIEW CEO of Zappos Shoes ACTUAL BUSINESS CASE	AMABILE'S POINT OF VIEW Professor at Harvard RESEARCH
1. Means to achieve productivity	Let employees have happiness and fun in the workplace	
2. Relationship of managers to employees		Guide employees to set goals/ measure their progress Goal and vision setter/supporter of goals
3. Guiding business principle		

STEP 2: Synthesize

Work with a partner to role-play this job interview for a management position at Zappos. Use the information to start and then continue the conversation.

Student A: You are the interviewer from Zappos. Ask questions on the three themes in the chart on the previous page. Find out whether this person could fit into your corporate culture.

Student B: You are the job candidate, a new graduate from Harvard Business School. Answer questions from Amabile's point of view. You studied her research, believe it, and want to work in a company that applies it.

Example

Student A: Thanks for applying for the Zappos position. As I'm sure you know, we really believe that employees do best when they are happy and having fun. This is key to our corporate culture. How do you feel about this for yourself?

Student B: Well, it sounds nice and could work, but I've studied with Amabile at Harvard, whose research. . . .

■■■■■■■■■■■■■■■■■■■■■■■■■■■■■■■■■■■■ *GO TO* MyEnglishLab *TO CHECK WHAT YOU LEARNED.*

3 FOCUS ON SPEAKING

VOCABULARY

REVIEW

The Progress Principle: Using Small Wins to Ignite Joy, Engagement, and Creativity at Work, by Teresa Amabile and Steven Kramer, emerged as one of the top customer's favorite business books on several online booksellers' websites.

Working with another student, fill in the blanks in the online customer reviews on the next page with the correct form of the words or phrases from the box.

autonomy	first-hand	revenue
bottom line	get (something) right	setbacks
chit-chats	incremental	stalled
cubicles	insights	worst-case scenarios
day in and day out	intangibles	
enduring	productivity	

Home • My Books • Recommendations • Explore

Customer Reviews

★★★★⯪ (28)   4.6 out of 5 stars   <u>See all 42 customer reviews</u>

Most Helpful Customer Reviews

98 of 100 people found the following review helpful
★★★★★ **A Brilliant Piece of Work** <u>Richard T. Sutter April 6th</u>

With *The Progress Principle*, Amabile and Kramer really **(1)** _____. Unlike many

other business books which are based on lighthearted anecdotes or half-baked research, the

authors gathered a huge volume of **(2)** _____ accounts to provide clear evidence

of the importance of "small wins" to boost **(3)** _____ which hopefully results in

increased **(4)** _____. One of my biggest takeaways was the authors' focus on the

importance of **(5)** _____ such as interpersonal support and recognition for good

work. These incentives don't cost a company a dime, yet they have a huge impact on

motivation. I have only one small complaint: It would have been nice if the authors had included

not just success stories, but also examples of failed attempts to motivate employees, in other

words some **(6)** _____. Learning from failures is useful.

Was this review helpful to you?   Yes   No

18 of 19 people found the following review helpful
★★★★★ **Progress on Progress** <u>Hyun Ju Kim April 4th</u>

This is one of the most important business books ever written. Based on rigorous evidence,

it offers deep **(7)** _____ into employee motivation and emotions. I must admit that

I was one of the 238 people who participated in the multi-year study, which tracked our

activities **(8)** _____. All 238 participants in the study worked in 26 project teams

at 7 companies in 3 different industries. At the end of each day, we sat in our

(9) _____ and emailed a diary entry to the authors who reported on our

achievements, our **(10)** _____, and even our casual **(11)** _____ next

to the water cooler. An engaging read from cover to cover. Highly recommend it!

Was this review helpful to you?   Yes   No

★★★★☆ **Ground-breaking research** <u>Mohammed Assaf</u> <u>August 28th</u>

This gem of a book presents a simple message: Companies can definitely improve their

(12) _____ not by pushing their employees to work harder or longer or

motivating them with promises of promotions and perks; rather, counterintuitive though it

may be, employees will be motivated most effectively if they feel they are making

(13) _____ progress step-by-step towards a goal. When their efforts are

(14) _____ or diverted, or when their managers refuse to give them the

(15) _____ to make decisions, employee productivity will be affected.

What truly inspires and motivates employees are "small wins" leading towards positive results.

The authors present a compelling and **(16)** _____ message that all managers

should follow.

Was this review helpful to you?   Yes   No

EXPAND

In addition to its unique corporate culture, Zappos is also famous for providing outstanding customer service to its millions of online shoe customers. Thousands of Zappos customers responded to an email asking them to provide feedback regarding the telephone conversation they had with the customer service representative when they ordered their shoes.

1 The following excerpts from these emails include idioms used frequently in business contexts. Notice the **bold-faced** phrase in each sentence and try to guess its meaning. Work with a partner and compare your ideas.

1. **MELANIE:** Tanya answered my call with a warm, "Hello. I am Tanya, and I am here to help you." Honestly, I was totally **(1) caught off guard** by this friendly and helpful attitude. Panicked and rushed, I had to get shoes immediately for my sister's wedding in three days and was clueless about what to buy. Tanya **(2) got the ball rolling** by asking me a lot of questions about my dress, wedding location, and so on. Then I asked Tanya a dozen questions in return. She **(3) fielded all of my questions** with patience and knowledge. She is living proof of Zappos's motto: "Delivering 'wow' through service."

   1. _____

   2. _____

   3. _____

(continued on next page)

Business Not as Usual   **135**

2. ANNA: No other online company compares to Zappos. It is simply **(4) in a league of its own**. I have ordered shoes, gloves, handbags—you name it—from Zappos and not a single customer service rep has ever **(5) dropped the ball**. I had some bad experiences with other online retailers and nearly decided never to shop online again. Clearly, Zappos's extraordinary customer service **(6) gives them an edge** over other online retailers.

4. _____

5. _____

6. _____

3. NASIR: Outstanding service! The very best! When it comes to customer service, there is no doubt that Zappos **(7) means business**. Every employee knows that great service affects **(8) the bottom line**. Last week, I had to call Zappos to return the sneakers I bought. Because of bad customer service experiences with many other companies, I just expected to **(9) get the runaround** and be transferred to several other people before someone could help me. Well, the opposite happened! The Zappos rep handled the call with efficiency as well as humor. On the call, I sensed the Zappos value to "create fun and a little weirdness." Now I am a Zapposholic!

7. _____

8. _____

9. _____

2 Work with a partner.

Student A: Ask Student B questions 1–5. Check Student B's answers with the correct answer in parentheses. ONLY look at your questions and do not write.

Student B: Cover the left column. Answer Student A's questions filling in the blank with one of the idioms in the box. Listen to Student A's questions carefully. Do not write. Then switch roles after question 5.

The first one has been done for you.

bottom line	field questions	give someone/something an edge
catch off guard	get the ball rolling	league of one's own
drop the ball	get the runaround	mean business

Student A

1. At Zappos, do employees always know what to expect, or does Hsieh surprise them sometimes? (catch the employees off guard)

2. Can you recall a time when you had to answer a series of questions from someone? (field a lot of questions)

3. What do you when a member of a team you're on doesn't do his share? (drops the ball)

4. What do you do when a salesperson fails to help you with a problem? (get the runaround)

5. In your opinion, what do you think most companies should do to stay profitable? (bottom line)

Now change roles.

6. How do you get a meeting started? (to get the ball rolling)

7. Besides Zappos, can you think of another online retailer that is a market leader? (league of its own)

Student B

1. Well, sometimes, he likes to do something new and _catch the employees off guard_.

2. Sure, once when I interviewed for a job, I had to _____.

3. Hmmm . . . good question. When a teammate _____, I usually try to find out what happened and help if possible.

4. Well, whenever I _____ from a salesperson, I try to find the manager to complain.

5. That's an easy one. To maintain their _____, most companies should simply not spend more than they earn.

6. OK. _____, I just say, "Let's start!" I also always start on time.

7. Sure. In the world of online bookselling, Amazon is clearly in a _____.

(continued on next page)

8. How did the coffee barista know the manager was serious about firing him? (meant business)

9. How does your favorite airline set itself above and beyond the others? (gives it an edge)

8. It was easy to tell he _____ when he walked in the shop and started yelling at the poor guy.

9. Flying National Air is a pleasure. Great customer service _____.

CREATE

Work with a partner to conduct this role play.

Student A: You are a business professor at Harvard Business School (HBS) and a close colleague of Teresa Amabile. You are going to teach a new course at HBS called " Passion, Productivity, and Profits in Business: Keys to Success." Although you know a lot about Amabile's research and agree with her conclusions, you would like to take a tour of Zappos in Las Vegas to learn more about the culture Hsieh has built.

Student B: You are a Zappos Insights Culture Magician, the official title of a tour guide who hosts visitors to Zappos's headquarters in Las Vegas.

First, write the conversation using the directions and the vocabulary in the chart. Then give a dramatic presentation of the conversation to the class.

CULTURE MAGICIAN	PROFESSOR
Greet the professor and state objectives of tour. *Hello, Professor. Glad you could come to Zappos. Now, to get the ball rolling, let me. . . .* **insights, first hand, field questions, get the ball rolling**	Express appreciation and state your goals for the tour. *Well, to begin, let me say thanks for having me. Here at Zappos, you've obviously gotten something right. I want to see how culture connects to productivity of your employees. Also, . . .* **get something right, productivity, revenues**
Give a quick introduction to the Zappos culture. **bottom line, enduring, in a league of our own**	Ask about the physical appearance of the offices—the decorations, the noises, etc. **cubicles, chit-chatting**
Answer the professor's question. **mean business, day in and day out, do favors**	Challenge the "fun atmosphere" by referring to Amabile's research. **by virtue of, drop the ball, give an edge**
Respond by defending Zappos. Also say you need to take a short break now in the tour. **throw in the towel, in the black, management guru**	Express appreciation for the information. **catch off guard, in the red, hit it out of the park**

■■■■■■■■■■■■■■■■■■■■■■■■■■■■■■■■■■■■ *GO TO* MyEnglishLab *FOR MORE VOCABULARY PRACTICE.*

GRAMMAR

1 Work with a partner. Examine the passage, which includes both **direct** and **indirect** speech. Then answer the questions that follow.

The interviewer, Kai Ryssdal, asked Tony Hsieh a question: "What role has your public profile played in Zappos's success?" He replied, "Well, I don't think my public profile has made the difference. As I have said, I have helped create a positive corporate culture. In addition, we actually have a separate entity called Zappos Insights, and we help other companies figure out their own values and develop their own strong cultures." Tony also reported that some of these companies had been suspicious of Zappos's values. They said, "OK, glad you have this strong culture, Zappos. Happy for you, but this would never work in another industry, such as a non-Internet company."

1. Why do you think some of the statements have quotation marks and some do not?

2. What do you think are some differences between the direct quotations and the other statements?

DIRECT AND INDIRECT SPEECH

To add variety and interest when you tell a story or report information, use a combination of direct and indirect speech. **Direct speech** is a quotation of someone's exact words. **Indirect speech** reports or tells what someone said without using the person's exact words. When you use indirect speech, try to vary the reporting verbs. Choose expressive verbs such as *complain*, *mention*, *remark*, *answer*, *reply*, *predict*, *deny*, *explain*, *wonder*, *question*, *add*, *respond*, *comment*, *observe*, and *continue*.

Look at the rules and examples for changing direct speech to indirect speech.

	Direct Speech	Indirect Speech
Statements Shift tense back (for example, from past to past perfect). Make appropriate pronoun and adverb changes.	The sleep researcher commented enthusiastically, "A daily power nap **can** enhance productivity."	The researcher commented **that** a daily power nap **could** enhance productivity.
Questions *Yes / No questions:* Do not use **say**. Use **if** or **whether**.	The CEO asked the sleep researcher, "**Will** a daily power nap interfere with nighttime sleep?"	The CEO asked the sleep researcher **if** a daily power nap **would** interfere with nighttime sleep.
Wh- questions: Do not use **say**. Use statement word order.	The CEO asked the researcher, "**When is** the best time of day for power napping?"	The CEO asked the researcher **when** the best time of day **was** for power napping.
Commands Use **not** + **infinitive** with negative commands or other imperative verb forms.	The sleep expert warned the employees, "**Do not drink** coffee or alcohol at lunch."	The researcher warned the employees **not to drink** coffee or alcohol at lunch.

2 Work with a partner. Read the interview transcripts on page 141.

Student A: Read Part One of the interview transcript silently. Then share the information you learned with Student B using direct and indirect speech and a variety of reporting verbs. (See the chart above.)

Student B: Read Part Two of the interview silently. After Student A has finished retelling Part One, retell the second part of the interview using direct and indirect speech and a variety of reporting verbs. (See the chart above.)

Then switch partners and roles. Finally, discuss your opinion of the information.

Part One

Su-Min Kim (CNN reporter):   Dr. Suarez, thanks very much for agreeing to this interview. I've heard a lot about your research.

Dr. Federico Suarez (sleep scientist):   It's a pleasure to speak with you.

Kim: OK. First question: Why are many companies encouraging their employees to nap during work hours?

Suarez: Well, there's been a lot of research done on the effects of exhausted workers. In fact, tired workers may cost businesses up to 150 billion dollars a year in lost productivity.

Kim: Really? That's hard to believe!

Suarez: Some studies have shown that to be true. In addition, a good nap can recharge both mind and body.

Kim: Should everyone stop drinking coffee and take a power nap instead?

Suarez: No, don't do that! Simply cut down on coffee AND take that nap.

Part Two

Kim: Excellent. Does that mean employers need to provide a special napping "office" equipped with a bed, soft music, herbal tea, and lavender aromatherapy?

Suarez: Well, they don't have to go that far. However, some companies, like Google, are offering napping rooms with special chairs, plants, and soothing blue paint on the walls.

Kim: I'll need to convince my own boss to do this. Remind me here: What are the main benefits again of napping?

Suarez: You need sleep to learn, sustain productivity, and do "on your feet thinking." Don't worry. Most employees won't need convincing. They will want to nap.

Kim: And when exactly is the best time for employees to nap?

Suarez: We haven't been able to pinpoint the exact "best time." However, I guess it's somewhere between 1 and 3 P.M., sometime after lunch.

GO TO MyEnglishLab FOR MORE GRAMMAR PRACTICE.

PRONUNCIATION

1 🎧 Look at the diagrams of the mouth, and listen to the words.

VOWELS

/æ/ c<u>a</u>t	/ɑ/ c<u>o</u>t	/ə/ c<u>u</u>t
Your mouth is open.	Your mouth is open wide.	Your mouth is almost closed.
Your lips are spread.	Your lips are not spread.	Your lips are not spread.

---

2 🎧 Listen to the words and repeat them.

	/æ/	/ɑ/	/ə/
1.	cat	cot	cut
2.	cap	cop	cup
3.	lack	lock	luck
4.	Nat	not	nut
5.	hat	hot	hut
6.	lag	log	lug

3 🎧 Listen to the words from Exercise 2 and circle the words that you hear.

4 Work with a partner.

1. Choose a set of words from Exercise 2 and say them to your partner. Your partner will check the shape of your mouth with the diagrams at the top of the page.

2. Say any word from Exercise 2. Your partner will point to the word. Then switch roles.

5 🎧 Listen and repeat the phrases. Then work with a partner. Write the phrase under the correct vowel pattern in the chart.

a challenging task	a savvy manager	happy customers
a candy company	a tough job	lack of money
a cultural struggle	consultants' money	love of company
a dozen brands	cultural values	lunchtime conversation
afternoon chit-chat	fun products	napping strategy

CUP–CUP /ə/–/ə/	CAP-CAP /æ/–/æ/	CUP–COP /ə/–/ɑ/	CUP–CAP /ə/–/æ/	CAP–CUP /æ/–/ə/
cultural struggle				

6 🎧 A *tongue twister* is a phrase with many similar sounds that is difficult to say quickly. Listen to these tongue twisters. Practice saying them as quickly as possible.

1. The bad boss banned bottles and batteries in the lab lunchroom.

2. Can't Connie cut the customer's conversation?

3. She says she sells success to access success.

4. Bigger business isn't better business but better business brings bigger rewards.

SPEAKING SKILL

MAKING A CONCESSION TO INTRODUCE A COUNTERARGUMENT

Notice the **bold-faced** and <u>underlined</u> words or phrases in the sentences.

- We discovered something we call the progress principle. **That may sound like "management speak" to you**, <u>but here's the thing</u>: It really is all about management.

- **Sure, cool perks are great. Who doesn't want gourmet food and game time?** <u>But</u> it's the feeling of getting somewhere that keeps people jazzed about what they do at work.

- **Some may think that a "Zappos-like" culture can only succeed in an Internet company**, <u>but they simply have not witnessed</u> the strong impact such a culture has had on non-Internet companies.

The bold-faced language exemplifies the speaker's concession. The speaker is saying, "I know you might be thinking *x*, but I have a different idea, *y*. This technique is often used for the purposes of:

- getting the listener's attention
- showing respect for the listener's opinion

The underlined language in each example sets up the contrast and introduces the counterargument. Once the speaker has gotten the listener's attention and shown respect for the listener's opinion, it is easier for the speaker to present the counterargument. This technique helps increase the likelihood of the listener understanding and agreeing with the speaker.

Look at the expressions below for making a concession and presenting a counterargument.

Making a Concession	Introducing a Counterargument
It may sound like . . .	But, here's the thing . . .
Sure . . . Who doesn't. . . .	But . . .
Some may think that . . .	But they simply . . .
It's understandable you think . . .	However. . . .
Some may say . . .	That said . . .

Work with a partner and follow the steps.

STEP 1: Select one of the companies with a unique culture. Read the list of characteristics that create the corporate culture for each company.

1. **Google** (http://www.google.com)

PERK OR INTANGIBLE	CULTURAL VALUE
fast-paced environment	speed produces results
free meditation classes several times/week	self-knowledge generates harmony
nap pods or small napping cubicles	sufficient rest enhances productivity
demanding bosses	nothing is impossible
dogs allowed at work	happiness promotes creativity

2. **Evernote:** technology company with over 330 employees offering award-winning digital tools for note-taking and saving information. (http://www.evernote.com)

PERK OR INTANGIBLE	CULTURAL VALUE
no offices or other status symbols	everyone is equally important
no desktop phones—cell phones only	efficiency improves business
unlimited vacation policy	just get the work done
short emails encouraged; long emails discouraged	excellent communication skills enhance productivity

3. **Terracycle:** global recycling company with over 100 employees operating in 20 countries. Their motto is "reduce, reuse, respect." (www.terracycle.com)

PERK OR INTANGIBLE	CULTURAL VALUE
building and offices made of recycled material built by employees	office itself should reflect core business model: reduce, reuse, respect
walls beautifully decorated with graffiti and other art provided by local artists	art inspires creativity and shows community support
discounted lunch for employees who eat together	teamwork promotes results
part-time "Director of Fun" to plan social events	happiness promotes creativity
financial transparency to all employees	everyone is equally important

STEP 2: Imagine you are recruiters for this company and have been asked to give a two-minute presentation about your company at a university job fair. With your partner, practice your presentation using the language of concession and counterargument. Take turns.

STEP 3: Work with a pair that has chosen a different company. Deliver your presentation to the other pair. Imagine that they are prospective employees whom you would like to recruit. Each partner in your pair must speak.

Example

Google

PERK OR INTANGIBLE	CULTURAL VALUE
1. fast-paced environment	1. speed produces results

GOOGLE RECRUITER: We know that with your skills, you can choose your company, but we want you to know that it's really great to work at Google. **It may sound like we have a very fast-paced environment**, and, in fact, we do, <u>but here's the thing: it really produces results</u>.

■■■■■■■■■■■■■■■ *GO TO* MyEnglishLab *FOR MORE SKILL PRACTICE AND TO CHECK WHAT YOU LEARNED.*

FINAL SPEAKING TASK

*In this activity you are going to give a short presentation about how to repair the corporate culture of a business whose revenue and profitability have plummeted over the past year. Moonbucks is an amalgam of actual companies. Play the role of consultants who have been hired to help repair the company culture. The new management team believes problems with company culture have caused the decline in business. Use the vocabulary, grammar, pronunciation, and listening and speaking skills that you learned in this unit.**

Follow the steps.

_____

*For Alternative Speaking Topics, see page 150.

STEP 1: Read the case and the brief description of the problem.

Brew Mountain Coffee, a small chain of family-owned coffee shops located in the heart of downtown San José, Costa Rica, has been a city landmark and popular tourist destination for three decades. A year ago, the owners, the Hernández family, sold the chain of 8 shops to the large coffee management corporation Moonbucks, based in São Paolo, Brazil. This large global coffee conglomerate, Moonbucks, manages coffee chains throughout Latin America and is a well-known competitor to Starbucks. Brew Mountain had been the pride and joy of San José, offering a friendly, warm atmosphere for tourists and residents to enjoy fresh roasted, environmentally friendly coffee along with local baked goods. The coffee, food, staff, and atmosphere all contributed towards differentiating Brew Mountain from the cookie cutter chains which the city council has fought hard to keep out of San José.

However, a year later, coffee isn't the only thing brewing at Brew Mountain. Trouble is brewing! Customers are complaining that Brew Mountain has changed and that Moonbucks has transformed Brew Mountain from a family-owned gem to a cold, corporate beverage shop. Employee morale is low; management insists on long shifts, few days off, and little scheduling flexibility. Employees even have to pay for their own coffee and snacks. Stressed and unhappy, baristas often make mistakes with drink and food orders, which annoys customers. Employees refuse to admit their mistakes and instead accuse each other or find ways to hide errors. Customers often witness chaos, unhappiness, and frustration behind the counter. Although the coffee quality has not declined, the overall atmosphere is cold and unwelcoming, an atmosphere completely different from the one created by the Hernández family.

As a result, the Brew Mountain chain is at risk of bankruptcy, and the new owners are desperate to repair the situation. Therefore, they have hired a team of consultants who specialize in advising companies on how to improve the corporate culture.

STEP 2: Work in groups of four. Use the figure of the Culture Web and the guiding questions on page 148 to brainstorm solutions that will help repair Brew Mountain's culture. The Culture Web, developed by Gerry Johnson and Kevan Scholes, is one approach to help companies create or repair a corporate culture. As you have learned, the corporate culture is simply "the way things are done" at a company and has a huge impact on the organization's success.

STEP 3: Present your "solution" to the Moonbuck's management. Your presentation must

- be between 3–4 minutes long.
- include no more than 8 PowerPoint™ slides with **no more** than 8 words on each slide. Use questions from at least three of the bubbles in the Culture Web on page 148. Be sure to include an introduction and conclusion. The slides should communicate the main themes or ideas about how to repair Brew Mountain's culture as you worked through the questions on the model.
- involve all members of the group.
- show passion and enthusiasm for your ideas.
- include ideas, vocabulary, grammar, and the speaking and listening skill topics from the unit.

Have fun!

STEP 4: As a class, vote on which consultancy group presented the best solution for saving Brew Mountain for the coffee-loving residents and tourists of San José!

Stories
What kinds of things do you want employees and customers to say about the company?

Routines
What kinds of daily routines or rituals do you need to have to represent the values?

Symbols
What kind of image (logo, brand) and atmosphere (office, website) do you need to create?

Culture Web

Organizational Structure
Is the organization rigid and hierarchical or is it flat and democratic? Explain why.

Control Systems
What kinds of controls and processes are there for incentives, quality, product development, etc.?

Power Structure
How are decisions made? By the top few, by all?

UNIT PROJECT

You will become a roving reporter and interview several people on the corporate culture in the business in which they work. Follow the steps.

STEP 1: Choose two different kinds of workplaces, such as a small family-owned business, large corporation, academic institution, etc. Try to arrange an interview with people at different levels in the company.

STEP 2: Work with a partner. Brainstorm a list of questions you would like to ask in your interview using the information you have learned in the unit. For example:

- Look at the cartoon above. What do you think it means? What are the unwritten rules in your company?

- How would you describe the culture of the company or business?

- Does your workplace have explicit corporate or business values? What are they? Do these values match the day in and day out realities? Why or why not? What kind of perks and intangibles are offered?

STEP 3: Conduct your interviews. Start your interviews like this:

- "Excuse me. I'm doing a brief survey for my English class on the topic of culture in the workplace. Could I ask you a few questions?"

- While you interview, take notes on the answers to the question.

STEP 4: Present a summary of your findings to the class.

ALTERNATIVE SPEAKING TOPICS

Choose one of the topics and follow the directions.

Topic 1

Look at the different elements that contribute to shaping a company's corporate culture. Number the items in order of importance from 1 to 10. Number 1 is the most important and number 10 is the least important. Then discuss the questions with the class. Use ideas, grammar, vocabulary, pronunciation, and the language for conceding and making a counterargument.

_____ unlimited vacation time as long as you get your work done

_____ perks such as free lunch, iPads, iPhones, housekeeping services, health club membership

_____ freedom to work at home

_____ vacation time according to need

_____ no specific job titles—everyone is equal

_____ social events such as employee picnics, parties, etc.

_____ monthly instead of yearly performance reviews

_____ no email on Fridays

_____ financial incentives such as profit sharing, raises, promotions

_____ "productivity coach" to help you learn how to be more productive

In what kind of workplace would you like to work? What elements in the workplace would help you be most productive and motivated?

Topic 2

Work in small groups. Read the expressions for paraphrasing and the quotes on the next page. Work together to paraphrase the quotes and then discuss them. In your discussion, use ideas, vocabulary, grammar, pronunciation, and speaking techniques from the unit.

Expressions for Paraphrasing

In other words . . .

The point she's trying to make is . . .

To put it another way . . .

What he's trying to say is that . . .

What she means is that . . .

- The first man gets the oyster, the second man gets the shell. —*Andrew Carnegie*

- Hire character. Train skill. —*Peter Schutz*

- To be successful, you have to have your heart in your business, and your business in your heart. —*Thomas Watson, Sr.*

- If you think you can do a thing or think you can't do a thing, you're right. —*Henry Ford*

- When you reach for the stars you might not quite get one, but you won't come up with a handful of mud either. —*Leo Burnett*

- Remembering that you are going to die is the best way I know to avoid the trap of thinking you have something to lose. —*Steve Jobs*

GO TO MyEnglishLab *TO DISCUSS ONE OF THE ALTERNATIVE TOPICS, WATCH A VIDEO ABOUT A GENEROUS BUSINESSMAN, AND TAKE THE UNIT 5 ACHIEVEMENT TEST.*

TOGETHER
Alone

1 FOCUS ON THE TOPIC

1. Look at the photo and the title of the unit. What does the title imply about the impact of technology today? Does the photo remind you of any experience you have had? Explain.

2. People all over the world are using many forms of social media to communicate. Some studies have found that social media may be changing us in important ways, for example, making it more difficult for us to pay attention for long periods of time and/or to pay attention to other people. Do these findings seem true for you? Explain.

3. Find a photo of a friend or relative. On a separate piece of paper, jot down some notes describing how the use of social media is making an impact on his or her life or on your relationship with this person. Share the photo and information with a small group. Discuss the pros and cons of the impact, as well as your predictions for future impact.

GO TO MyEnglishLab TO CHECK WHAT YOU KNOW.

VOCABULARY

🎧 Read and listen to the online letters and responses about the relationship between communication problems and the use of technology. Pay attention to the **bold-faced** words and phrases. Then read the list of definitions that follows. Work with a partner. Write the number of the bold-faced word or phrase next to its definition.

AskAnnie

Home | Advice | Articles | Links

Old Friends by Ali – May 18th

Hi Annie,

I hope you can help me. When I walk around my neighborhood, I often see familiar faces from junior high and high school. Some of these people are simply distant friends on my social media sites. Do I really need to stop and say hello to them, even though we haven't communicated face-to-face in years? I really don't have the **(1) capacity** to develop relationships with people from my past. And furthermore, I'm not **(2) seeking intimacy** with anyone at the moment either.

Dear Ali,

(3) Given that it is always nice to be polite and smile, it can't hurt for you to say hello to them. But if you were never friends with these people anyway, you really don't have to do anything. However, you never know when you might end up having **(4) to collaborate with** these neighbors on some community project, so you might as well smile at least.

| REPLY | BACK | RETURN TO ASKANNIE-ONLINEADVICECOLUMN.COM |

A Keyboard Wedding by Anonymous – June 26th

Dear Annie,

I know what I am going to say is going to be hard for you to believe, but it's true. I am simply **(5) overwhelmed** by shock. We have just been invited to view a wedding online. In other words, we are not invited to go to the wedding; rather, the invitation is for an "online viewing." Eight months ago, we attended the "real" wedding of the bride's sister and, of course, we gave a gift. Do you think we need to give a gift for this invitation to a virtual viewing?

Dear Anonymous,

Wow! My immediate natural response several years ago would have been, "Yes, you have been invited to a wedding, so give a gift." However, I advise you to **(6) throttle back**, take a deep breath, and reflect. You need to make a **(7) conscious choice** here. Think about your relationship with the soon-to-be couple. I've never heard such a thing before and am also surprised by the **(8) velocity** in which the Internet is taking over nearly every aspect of our lives.

| REPLY | BACK | RETURN TO ASKANNIE-ONLINEADVICECOLUMN.COM |

Distant Dad by Jenny – August 10th

Dear Annie,

This morning, I was standing in a long line in my small cozy local coffee shop patiently waiting to place my cappuccino order. I suddenly heard the high-pitched squeals of an adorable two-year-old girl, "Daddy! Daddy! Look what I made! Come see what I drew! Daddy, Daddy, I made a beautiful picture for you." I looked back and saw "Daddy," about a foot away, absorbed in a cell phone conversation, ignoring his child. I was dying to run over and shout, "Excuse me. **(9) Get a grip**, and pay attention to your child!" Annie, I see this all the time everywhere. Should I have intervened?

Dear Jenny,

Sad to say, but your story clearly demonstrates the **(10) degradation** of our relationships, even between parents and children. Unfortunately, **(11) the horse is out of the barn**, and cell phones are here to stay. The father has clearly **(12) ratcheted down** the quality of the time he spends with his little daughter. So, what should you do? Follow your instincts. Use humor if possible or even better, walk over and look at the kid's picture yourself. Maybe he'll see your example and next time **(13) tuck** his cell phone **away** in his pocket and pay attention to his kid!

| REPLY | BACK | RETURN TO ASKANNIE-ONLINEADVICECOLUMN.COM |

_____ **a.** admitting that

_____ **b.** decline

_____ **c.** reduced

_____ **d.** deliberate decision

_____ **e.** ease off; take something easy

_____ **f.** gain control

_____ **g.** looking for close companionship

_____ **h.** overcome

_____ **i.** potential

_____ **j.** put away securely

_____ **k.** speed

_____ **l.** the event or change has already occurred

_____ **m.** work together

■■■■■■■■■■■■■■■■■■■■■■■■■■■■■■ *GO TO* MyEnglishLab *FOR MORE VOCABULARY PRACTICE.*

Together Alone 155

PREVIEW

John Moe, host of a radio show on technology, interviews MIT Professor Sherry Turkle, author of *Alone Together: Why We Expect More from Technology and Less from Each Other*. To start the interview, Moe admits his house is unusually "low-tech."

🎧 Work with a partner. Predict what examples he might give to illustrate that his house is low-tech. Then listen to the excerpt to verify your predictions.

1. *There's no computer visible in the house when you walk in.* _____

2. _____

3. _____

4. _____

MAIN IDEAS

🎧 Listen to the interview between John Moe and professor and author, Sherry Turkle. In your own words, complete the sentences with the main idea of each part. Then work with a partner and compare answers.

Part One

According to Moe, the focus of Turkle's book is about how we _____ to

_____ and how we are going to _____ given that
    (2)   (3)

_____.
    (4)

Part Two

Turkle says that she is not *for* or *against* technology. She thinks that the most important thing

people need to create is _____ where _____.
                            (5)   (6)

Part Three

Turkle's research shows that a lot of people are overwhelmed by email messages from

others who expect immediate answers. Therefore they _____ and
                                          (7)

_____. Turkle also thinks that amount and speed of technology cause
    (8)

_____.
    (9)

DETALS

Listen to the interview again. Read the sentences and write **T** (true) or **F** (false). Correct the false statements. Then discuss your answers with a partner.

Part One

_____ 1. Turkle thinks that, as a society, we are doing a good job at managing the technology in our lives.

_____ 2. She believes that we will continue to be addicted to technology as long as it continues to exist.

Part Two

_____ 3. Moe asks Turkle whether or not our use of technology will naturally decrease or if we will have to discipline ourselves to reduce our use.

_____ 4. Turkle believes everyone should go on a strict "technology diet" and simply unplug.

_____ 5. On Facebook and Twitter, Moe interacts with about four people each day, in addition to his family.

Part Three

_____ 6. Turkle is not worried about people who use social networks to enhance their relationships.

_____ 7. Turkle's research has explored the use of technology among families and professionals.

_____ 8. Most people expect an answer to an email within a day or two.

_____ 9. Turkle behaves just like the people she is complaining about. She herself gives simple answers to simple questions.

_____ 10. Turkle says our work performance is being degraded due to the amount of email we receive.

GO TO MyEnglishLab *FOR MORE LISTENING PRACTICE.*

MAKE INFERENCES

LISTENING FOR STANCE

In the interview, Professor Sherry Turkle argues strongly that we are not managing our relationship with technology effectively. Turkle knows that her point of view on this hot topic is debatable, complex, and controversial. Therefore, she takes a firm stance on the issue. She is not afraid to tell John Moe, the interviewer, and the listening audience what she thinks.

Speakers, including Turkle, take a strong stance by using a variety of techniques, sometimes in combination, such as

- repeating language
- using a high-pitched and loud tone of voice
- citing of research, facts, or evidence to support a position
- refuting commonly held beliefs
- defining a point of view by saying what it is not

🎧 Read and listen to this excerpt and check (✓) the technique(s) Turkle uses to present her firm stance. Explain the reasons for your decision. Then read the explanation.

Example

TURKLE: It's not a question of saying "the horse is out of the barn" or "we're addicted." I mean this is with us to stay. And we have to learn to be a partner with it in a way that we get it right.

- repeating language
- using a high-pitched and loud tone of voice
- citing research, facts, or evidence to support a position
- ✓ refuting commonly held beliefs
- ✓ defining a point of view by saying what it is not

In this example, Turkle uses two techniques for taking a firm stance: (1) she refutes a commonly held belief and (2) defines a point of view by saying what it isn't. She suggests that most people are saying don't bother with trying to change our relationship with technology because everyone knows it's too late. We are all addicted anyway. Turkle contradicts this and says, "This is with us to stay, so we had better figure out how to work with it." She also defines something by saying what it's not: "It's not a question of X or Y."

🎧 Listen to each excerpt. Check (✓) the technique(s) Turkle uses to take her firm stance. Explain the reasons for your decision.

Excerpt One

1. _____ repeating language

   _____ using a high-pitched and loud tone of voice

   _____ citing research, facts, or evidence to support a position

   _____ refuting commonly held beliefs

   _____ defining a point of view by saying what it is not

Explanation: _____

Excerpt Two

2. _____ repeating language

   _____ using a high-pitched and loud tone of voice

   _____ citing research, facts, or evidence to support a position

   _____ refuting commonly held beliefs

   _____ defining a point of view by saying what it is not

Explanation: _____

Excerpt Three

3. _____ repeating language

   _____ using a high-pitched and loud tone of voice

   _____ citing research, facts, or evidence to support a position

   _____ refuting commonly held beliefs

   _____ defining a point of view by saying what it is not

Explanation: _____

EXPRESS OPINIONS

Many listeners reacted to John Moe's interview with Sherry Turkle. They posted their short comments online. Below are a few of these comments.

Read several reactions and decide whether you agree or disagree. Write **A** (agree) or **D** (disagree) in the blanks. Work in groups of three to compare answers and defend your choices.

You must be signed in to leave a comment.   **Sign in / Register**

COMMENTS

_____ 1. It's important to be "always on and always available." Technology allows us to do that.
— P. W., a day ago

_____ 2. Social media are causing us to lose the ability to make simple, genuine connections with other people. We end up "being there, but not there."
— Jay E., a day ago

_____ 3. Digital communication, including email, can be just as deep and "meaty" as face-to face communication. It depends on how you use it.
— ahaigh3127, a day ago

_____ 4. I'm like Moe, the guy who interviewed Sherry Turkle. At certain times of the day, I unplug—except for my phone.
— SAC3456, 2 days ago

_____ 5. The only way to control the volume and velocity of email is by going on a strict "digital diet." A natural throttling back is impossible.
— R. H., 2 days ago

■ ■ ■ ■ ■ ■ ■ ■ ■ ■ ■ ■ ■ ■ ■ ■ ■ ■ ■ ■ *GO TO* MyEnglishLab *TO GIVE YOUR OPINION ABOUT ANOTHER QUESTION.*

VOCABULARY

1 Read this passage on Internet identity. You will hear the **bold-faced** words in the next listening selection. Notice them as you listen.

Who are you? To answer that question, we think of our identity—the pieces of ourselves that define who we are. These include our race, gender, date of birth, looks, religion, culture, and so on. Many parts of our identity are fixed and cannot be changed. However, the online world offers another option. We now have the freedom to choose an identity and select from a variety of multiple **personas**. Many people are asking an important, prominent question: Who has the right to control this online identity?

Authentic Identity   Facebook® and other social media tools say that people should use their real and authentic identity on the Internet. This means using your own name and other identifying information. In other words, we should have the same identity in the online and offline worlds. In fact, in their view, it is a crime to create a fake or false identity, or to pretend to be someone else, an **impersonator**.

Invented Identity   On the other hand, other social media companies, such as Twitter®, believe that web users should be free to use invented identities if they want. People should be able to use pseudonyms, or false names, to hide their authentic identity. In other words, these companies are **advocates** of alternate identities or Internet **pseudonymity**. They say that being able to hide, being anonymous, or unknown, is important for freedom of speech. Having a pseudonym or a fake name guarantees that no one can find you. You can be anonymous, or unknown. At times, people choose **anonymity** to escape or avoid a problem or, at worse, a highly sensitive and serious political crisis or **debacle**. These free speech supporters disagree with Facebook® supporters who believe each of us should be real or authentic online just as we are in the offline world.

2 Match the words on the left with the definitions or synonyms on the right. Write the corresponding letter in the blank.

_____ **1.** personas   **a.** disaster

_____ **2.** impersonator   **b.** assumed identities

_____ **3.** advocates   **c.** condition of disguised identity

_____ **4.** pseudonymity   **d.** someone who pretends to be someone else

_____ **5.** anonymity   **e.** supporters

_____ **6.** debacle   **f.** condition of being unknown

COMPREHENSION

🎧 Read the items on the left. Then listen to the short commentary presenting two opposing views on Internet identity. Match the first half of each statement on the left with the corresponding second half of the statement on the right. Write the letter in the blank. Then listen again to check your answers.

1. The key issue is: Can we have multiple personas or identities or _____?

2. The issue of online identity has gained prominence or importance because _____.

3. Facebook® deactivated the page of Salman Rushdie, the famous writer, because they thought _____.

4. They asked Rushdie, a well-known Indian writer, to prove _____.

5. In support of free speech, companies like Twitter® favor Internet pseudonymity which means a situation in which _____.

6. Other companies, like Google® and Facebook®, support _____.

7. On the one hand, advocates of free speech favor _____.

8. On the other hand, advocates of safety, fairness, civility are in favor of _____.

a. he was not Rushdie, but an impersonator

b. users can craft their own identities

c. authenticity

d. an open, safe, authentic online experience

e. pseudonymity online

f. his identity and use his real name

g. a single authentic one

h. so much of our lives is happening online

GO TO MyEnglishLab FOR MORE VOCABULARY PRACTICE.

LISTENING SKILL

IDENTIFYING SIGNALS FOR OPPOSING PERSPECTIVES OF AN ISSUE

In the second listening selection, the Global Ethics Corner speaker presents two sides of the issue: Who should control our identity on the Internet? In this succinct two-minute presentation, the speaker uses linguistic clues to signal or suggest that there are two opposing points of view followed by words and phrases that express those two perspectives.

🎧 Read and listen to this example. Then answer the questions and read the explanation.

Example

SPEAKER: Who should control your identity on the Internet? Should you be free to pick and choose among multiple personas? Or should you be expected to adhere to a single, authentic identity online, as you would offline?

1. What sentence structure does the speaker use to signal there are two points of view?

_____

2. What words or phrases are used to express the two points of view?

_____

In this example, the speaker uses two questions to signal that there are two points of view. She also uses the word "or" to set up the contrast between the perspectives. The phrases "free to pick and choose" and "expected to adhere to" then express those opposing points of view.

🎧 Listen to the comments. Identify the linguistic clues used to signal and express opposing points of views.

Excerpt One

1. What sentence structure signals that there are two points of view?

_____

What are the words and/or phrases that express the two points of view?

_____

Excerpt Two

2. What sentence structure signals that there are two points of view?

_____

What are the words and/or phrases that express the two points of view?

_____

(continued on next page)

3. What sentence structure signals that there are two points of view?

_____

What are the words and/or phrases that express the two points of view?

_____

GO TO MyEnglishLab **FOR MORE SKILL PRACTICE.**

CONNECT THE LISTENINGS

STEP 1: Organize

The speakers in both Listenings One and Two commented on issues arising from the role of the social media in our daily lives. Look at the list of issues and check (✓) which speaker identified the issue as a "potential problem" in our lives.

POTENTIAL PROBLEMS	TURKLE	GLOBAL ETHICS PRESENTER
Overusing social media sites		
Substituting social media for face-to-face communication with one's parents or children on serious issues		
Creating a pseudonym instead of using your real name on a social media site		
Responding to email immediately without thinking		
Discussing complex political issues on Twitter™ using real names		

Work with a partner. Look at the cartoons. Discuss the questions below them using the information from the chart on the previous page and the two listening selections.

VALERIE THRIVED IN AN INTERNET COMMUNITY THAT HAD NO IDEA THAT SHE WAS A CHICKEN...

"How am I? I don't know, let me check Google."

1. What is the message of each cartoon?

2. Look at the chart on the previous page. How do the messages from each cartoon connect to the ideas expressed by Turkle and the Global Ethics presenter?

3. Do the cartoonists favor authentic identity or invented identity on the Internet? How do you know?

4. What would Sherry Turkle say about the message of each cartoon? Explain.

GO TO MyEnglishLab TO CHECK WHAT YOU LEARNED.

VOCABULARY

REVIEW

More and more people are studying the impact of social media. These excerpts have been taken from data collected by some of these researchers. Complete the sentences with the appropriate form of the words and phrases in the box above each excerpt.

debacle	make a conscious choice	overwhelm	seek intimacy

1. For years I only occasionally carried my mobile phone with me, just in case I needed to make a call or receive a call. But now, my phone is like an additional arm, finger, or hand. It is with me all the time. I have to _____ to leave it behind, in order to find a few moments of peace and quiet. I often feel _____ by needing to be in touch with so many people all day long. At work, my colleagues and I are constantly emailing and texting each other. Our communication is fast and frequent, so much so that I worry one day there will be a huge _____ at work, because I'll say the wrong thing to the wrong person in the wrong way. It's an accident waiting to happen. I fear I'm _____ in technology and developing too many virtual connections instead of making real-life connections.

capacity	get a grip	given that	tuck away

2.  Look. The whole message thing has the

_____ to bring about a bit of anxiety.

For example, texting brings "social pressure" because if I text

someone and he doesn't get back to me right away, I take it hard.

My friends tell me to _____ and ignore it because the system doesn't

work that way. Maybe the person has just _____ his phone in his

pocket or something, but I don't buy it. _____ everyone is "on" his

or her phone all day and all night, there is no such thing as simply not being available.

advocate	collaborate	impersonator

3. I'm beat after work so I look forward to going online to play

games in which I have created an avatar and turned myself into

someone else. I don't know who any of my friends are in the real

world. In the fictional online space, I'm Roger instead of

Rajit. By day, I am an architect, but by night, I am a world-renowned tennis player

_____, Roger Federer. It's no big deal really. We are just role-playing

games and _____ with each other on different kinds of stuff. I'm a

huge _____ of these "communities" and "worlds" because my life

there is so much more interesting than my real life.

(continued on next page)

anonymity	degrade	velocity

4. I'm a respected professional who has had to hire a service to manage my reputation online. A while ago, when I worked for a different company, I posted some negative comments about a client online. I thought my comments were _____, but the client has figured out that it was me. Now my boss is furious with me because we could lose this client. The _____ with which a reputation can be _____ is positively frightening. No wonder these online reputation management services are becoming a big business.

EXPAND

Social media is giving us the opportunity to connect with anyone, anywhere, and anytime. We need vocabulary to discuss this new phenomenon. As these tools become more prevalent, vocabulary to allow us to discuss the impact social media has on our lives is also emerging.

1 Words and their opposites are often used when discussing the impact of social media on our lives. Look at the list of words below. Write down what you think the opposite of the word might be. Work with a partner. Then, check the list of words in blue on the next page. Can you find a different, or better choice, than the one you made? Write the blue word next to your original guess.

	OUR GUESS	BLUE WORD
advocates		
anonymity		
distracted		
isolated		
narcissistic		
social		
solitude		
superficial		
transparent		
virtual		

Blue Words

authentic	fame
companionship	focused
connected	hidden
critics	real
detached	unselfish

2 Enrique Gonzales, a young entrepreneur, has recently launched a hugely popular social networking site, GlobalConnect.com. Enrique recently sat down with reporter Jason Lin to talk about his new venture.

Read each exchange between Jason and Enrique. Use the context to help you understand the meaning of the **bold-faced** words in Lin's remarks. Choose the best blue word from the box above that contrasts with the **bold-faced** word and fill in the blank in Enrique's comments. Then, in pairs, looking at each other, read the conversation aloud with feeling. Notice how the use of opposites helps maintain the conversation.

1. **JASON LIN:** Enrique, thanks for spending some time with me. I've heard that on your site users can do everything they do on the most popular sites, plus find a date, play games, and write movie and book reviews. No one in the world can ever feel **isolated** when they log onto GlobalConnect.

    ENRIQUE GONZALEZ: That's correct. No user will be isolated. They can always be

    _____ with anyone anywhere in the world, not only
    (1)
    with their own personal circle of friends, which is what most sites offer.

2. **JL:** I see. I guess for online dating then, users have a huge pool to draw from. I met my wife on an online dating site, so I am an **advocate**.

    EG: Me too. I just got engaged to a woman I actually met on GlobalConnect. Imagine that! Start a business and get a wife. Two for one. Anyway, I know that _____ of online dating
    (2)

    (continued on next page)

worry about users misrepresenting themselves and creating false identities.

3. **JL:** Right. And there are some people who use the sites to hide who they are and create **anonymity**. They don't want anyone to know their real identities.

    EG: Yes, indeed. We have some well-known actors on our site who are actually choosing anonymity to escape _____ and
(3)
online paparazzi.

4. **JL:** I imagine you draw a number of people who prefer dating in the **virtual** world because it is less threatening.

    EG: Uh-huh. Most of these people have given up looking for someone in the _____ world and are pretty much hooked on
(4)
online dating.

5. **JL:** Well, even though I am a reporter and like to speak to people, I really treasure my **solitude** and time alone, so I found online dating had advantages in this respect.

    EG: Yes, the online dating feature on my site attracts people like you who prefer to be alone, but are really looking for a bit of

_____.
(5)

6. **JL:** A lot of the real dates I had were just empty and **superficial**.

    EG: Mine too. My online conversations with my sweetheart, Diana, were much more _____ and interesting than those I
(6)
had had in the real world.

7. **JL:** I'm curious about something. How open or **transparent** do you encourage your users to be when they create their profiles? Tell all?

EG: Well, it is up to them. But it is not great if they have kept certain important things about themselves _____ and (7) reveal those later when it might be too late.

8.   **JL:** Too late? You mean if someone comes across online as someone who is super friendly, gregarious, and very **social**, but in the real world is different?

EG: Indeed! Imagine finding out later that Little Miss Friendly is really Little Miss _____. (8)

9.   **JL:** Or, even worse, if the person presents himself as being caring and giving, but is really **narcissistic**.

EG: Holy cow! Too right. Frequently, we notice that people pretend to be _____ and considerate, but they are really self- (9) centered in real life.

10.   **JL:** Enrique, I heard that while you were trying to launch GlobalConnect you were working as an investment banker, running marathons, taking care of your aging mother, and playing bass in a rock band. Quite impressive! How did you manage not to get **distracted** with all of these things?

EG: Well, my daily meditation has taught me to stay _____ and to appreciate the unseen connection (10) between all people and things in the world. That is my mission.

CREATE

1 Look at the words and phrases in the box.

advocate	distracted	overwhelmed	superficial
anonymity	impersonator	persona	transparent
collaborate with	isolated	seek	velocity
conscious choice	narcissistic	solitude	virtual

2 Work in groups of four. As a group, choose one of the debate topics below. Divide your group into pairs. Each pair should choose either the Pro or Con position of the topic. Brainstorm supporting arguments for your position statement. Use as many vocabulary items as possible to state and develop your arguments.

With your partner, present your position statement and argument to the other pair. As you listen to the arguments, check (✓) the words from the box that you hear. Then practice your arguments again with two more pairs.

Debate Topic One: Online Dating

Pro position statement: Online dating is a great way to meet people and seek companionship.
Con position statement: Online dating is dangerous because you can easily be misled by a fake profile.

Debate Topic Two: Control of Online Identity

Pro position statement: People have the right to control their online identities.
Con position statement: Any website has the right to impose rules on the individual's use of anonymity.

GO TO MyEnglishLab *FOR MORE VOCABULARY PRACTICE.*

GRAMMAR

1 Work with a partner. Examine the short conversations and discuss the questions that follow.

Q: Is your wife going to quit texting while driving?
A: No, but **I wish she would**. It's dangerous and illegal.

Q: Are your kids addicted to online video games?
A: Yes, unfortunately, but **I really wish they weren't**. They're not doing enough homework.

Q: Do you know how I can stop checking my social networking sites so much?
A: No, but **I wish I did**. It's a complete waste of time.

Q: Did you start dating online after your divorce?

A: Yes, and **I wish I hadn't**.

1. How are the first three bold-faced phrases similar?
2. How is the last bold-faced phrase different from the first three?

WISH STATEMENTS—EXPRESSING UNREALITY

Use the verb *wish* when you want to express unreality—a desire for reality to be different or a regret that it was not different. The verb forms and structures used in the clause after *wish* can express future, present, or past situations.

Wish Situation	Examples
PRESENT AND FUTURE WISH Use *wish* + **would** or *could*.	• **A friend of mine wishes she could get rid of her cell phone,** but she can't because she is totally hooked on texting. • I know. **I wish she'd turn her phone off.** The constant texting is driving me crazy.
PRESENT WISH Use *wish* + past form of the verb.	• The problem is out of control. **I just wish people didn't feel compelled** to respond to texts so quickly.
PRESENT WISH (VERB *TO BE*) Use past form: *wish* + *were*.	• In a way, **I wish texting weren't so cheap** because then people wouldn't use it so much. • You've got it. **If it were more expensive,** we wouldn't rely on it as much.
PAST WISH Use *wish* + *had* + past participle.	• Social media sites have their pluses, but **I wish they hadn't become** so popular. They can be dangerous. • Don't be ridiculous! I'll bet **you just wish you'd predicted** the trend and started your own Facebook™! • Yeah, I guess so. But more than that, **I just wish I hadn't been so careless** and **revealed** so much on my Facebook™ page. I didn't get the job I had applied for.
PAST WISH: *COULD HAVE* Use *wish* + *could have* + past participle.	• Sorry to hear that. Couldn't you convince the manager that the issue was important? No. **I wish I could have,** but the guy wouldn't listen.

GRAMMAR TIP: The tense of the verb "wish" does not affect the tense of the verb in the clause following "wish." In spoken informal English, we often use short answer phrases with *wish* statements. (See the phrases in Exercise 1.)

2 Work with a partner.

Student A: Ask Student B questions 1 through 6. Check Student B's answers with the correct answer in parentheses.

Student B: Cover the left column. Answer Student A's question using a short-answer *wish* statement. Then switch roles after question 6.

Student A	**Student B**
1. Will your colleague promise not to text during the business dinner? (No, but I wish he would or could.)	1. No, but I wish he _____.
2. Does your colleague always keep his phone on the table during these dinners? (Yes, and I wish he didn't or wouldn't.)	2. Yes, and I wish he _____.
3. Are you still planning to tuck away your phone during the dinner? (Yes, but I wish I weren't.)	3. Yes, but I wish I _____.
4. Couldn't you get a reservation at the "no cell phone policy" restaurant that just opened? (No, but I wish I could have.)	4. No, but I wish I _____.
5. Did they know that the restaurant gives customers a 10% discount off their meal if they give up their phones? (No, but they wished they had.)	5. No, but they wish they _____.
6. Is it really true that his business was hurt by the "no cell phone policy?" (Uh-huh, and he wishes it hadn't been. He liked the policy.)	6. Uh-huh, and he wishes it _____. He liked the policy.

Now switch roles.

7. Is he planning to post his negative comments on their website?

   (Yes, but I wish he wouldn't.
   He'll never be able to delete them.)

8. I noticed that your online profile is outdated.

   (Yes, and I wish it weren't. I have to update it.)

9. Does she know how to set the privacy controls on the site?

   (No, but she wishes she did. She wants to protect her identity.)

10. Did he create a pseudonym for political reasons?

    (Yes, and he wishes he hadn't.)

11. It's too bad you couldn't protect your online identity before it was revealed.

    (Uh-huh, but I wish I could have.)

12. Were you able to find a way to stay in touch with your friends without using social media?

    (No, but I wish I had or could have.)

7. Yes, but I wish he _____.
   He'll never be able to delete them.

8. Yes, and I wish it _____. I
   have to update it.

9. No, but she wishes she
   _____. She wants to
   protect her identity.

10. Yes, and he wishes he _____.

11. Uh-huh, but I wish I _____.

12. No, but I wish I _____.

GO TO MyEnglishLab FOR MORE GRAMMAR PRACTICE.

PRONUNCIATION

EXPRESSIVE INTONATION

Intonation is the melody of language that communicates feelings and attitudes in order to convey a certain meaning. Intonation can aid communication and help engage the listener, but it can also prevent understanding.

🎧 Read and listen to the way Sherry Turkle conveys her position or stance on the topic of technology use.

Examples

TURKLE: Turkle says "unplug." And I am not saying that. It's not Turkle says "unplug." It's Turkle says "Get a grip. Think." It's Turkle says "reflect."

TURKLE: That's great. That's not what I am talking about. If you don't have a problem, I'm not talking about you.

TURKLE: In other words, people are asking simpler questions in order to the get the answer. And I am starting to give simpler answers in order to be able to give an answer.

In the first two examples, Turkle uses a varied pitch with short, clipped phrasing in order to express a strong opinion as well as a hint of annoyance and frustration. However, in the third example, she uses a lower, flatter, and heavier stress level. Here she is expressing a calmer, more controlled, and less frustrated attitude.

1 🎧 Listen to the speaker say the phrase "Control your identity." Read the description of the intonation and its interpretation.

	INTONATION	INTERPRETATION
Control your identity.	varied pitch from extreme high to low with clipped phrasing	annoyed and frustrated
Control your identity.	low, flat, heavy stress	mildly annoyed and frustrated
Control your identity.	mid-level pitch, flat, soft	indifferent, matter-of-fact
Control your identity?	very high, rising pitch	disbelief, surprise

2 🎧 Listen to the dialogues and interpret how Student B is feeling. Circle the correct word.

1. **A:** Remove your phone from the table.

   B: Do I have to?

   very annoyed   mildly annoyed   indifferent   surprised

2. **A:** I didn't hear her. What did the professor say?

   B: She said we need to put away our cell phones during class.

   very annoyed   mildly annoyed   indifferent   surprised

3. A: I think you'd better check your identity by Googling yourself daily.

    B: Daily? Are you kidding?

       very annoyed   mildly annoyed   indifferent   surprised

4. A: We can't hire him. He's not who he says he is.

    B: Seriously? We spent so much time interviewing that guy. What a waste of time.

       very annoyed   mildly annoyed   indifferent   surprised

5. A: What's wrong?

    B: I just read an article about how to manage our online identities. Yet another thing I have to worry about!

       very annoyed   mildly annoyed   indifferent   surprised

6. A: Hey. Check out this text from my grandmother.

    B: Your grandmother texts? She's nearly 100!

       very annoyed   mildly annoyed   indifferent   surprised

3 Practice the dialogues from Exercise 2 using the correct intonation. Then change partners. Practice the dialogues again choosing a different feeling or attitude and have your partner guess your feeling.

4 Practice the dialogue below with your partner. Follow the intonation cues in parentheses. Change partners and practice again.

A: Hi, Paul. What's up?

B: Well, Sally just sent me a text. She's canceling our plans for the concert tonight. (mildly annoyed)

A: No way! She sends you a text to tell you that? (surprised)

B: Yeah. Especially given that the tickets cost a fortune, it's unbelievable she didn't have the courtesy to at least call me. (very annoyed)

A: Hey, get a grip! Maybe she just got distracted and forgot until now. (indifferent)

B: I doubt it. She just texts me whenever because it's easier for her. Sometimes she can be so narcissistic! (mildly annoyed)

A: You're right. I'm an advocate of texting when there just isn't time to talk, but in this case it's just so superficial. My girlfriend does it too. (mildly annoyed)

B: Yeah. Sometimes I feel like she makes a conscious choice to be detached. (very annoyed) Anway, ya wanna go to this concert with me?

A: Sorry buddy. Not trying to be anti-social, but I've got plans. Maybe next time.

SPEAKING SKILL

BUILDING ON OTHERS' IDEAS

To get people to listen and collaborate effectively, you need to **build and expand on the ideas of others**. This list of useful expressions can be used in academic or professional meetings and discussions.

- **To add to your idea**, I think students socialize differently online than they do when they are face to face.

- **Not only that, but I would also say that** people interact more creatively when they interact face to face.

- **Your point makes me think of** another issue, which is the trend toward texting instead of emailing.

- **Another thing I'd like to bring up is** the fact that a lot of people are really rude when they text at inappropriate times.

- **You speak of** needing to stay connected 24/7; **then, can I also assume that** you never tuck your phone away?

Work with a partner.

Student A: Read each of the first four opinions aloud.

Student B: Cover the left column. Build upon, add to, and expand on what your partner has said. Use the expressions listed above. Support your opinion with a few other statements. Then switch roles after item 4.

Example

STUDENT A: Non-stop texting degrades our face-to-face interactions.

STUDENT B: Not only that, but I would also say that incessant texting disrupts continuity of thinking.

Student A	Student B
1. Texting, emailing, and posting let us present the self we want to be. We can edit who we really are.	1. To add . . .
2. Schools should teach a course on "How to manage your online identity" because not knowing can be dangerous.	2. Not only that . . .
3. Online anonymity is very liberating. It allows us to push limits and act in ways we wouldn't act "IRL" (in real life)	3. Your point makes me think . . .
4. Online interactions can be dangerously misunderstood because there is no tone of voice or body language.	4. [your own idea]

Now switch roles.

5. Internet freedom is essential for an open and democratic society.

6. We have time to do everything these days, except think.

7. In the future, identity will exist primarily online.

8. Spending thousands of dollars to manage my online reputation is really not worth it.

5. Another thing . . .

6. You speak of . . .

7. [your own choice]

8. [your own choice]

■■■■■■■■■■■■■■■■ *GO TO* MyEnglishLab *FOR MORE SKILL PRACTICE AND TO CHECK WHAT YOU LEARNED.*

FINAL SPEAKING TASK

In this activity, you will have a group discussion in order to recommend a set of policies on the use of electronic communication in classes at a university. Use the vocabulary, grammar, pronunciation, and listening and speaking skills that you learned in the unit.*

Follow the steps.

STEP 1: Read the following scenario.

Situation

The English Language Department at the university in your city has been one of the most popular and well known English language departments in the country. However, recently, faculty and administrators have noticed a distinct correlation: As e-communication in the classroom has increased, final test scores have decreased. The difference is dramatic and notable. Students, professors, and administrators are concerned. The issue has been a topic in the local and national media, too. The university administration has decided to establish three task forces to make these policy recommendations.

(continued on next page)

---

*For Alternative Speaking Topics, see page 182.

STEP 2: Look at the roles and the key issues of each group.

Roles and Key Issues

STUDENTS	FACULTY	ADMINISTRATORS
• need to have phones to stay connected • consider phones an "extension of their hands" • feel anxious without their phones • use phones/tablets for study purposes, e.g., to look up information, take notes • prefer not to have phones in class: result of recent student poll	• consider phones distracting and limiting in classroom interactions • believe they must differentiate between planned, purposeful use of technology in teaching and casual, social use • note that getting a grip on technology is an important skill for life	• see correlation between rise in e-devices and decrease in learning outcomes • fear that poor exam scores will affect reputation of the English Department and the whole university • worry about limiting freedom of speech

STEP 3: Work in three large groups: students, faculty members, or administrators. Choose a leader and a note-taker.

STEP 4: Look again at the issues for your group. Generate and build upon each other's ideas. Use "wish" to express regrets you may have about the pre-electronic days. Make sure the note-taker writes down the main points. Use expressions such as:

- Not only that, but I would also say that . . .
- Your point makes me think of . . .
- Another thing I'd like to bring up is . . .
- OK, and to add to that idea I'd say . . .

STEP 5: Discuss the key areas on which decisions need to be made in order to make the policy recommendations. Be creative. Include recommendations about:

- the presence of devices (phones, laptops, computers, etc.) in class
- the appropriate time and place for texting, blogging, using social media in class
- incentives to encourage compliance with the policies
- discipline measures to enforce policies

STEP 6: Form new groups of three: one student, faculty member, and administrator. Discuss the issues from your points of view. Support your ideas with passion and conviction giving reasons for your ideas. Build on ideas and use "wish" to express regrets.

STEP 7: Come together as a whole class. Report your group's recommendations. Support your position with reasons for your decisions. Vote on the most creative and well thought-out policy recommendations. Use some of these expressions when you report:

- We urge you to . . .
- We recommend that . . .
- What we suggest is that . . .

UNIT PROJECT

In this activity, you will play a roving reporter and interview several people about their opinions on the topic of the use of social media and its impact on our lives.

STEP 1: On the Internet, look for research studies that relate to the impact of social media on our lives. Read one or two of these studies. Take notes.

STEP 2: Choose eight different people, two in each of the following age groups:

15–18

18–30

30–50

50 +

STEP 3: Work with a partner. Brainstorm a list of questions that you would like to ask in your interview. For example:

- Tell me about your texting habits? How often? When? Where? Why?
- What do you think about Facebook™, Instagram™, Twitter™, and other forms of social media? Do you use them? How and how often?
- Have you thought about your online reputation? What do you do to protect or manage it?

Add other questions.

STEP 4: Conduct your interviews. Start your interviews like this:

"Excuse me. I'm doing a brief survey for my English class on the topic of social media. May I ask you a few questions?"

While you interview, take notes on the answers to your questions.

STEP 5: Present a summary of your findings to the class.

ALTERNATIVE SPEAKING TOPICS

Choose a topic. Use ideas, vocabulary, grammar, pronunciation, and expressions for building on others' ideas.

Topic 1

Work in a small group. Look at the comments made by Sherry Turkle on her Twitter™ page. First, use your own words to paraphrase the comments. Then discuss whether you agree or disagree with them and why.

1. "If you don't teach your children how to be alone, they'll only always know how to be lonely." @STurkle _1:28 PM 22 Feb_

2. "It's teenagers who say, 'My parents text at the dinner table.'" @STurkle on how children also want sacred spaces. _1:34 PM 22 Feb_

3. "The greatest gift you can give your child is to walk out of the house without your phone. Show your child what that looks like!" @STurkle _1:41 PM 22 Feb_

4. "Whether or not we want robots caring for our elderly will be one of the most humanistic conversations we're going to have." @STurkle _2:17 PM 22 Feb_

Topic 2

Look at the list of forms of communication in the list on the right. Think about the ways you most like to communicate with the people in each of the labeled circles. Draw lines connecting your preferred communication methods on the right with the people in green. Then share the results with a partner and explain.

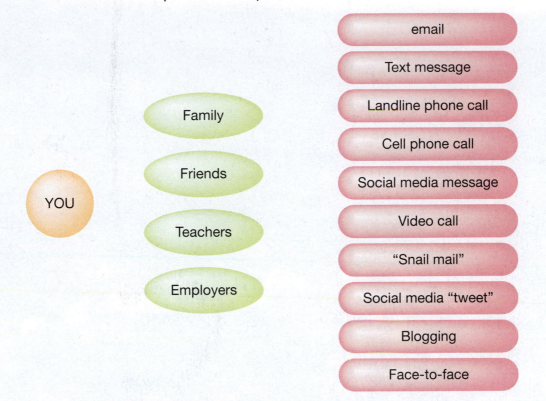

Topic 3

What do you think happens to your online identity when you die? Would you like to keep your identity open and available to friends and family, or would you prefer to erase it? For example, Google™ has a feature which allows you to plan your "digital afterlife." Would you use this tool? Why or why not? What kinds of decisions do you think you would make?

GO TO MyEnglishLab *TO DISCUSS ONE OF THE ALTERNATIVE TOPICS, WATCH A VIDEO ABOUT SOCIAL MEDIA, AND TAKE THE UNIT 6 ACHIEVEMENT TEST.*

LEARNING THROUGH THE Arts

1 FOCUS ON THE TOPIC

1. Look at the photo and the title of the unit. The *arts* refers to all the arts: music, painting, sculpture, theater, dance, and so on. For children, what might be the benefit of participating in the arts, for example, learning to play a musical instrument?

2. Think about your early educational years. Were music and art lessons available in your school? How important were they in the overall school program? Outside of school, what other music or art training have you had?

3. Think about your life today. What role do music and art play in your life? Has learning to play an instrument or participating in another arts activity enriched your life or the life of someone you know? How?

4. José Antonio Abreu, founder of an innovative arts education program in Venezuela, often says, "A child who has a clarinet in his hand will not pick up a gun." What does he mean? Do you agree? Why or why not?

GO TO MyEnglishLab *TO CHECK WHAT YOU KNOW.*

VOCABULARY

🎧 Read and listen to the description of a fictional international policy group whose mission is to research and promote arts education all over the world. Pay attention to the **bold-faced** words and phrase. Then read the list of definitions that follows. Work with a partner. Write the number of the **bold-faced** word or phrase next to its definition.

 Arts Education Policy Institute

Mission

Arts Education Policy Institute is an international organization dedicated to the understanding and promotion of the **(1) tangible** benefits of arts education. We are a **(2) diverse** group of researchers, policy makers, business people, artists, musicians, and educators. We aim to draw attention to the potential benefits of arts education for young people who may not **(3) have access to** arts programs inside or outside of school. Unlike youth in **(4) affluent** communities, young people living in low socioeconomic situations don't **(5) have the means** to afford high-quality, private arts programs to supplement their regular school curriculum.

Research

Although we're still **(6) refining** key findings, **(7) preliminary** data from several studies indicate that children who **(8) are engaged** in the arts, either in or out of school, demonstrate positive outcomes associated with academics, career, and community. When arts are **(9) infused** into the curriculum, children tend to perform better academically on standardized tests in math and reading. One of our studies also indicated that children who participate in long-term, intensive arts education programs tend to demonstrate skills critical to success in the workplace. For example, employers have noted that these children show **(10) persistence**—the ability to stick with a task and not give up. They also tend to be creative risk takers willing to be imaginative and **(11) venture outside the box**. Finally, arts programs often **(12) instill** certain **values** that can help build strong schools and communities. The arts help children see the world from different perspectives, accept differences in others, and encourage positive social interaction.

President's Statement

I visited a school last week and interviewed a 14-year-old about an innovative theater program which had just begun at his school. I asked him why most children don't like school. He said, "School **(13) gets a bad rap** because there's a lot that's kind of boring and repetitive. But these days, it's not such **(14) a drag**. The theater program is pretty cool!"

Our **(15) core** message is simple: Arts education is a transformative experience which can **(16) alter** many aspects of a child's life: school, home, and community. We ask you to support the work of our association. Thank you very much.

_____ **a.** added

_____ **b.** a bore

_____ **c.** are involved deeply

_____ **d.** be creative or original

_____ **e.** change

_____ **f.** concrete; real

_____ **g.** have the money

_____ **h.** have the opportunity

_____ **i.** initial

_____ **j.** introduce worth

_____ **k.** key

_____ **l.** modifying; improving

_____ **m.** receives unjustified criticism

_____ **n.** stamina

_____ **o.** varied

_____ **p.** wealthy

■■■■■■■■■■■■■■■■■■■■■■■■■■■■■■■■■■ *GO TO* MyEnglishLab *FOR MORE VOCABULARY PRACTICE.*

PREVIEW

You will hear an interview from the radio news program *KUOW Presents*.

🎧 Work with a partner. Studies have shown that kids who are involved in the arts do better in school. Why? What can they learn from participation in activities in music, painting, theater, or dance? List the benefits below. Then listen to a short segment of the interview to verify your predictions.

_____   _____

_____   _____

_____   _____

MAIN IDEAS

Listen to the interview divided into three parts. After each part, write the main idea in a complete sentence using the key words given. Compare your answers with those of another student to refine your understanding of the main idea.

Part One

Key words: involved in / do better

_____

Part Two

Key words: have the means / literacy skills

_____

Part Three

Key words: infuse / data / creative process / discipline processes

_____

DETAILS

Listen to the interview again. After each part, write your answers to the questions. Then compare your answers with those of another student to refine your understanding of the details that support the main ideas.

Part One

1. According to an informal poll, what do most kids think about school?

    _____

2. According to some scientists, if kids are involved in the arts, what effect might that have on the brain?

    _____

3. How convincing, or solid, is the data linking the impact of the arts on learning?

    _____

Part Two

4. Roxhill Elementary School has a diverse student body. What makes it diverse?

   _____

5. What is the socioeconomic background of the student population of Roxhill?

   _____

6. Why did the principal at Roxhill agree to participate in a pilot program to use the arts to teach literacy?

   _____

Part Three

7. During intensive summer training sessions, what do the teachers study?

   _____

8. How do they apply their summer training to their teaching during the year?

   _____

9. The children are acting like snakes in a dramatic activity. What is the purpose?

   _____

10. Why does the principal, Carmela Dellino, believe that the arts program increases student learning?

    _____

11. The U.S. Department of Education is funding this program. How much money did they give to the Arts Impact program? Why?

    _____

12. The artistic process involves a number of things which are part of other academic disciplines. What are these?

    _____

■■■■■■■■■■■■■■■■■■■■■■■■■■■■■■■■■■■■■■■ GO TO MyEnglishLab FOR MORE LISTENING PRACTICE.

MAKE INFERENCES

INFERRING THE REPORTER'S PURPOSE FOR EXAMPLES

In her radio interview, the reporter, Marcie Sillman, uses examples in order to engage and maintain her audience's interest. These examples add variety in both sound and style. A close look at these examples can reveal the particular purpose for each one:

- set the context for the report: establish where the report is taking place

- add credibility: make a conclusion or assumption more believable

- "paint a picture": help listeners "see" what they are hearing.

🎧 Read and listen to this excerpt, which opens the broadcast, and select the specific reason Sillman might have used this example. Then read the explanation.

Example

SILLMAN: If you took an informal poll, most kids would probably tell you that school is a drag. [*rap song*] I'm Marcie Sillman. Why does school get a bad rap?

The main function of this audio example in the radio broadcast is to:

a. set the context

b. add credibility

c. paint a picture

The answer is *a*. The broadcaster has us listen to an excerpt of a rap song about kids feeling bored in school. With this example, we can infer that she wants to establish the context of school. We can also infer that she uses this catchy rap about being bored in school to contrast with the engagement kids feel when they have good arts education in school.

🎧   Listen to each excerpt. Make an inference about the reporter's specific purpose for including this example. Work with a partner. Share your answers and explain your reasons.

Excerpt One

1. In the United States, students from poor families can receive free food at school. We can infer that the reporter chose this audio example mainly to:

    a. set the context   **b.** add credibility   **c.** paint a picture

Excerpt Two

2. We can infer that the reporter chose this audio example mainly to:

    a. set the context   **b.** add credibility   **c.** paint a picture

Excerpt Three

3. We can infer that the reporter chose this audio example mainly to:

    a. set the context   **b.** add credibility   **c.** paint a picture

EXPRESS OPINIONS

Follow the steps for noting and summarizing opinions.

STEP 1: Look at the questions in the left column of the chart. Quickly jot down your answers in the second column. Then circulate in the classroom and find two other students. Write their names in the top row, ask the questions, and take notes on their answers. Spend no more than three minutes with each of your classmates.

QUESTIONS	YOU	1:	2:
Do you believe that participating in the arts can alter your brain? Why or why not?			
Do you think it's a good idea to use the "arts" to teach literacy skills? Why or why not?			
Should arts education be a part of a mandatory "core curriculum" in schools, or simply an optional extra? Explain please.			
Who should pay for arts education in schools: parents, if they want their kids to have it? The community? The government?			

STEP 2: Find two other students with whom you didn't speak and summarize your results. Write your summaries on a separate piece of paper.

GO TO MyEnglishLab **TO GIVE YOUR OPINION ABOUT ANOTHER QUESTION.**

VOCABULARY

In Listening Two, author Tricia Tunstall introduces *El Sistema*, a national music education program developed in Venezuela. She is interviewed about her book, called *Changing Lives: Gustavo Dudamel*, El Sistema, *and the Transformative Power of Music*. This program has inspired the growth of similar programs worldwide.

1 🎧 The **bold-faced** words and phrases will appear in the next listening selection. Notice them as you read and listen to what a twelve-year-old cellist has to say about her experience in *El Sistema*.

> Everyone always asks me what motivates me to practice so much when I could be doing other things like hanging out with my friends, watching TV, or just doing nothing. Well, my **incentive** is to get better and better at the cello, so I can teach the younger kids. *El Sistema* has **equipped** me with a strong **sense of accomplishment**. I now think I'm pretty **adept** at bowing, a really important skill to play the cello. Although my parents are pretty happy I am active in the orchestra, they are really happier that I just haven't **fallen into the trap of** laziness!

2 Match the words or phrases on the left with the definitions or synonyms on the right. Write the corresponding letter in the blank.

_____ **1.** incentive

_____ **2.** equipped

_____ **3.** sense of

_____ **4.** adept

_____ **5.** fall into the trap of

a. skillful

b. do something unwise that at first seemed like a good idea

c. motivation

d. prepared

e. feeling of

COMPREHENSION

🎧 Listen to the interview with the author, Tricia Tunstall. As you listen, check (✓) the statements that are true. There may be more than one correct answer. Compare your answers with those of another student.

1. *El Sistema* . . .

_____ promotes orchestra playing to develop young people.

_____ aims to produce professional musicians.

_____ equips youth to be productive members of society.

2. The children who participate in the *El Sistema* program . . .

_____ come from impoverished areas of Venezuela.

_____ must give up their guns and gangs.

_____ learn social as well as musical skills.

3. Participating in an orchestra helps children . . .

_____ develop a sense of self-esteem.

_____ learn how to teach their parents how to play an instrument.

_____ escape poverty by becoming instrument makers.

■■ *GO TO* MyEnglishLab *FOR MORE VOCABULARY PRACTICE.*

LISTENING SKILL

NOTICING PERSUASION WITH PARALLEL STRUCTURE

In this interview, Tunstall presents a compelling portrait of the inspiring music education phenomenon, *El Sistema*. In order to make a convincing argument for the benefits of *El Sistema*, she uses parallel structure: the repetition of the same grammatical structure to reinforce, enrich, and emphasize.

🎧 Read and listen to the example. Then complete the sentences and read the explanation.

Example

TUNSTALL: This program, as you said, produces many extraordinary musicians. But most of the graduates of *El Sistema* do not become musicians. What they do is go out into the world equipped both mentally and psychologically and emotionally to be productive, uh, contributing citizens, and to have flourishing lives.

Tunstall uses three adverbs: mentally, _____, _____,

She uses this parallel structure to stress that the goal of *El Sistema* is _____

The three adverbs are *mentally*, *psychologically*, and *emotionally*. Tunstall repeats three adverbs (parallel structure) in order to emphasize her message that the focus of *El Sistema* is to produce citizens who are healthy in every way.

(continued on next page)

🎧 Listen to the excerpts from the interview. Identify the items in parallel structure, or the repeated element. Write a short statement summarizing the purpose for using this element. Use the "sentence starters" to guide you.

Excerpt One

1. Turnstall uses five noun phrases: She says that a child learns not only how to harmonize musically, but how to harmonize socially—_____, _____, and _____.

She uses this parallel structure to stress that the ensemble offers . . .

_____

Excerpt Two

2. Turnstall uses three noun + noun phrases: a sense of self esteem, _____, and _____.

She uses this parallel structure to emphasize that playing an instrument . . .

_____

Excerpt Three

3. Turnstall repeats four *so* + adjective phrases: so attractive, _____, _____, and _____.

She uses this parallel structure to strengthen her view that these programs really provide . . .

_____

■■■■■■■■■■■■■■■■■■■■■■■■■■■■■■■■■■■■■■ *GO TO* MyEnglishLab *FOR MORE SKILL PRACTICE.*

STEP 1: Organize

Listening One presents a local arts education program, Arts Impact, based in Seattle, Washington, in the USA. Listening Two presents a large-scale national arts program, *El Sistema*, in Venezuela.

Complete the chart with your notes on key features of both programs.

	LISTENING ONE: ARTS IMPACT IN ONE SCHOOL IN SEATTLE, WASHINGTON	LISTENING TWO: *EL SISTEMA* IN COMMUNITIES THROUGHOUT VENEZUELA
Art(s) that are taught	theater, dance, music, visual arts	
Socioeconomic status of children in program		
Objective of arts education program		youth development / social community development
Impact of arts education program		

STEP 2: Synthesize

Use the information in your chart to prepare a two-minute mini-lecture. Work with a partner. One student chooses Arts Impact, while the other chooses *El Sistema*. Take a few minutes to plan your mini-lecture.

Try to answer these questions:

- What are the goals of the program?
- Whom does it serve?
- How does it work in practice?
- What are the pros and cons of the program to arts education?
- What benefits, other than the stated goals, might children, parents, and teachers expect?

Present your mini-lecture to your partner. If time permits, switch partners and give your talk again.

GO TO MyEnglishLab *TO CHECK WHAT YOU LEARNED.*

VOCABULARY

REVIEW

El Sistema, the world-renowned Venezuelan music program, has inspired other countries to create similar programs. *El Sistema* founder, José Antonio Abreu, conducts large meetings to spread the word.

Imagine a panel discussion with Abreu and Lennar Acosta, a clarinetist and the director of one of the "nucleos," or music schools in Venezuela. Over 500 educators, musicians, government officials, and parents are gathered at the *Palacio de Bellas Artes* in Mexico City to learn more about *El Sistema*.

Palacio de Bellas Artes

Read quickly the following transcript of a portion of the panel discussion. Then work with a partner and complete the transcript using the correct form of the words or phrases listed below from Listenings One and Two. Finally, listen to the transcript to check your answers.

access to	(a) drag	incentive	preliminary
adept	engage	infused	sense of accomplishment
affluent	fallen into the trap of	instill values	tangible
diverse	have the means (to)	persistence	venture outside the box

MODERATOR: Good afternoon. Maestro Abreu and Mr. Acosta—it is an honor to have you here in Mexico. Maestro, why *El Sistema*? You started this unusual program with 11 young musicians in an abandoned parking garage. What drove you to _____ and create such an extraordinary social

(1)

program?

MAESTRO ABREU: Like many countries, Venezuela had music schools and conservatories

for the _____, so music was an exclusive experience.

(2)

But for me, music's a universal right; my dream was to provide

_____ thousands of children in disadvantaged areas. I hope

(3)

for a world full of orchestras!

MODERATOR: So, kids who would never _____ take music lessons would

(4)

be able to participate. What's the role of the orchestra in *El Sistema*?

ABREU: It's the soul of the program. At age 2 or 3, children start to attend a local

nucleo. After school, they practice together 6–7 hours a day, 6 days a week.

Through this practice, the children learn about discipline, teamwork, and

_____. We now have more than 200 orchestras and dozens

(5)

of choruses performing a _____ array of musical genres.

(6)

MODERATOR: Thank you, Maestro. Now Mr. Acosta, you're the director of one of the

largest *nucleos* in Venezuela, *Los Chorros*. I understand this *nucleo* started

as a facility for delinquent and abandoned kids, and that you were one of

them.

LENNAR ACOSTA: Yes, at the age of 12, I had already _____ crime. I was put

(7)

in *Los Chorros* not for protection, but for punishment. Then Maestro

Abreu turned the facility from a detention center into a *nucleo*.

ABREU: When I first met Lennar he was a troubled teen with no apparent talent.

Clearly, he thought playing music was really just _____.

(8)

However, after offering him a few instruments, we handed him a clarinet

and he seemed to be an adept clarinetist. He worked diligently and, as he

(continued on next page)

improved, his _____ (9) grew, which provided the necessary

_____ (10) to audition for the most prestigious youth orchestra

in Caracas, the Simón Bolívar Orchestra. Eventually, he returned to *Los*

Chorros to be the director, a very _____ (11) result of all his

hard work, for sure!

MODERATOR: Maestro, tell me the truth! Is Lennar the exception or the rule?

ABREU: Although he's exceptional, he's the rule. Come walk the halls of *Los*

Chorros. They're _____ (12) with the sounds of exquisite

music. Not only will you hear the magic, but you'll also witness the

way the teachers _____ (13) and motivate the kids with

humor and energy. The teachers, former students themselves, aren't just

technical instructors; they're friends, mentors, social workers striving to

_____ (14) of solidarity, tolerance, and peace.

MODERATOR: OK. So what's next?

ABREU: Well, currently we're working to launch *nucleos* in the poorest areas of

Venezuela where children have nothing—barely one meal a day, no water,

no electricity. They search garbage dumps for stuff to sell so they and their

families can eat. We're studying _____ (15) data that show even

in these impoverished areas, the children are showing motivation, growth,

and determination to transform their lives.

ACOSTA: Maestro has often said, "Culture for the poor must never be poor culture."

I'm a product of his dream.

MODERATOR: Sadly, we're out of time, but thank you both so much for being here today.

EXPAND

1 Work with a partner. Read the sentences. Many words have more than one meaning. Write **Lit.** next to the sentence if the **bold-faced** word or phrase is being used in a **literal** way, and write **Fig.** next to the sentence if it's being used in a **figurative** way. Then using the context clues, explain how the two words differ.

1. a. _____Fig._____ Early experiences with art and music might be having some effect on children knowing how to **attack** academic content.

   b. _____Lit._____ The army **attacked** the opposing forces.

   Explanation: In a, "attack" is used in a non-physical way. It's not a literal attack. The word creates a picture in your mind. In this sentence, "attack" means "set to work on" or "approach." In contrast, in b, "attack" is used in a physical way. Here, it is a literal attack. It means "used violence against."

2. a. _____ After the performance, the audience gave the singer **a big hand**.

   b. _____ The pianist's **big hands** allowed him to play the difficult chords in romantic music.

   Explanation: _____

   _____

3. a. _____ The snake **rattled** loudly as it moved through the dense plants next to the path.

   b. _____ The clarinetist's nerves were **rattled** as he had never performed a solo before such a large audience.

   Explanation: _____

   _____

4. a. _____ The singer's throat was hurting her, so she **infused** some tea with fruit and drank it slowly.

   b. _____ The award-winning theater arts program from China was **infused** with imagination, tradition, and culture.

   Explanation: _____

   _____

(continued on next page)

5. a. _____ The pianist's hand was **scarred** after he burned it.

   b. _____ The father forced his child to practice ten hours a day. That experience was painful and **scarred** the child for life.

   Explanation: _____

   _____

6. a. _____ The orchestra director **blew up** when his flight was delayed for no apparent reason. He risked being late for his own performance!

   b. _____ Police suspect that the terrorist group may **blow up** another car.

   Explanation: _____

   _____

2 Work with another student.

Student A: Ask Student B questions 1 through 4.

Student B: Cover the left column. Answer Student A's questions. Respond in as much detail as possible, using the cues given and incorporating figurative language as much as possible. Switch roles after question 3.

Student A	**Student B**
1. When was the last time you went to a concert or show and gave the performers **a big hand**? Describe the performance.	1. Hmm. Let me see . . .
2. What is your strategy for **attacking** new material in English?	2. Well, . . .
3. Do your nerves ever get **rattled** before you have to give a presentation in English?	3. Yes, . . .

Now switch roles.

4. Have you ever **infused** drama or theater into your work or studies?	4. Of course. One time . . .
5. When was the last time you **blew up** at someone? What happened?	5. Hmm. I'm not sure I remember all the details, but . . .
6. Very scary movies often frighten young children out of their wits. Do you think these experiences **scar** them for life? Why or why not?	6. Let me see . . .

CREATE

Form teams of two to four players. All teams will play the game described below.

WORD GAME: CLEAN THE BOARD

Object of the game: To be the first team to "clean the board," or remove all cards from the large piece of paper, the "game board."

How to Play the Game

1. Each team copies the game board onto a larger piece of paper. It should have two columns and three rows as shown in the picture below.

2. Each team chooses six words or phrases from the list and writes each one on a small card. Place them face up over a different box on the team's game board. Each team should choose different words or phrases from the list.

access to	equipped	persistence
adept	fall into the trap of	preliminary
affluent	have the means to	rattled
(a) drag	incentive	sense of accomplishment
diverse	infused	tangible
engage	instill values	venture outside the box

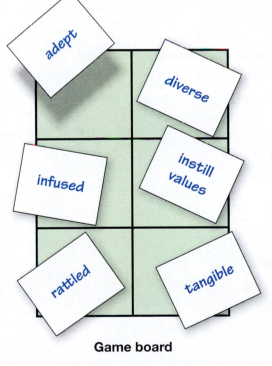

Game board

3. All teams play at the same time. The object is for each team to clean its board as quickly as possible. This is how a team works to clean the board:

- One student on each team asks the teammate(s) a question that tries to get another teammate(s) to say one of the words on the board. The teammate must answer the question using the word.

- If the teammate(s) choose a correct word to answer the question, the card from the board is removed.

Example

TEAMMATE ONE: What is something you are really good at?

TEAMMATE TWO: Actually, I think I am pretty *adept* at playing an electronic keyboard.

A correct word, *adept* was chosen, so Teammate One removes the word from the board.

(continued on next page)

4. The winning team is the one that cleans the board (removes all its cards) first.

5. Play again. Start over using different words from the list.

GO TO MyEnglishLab FOR MORE VOCABULARY PRACTICE.

GRAMMAR

1 Work with a partner. Examine the sentences and discuss the questions that follow.

- In one ensemble, a group of three-year-olds **was given** singing lessons while another group of four-year-olds **was selected** for violin lessons.

- Major research on the impact of arts education **has been conducted** by UNESCO and other international agencies.

- A mistake **was made** in the printed program. The sonatas by Mozart **will not be played**.

- Before the concert, we **had** the piano **tuned** and **got** the lights **repaired**.

1. In each sentence, why do you think the speaker chooses the passive voice for the verbs?

2. In the last sentence, who is performing the action?

THE PASSIVE VOICE AND THE PASSIVE CAUSATIVE

How to Form the Passive Voice

The **passive voice** is formed by using a form of the verb *be* plus the past participle of the main verb. The verb *be* can be used in any tense, as illustrated below.

SUBJECT	FORM OF THE VERB *BE*	PAST PARTICIPLE	COMPLEMENT
The students	**are**	**given**	a well-rounded education
His self-esteem	**was**	**enhanced**	
The program	**will be**	**canceled**	
The curriculum	**is going to be**	**improved**	
The pieces	**must be**	**practiced**	
The neurons	**might have been**	**stimulated**	
Spatial reasoning	**is being**	**improved**	

When to Use the Passive Voice

The passive voice is used when you:

- want to emphasize the object of the action, not the actor
- do not know the actor
- want to avoid mentioning who performed the action or to avoid blaming anyone
- want to report an idea or fact

Passive Causative

The **passive causative** is used to speak about services arranged.

It is formed with the verbs *get* or *have* plus the past participle of the main verb.

Ms. Diaz is organizing an art exhibition of her students' work. With special funds collected for this purpose, she **had** the paintings **mounted** on special paper. She also **had** the works **framed**. Finally, she **got** the school lobby **cleaned** and **set up**.

2 Complete the paragraphs with the appropriate forms of the verbs provided. Choose active or passive forms, including passive causative. Keep in mind that some verbs cannot be used in the passive voice. Then discuss your reaction to the study.

PIANO OR COMPUTER: WHICH BOOSTS INTELLIGENCE?

In recent years, there has been exciting research about the effects of musical training on intelligence. Currently the effects of piano lessons on young children _are being researched_
1. (research)
by Frances Rauscher of the University of Wisconsin.

Whether children can learn more from a piano keyboard or a computer keyboard _____. A report on this
2. (study)
research recently _____
3. (appear)
in the journal *Neurological Research*. It said

that certain aspects of a child's intelligence

_____ by musical training,
4. (can / enhance)
particularly by piano study. Spatial reasoning

skills _____ by work on a
5. (can / improve)
piano keyboard, but not on a computer keyboard.

In one of Rauscher's studies, 78 young

children _____. They
6. (involve)
_____ into four groups
7. (divide)
of subjects. Some of the children took

piano keyboard lessons, some computer

lessons, and others _____
8. (receive)

(continued on next page)

group-singing lessons. No special training

_____ for the fourth group.
　　　9. (provide)

By the end of six months, the piano keyboard

children _____ instruction
　　　　　　10. (give)

in muscle coordination, simple compositions,

and musical literacy. Rauscher claimed that

the children _____ enough
　　　　　　11. (give)

training to be able to play simple pieces such as

Beethoven's "Ode to Joy."

　　The final step in the research

_____ of a test of
　　12. (consist)

analytical reasoning skills. Rauscher

_____ the results

_____ by research assistants.
　　13. (collect)

Then she _____ the

data _____ by a highly
　　　14. (analyze)

sophisticated computer program. An important

finding _____. The children
　　　　15. (emerge)

who _____ in piano keyboard
　　　16. (instruct)

training scored significantly higher on the test

than the children in the other three groups.

Therefore, Rauscher _____
　　　　　　　　17. (conclude)

that, regardless of the fact that a keyboard

_____ for the computer group,
　　18. (use)

the children who used a piano keyboard still

_____ higher on the test.
　　19. (score)

　　The research underscores the fact that the

piano _____ to be the critical
　　　20. (seem)

ingredient. In musical training, the brain circuits

_____ in such a way that
21. (may / stimulate)

certain nerve pathways _____.
　　　　　　　　　　22. (strengthen)

Nevertheless, in order to confirm these results,

Rauscher _____ the study
　　　　　　23. (repeat)

_____ by other researchers.

3 Work with a partner.

Student A: You are a reporter for *Music Times Newsletter*. You are writing a profile about Gustavo Dudamel, the conductor of the Los Angeles Philharmonic and the Simón Bolívar Orchestra of Venezuela. To gather data, you are interviewing Dudamel's mother, Solángel Ramírez Viloria. Cover the right column. Read the questions in the left column. Change the **bold-faced** verbs to the passive voice as you read.

Student B: You are Dudamel's mother. You have watched your son emerge to be one of the most famous conductors in the world. Cover the left column. Read the responses in the right column. Change the **bold-faced** verbs to the passive voice as you read. Listen carefully, look at each other as much as possible, and read your lines with feeling.

Student A

1. Thanks so much for taking the time to speak with me, Señora.

2. So, how **be** Gustavo's interest in violin **spark**?

3. Why a violin? I heard Gustavo's father was a trombone player? **Be** he **give** a trombone to try?

4. **Be** he **push** to **play**?

5. Do you mean he **be** /**not** / **discover** for 7 years?

6. Amazing. Now he is a world famous, globe-trotting conductor. How **have** his career **be** / **manage** since he's become a star?

7. I hear now that the Simón Bolívar Orchestra may **have** / **be** / **select** to perform at the unique National Center for Performing Arts, a.k.a. "The Bird's Egg" in Beijing.

8. Well, good luck then to Gustavo and his musicians. You have a brilliant son! Thanks so much for your time.

Student B

1. Oh, it's my pleasure.

2. Well, he seemed to love music since he was a tiny baby. But I think he **might** / **inspire** when he **give** a violin at the age of 6.

3. Sure, but he couldn't play it because his arms were too short, so he turned to the violin when he joined *El Sistema*.

4. Absolutely not! He **encourage**, but not **push**. He had been participating in *El Sistema* for over 7 years before he **identify** as a gifted musician.

5. Yes. he **might** / **notice** earlier, but *El Sistema* teachers really focus on helping all the kids, and not just identifying and nurturing a star.

6. Well, he is still a performer who **have** to **have** all his performance details **handle**. Before a concert, he **have** to **have** his violin **repair**. He always **get** his suit **dry-clean** and **have** photos **take**. There's a lot that **must** / **do**.

7. Yes, at this time the orchestra **be** / **consider** to play at the Beijing Music Festival. If it **be** / **choose**, it'll be the first Latin American orchestra ever to **have** / **invite** to play at this very popular event.

8. Thank you for speaking with me. Hope to see you at one of Gustavo's performances soon.

GO TO MyEnglishLab *FOR MORE GRAMMAR PRACTICE.*

PRONUNCIATION

JOINING FINAL CONSONANTS

Words that end in consonants join to following words in different ways.

- When the next word starts with a vowel: Join the final consonant and vowel clearly.

  Self-esteem   works in progress

- When the next word starts with the same consonant or sound: Hold one long consonant. Do not say the consonant twice.

  Art teachers   enhance skills

- When the next word starts with a different consonant: Keep the final consonant short. Hold it, and then immediately say the next word.

  extreme poverty   attack problems

1 🎧 Listen and repeat the phrases. Then practice saying them with a partner. Pay attention to how you join the two words.

1. music appreciation

2. art education

3. critical ingredients

4. parental involvement

5. music class

6. top performance

7. abstract topics

8. recent studies

9. reap benefits

10. instill values

2 🎧 Listen, and repeat the phrases. Using the rules for joining consonants, mark each phrase: ⌣ or ⌢ or). Then complete the sentences with the correct phrases. Compare your answers with those of a partner. Take turns saying the sentences.

an interactive approach	peer review
boost brain power	research challenge
a critical ingredient	self-esteem

1. The researchers found that music has a general effect of improving a child's self-image and _____.

2. Just how and why music and art enhance certain mathematical skills continues to be a _____.

3. Arts education seems to be _____ in improving analytical reasoning.

4. Studies done in the past seven years indicate that studying music and art can significantly _____.

5. Communication, discussion, and involvement are hallmarks of _____ to education.

6. _____ is a typical activity in music classes in which kids help and teach each other.

SPEAKING SKILL

SPEAKING PERSUASIVELY WITH PARALLEL STRUCTURE

Notice the **bold-faced** words or phrases in the sentences.

- He is learning in ensemble which is very important because in the orchestral ensemble you learn not only **how to harmonize musically, but how to harmonize socially—how to become a contributor, how to cooperate with other people, how to work together for one common goal.**

- Playing an instrument and learning and getting better at the instrument also really gives a child **a sense of self-esteem, a sense of mastery, a sense of accomplishment** that he or she may not have gotten anywhere else in his or her life either at school or in the home.

- To learn a skill, artists need to show **persistence, courage,** and **risk-taking**.

(continued on next page)

The bold-faced expressions exemplify parallel structures: repeated patterns of words or phrases that give emphasis. Two or more words or phrases can be linked in a variety of ways to help you persuade others of your point of view. All words or phrases must follow the same grammatical pattern.

The speakers in Listenings One and Two use this device to help make their arguments more persuasive.

Work with a partner. Play the following roles.

Student A: Cover the right column. You are a cellist auditioning for the Simón Bolívar Orchestra in Venezuela. You are practicing for your interview with your friend. Read to Student B a few of the reasons you think you should be chosen.

Student B: Cover the left column. Show Student A how to be more persuasive. Restate Student B's reasons using parallel structure.

Switch roles after statement 3.

Student A	Student B
1. By playing in the ensemble, I realized music was fun, inspirational and it relaxed me.	1. Hold on. You could be more persuasive by saying it this way: By playing in the ensemble, I realized music was fun, inspirational, and relaxing.
2. My teachers helped me develop a sense of accomplishment, my self-esteem grew, and I developed mastery.	2. Why don't you try this:
3. With my mastery of diverse styles, unique compositions and I have a great sense of rhythm, I know I can make a strong contribution to the orchestra.	3. Um, let's see. Try this:

Now switch roles.

Student A	Student B
4. When I am not practicing, I participate in a community theater group and I watch movies, and enjoy reading.	4. Hold on. You should try it this way:
5. Trust me when I tell you that I can perform under pressure and I am adept at improvising and at memorizing.	5. For more emphasis you could say this:
6. I am very persistent, and I am confident I will do well in the orchestra with my natural talent and my strong technical skills.	6. Be more persuasive. Try this:

■■■■ ■■ ■■■■ ■■ ■■■ ■ ■■ GO TO MyEnglishLab FOR MORE SKILL PRACTICE AND TO CHECK WHAT YOU LEARNED.

FINAL SPEAKING TASK

In this activity, you will lead a task force meeting about the role of arts education in government schools and the funding for it. Use the vocabulary, grammar, pronunciation, and listening and speaking skills that you learned in the unit.*

Follow the steps.

STEP 1: Read the background information and case study based on a real news report.

Background

In many countries around the world, government schools—that is, publicly-funded local schools—are administered and financed by both federal (national) and state governments. These government officials determine the school budget, which is the yearly financial plan of how money will be allocated to the local schools.

The costs to fund public school education has been rising, and the federal governments are contributing less to the individual states. Therefore, many states are struggling to maintain a high-quality educational program for their local schools.

Case Study: State Government Proposes Drastic Cuts in Arts Program

One state in a country in Latin America is in the process of developing its yearly budget. However, this year the state must work with 30 percent less money than it has had in the past. In order to save money, state officials have already decided on a number of actions:

- mandatory early retirement for 2,000 teachers
- elimination of physical education classes in the middle schools and high schools
- elimination of English language instruction in primary schools (kindergarten through sixth grade)

However, now state officials are saying that these cuts are not enough. Now they have proposed the elimination of all art and music classes from elementary schools.

Parents are outraged. Angry discussion can be heard everywhere throughout the towns: on downtown streets, in supermarkets, at the community centers and football fields, and so on. Parents are demanding that state officials reconsider their decision.

Because of all the complaints, the board has agreed to hold open forum meetings to discuss the proposal. It has invited representatives from three groups to attend the meetings: (1) parents, (2) art and music teachers, and (3) state school officials.

---

* For Alternative Speaking Topics, see page 212.

STEP 2: Prepare for the meeting. Everyone in the class should choose a role: parent, teacher, or state school official. Divide into groups of students who are all playing the same role. In your role groups, study the descriptions that follow, and brainstorm other supporting arguments. Write your arguments on separate pieces of paper.

Parents

- want to keep art and music classes in the school curriculum

- cannot afford to pay extra to provide private art or music lessons

- feel art and music instruction inspires appreciation of the arts, provides a break from academic instruction, and builds persistence, courage, and discipline

Art and Music Educators

- feel music is a universal human right and the goal of arts education should be to "make music and make citizens"

- feel that it's important for children to participate in a musical community infused with joy, and a sense of dignity

- feel that arts instruction can improve 21st century skills such as creativity, collaboration, and critical thinking

State School Officials

- feel that art and music instruction is a frill, a non-academic extra without the rigor or importance of math, science, or reading

- feel pressure from the federal government to improve scores on all standardized exams so there is no time in the curriculum for arts education

- think parents should be responsible for this extra activity

STEP 3: Conduct preliminary meetings of three students each: one parent, one arts educator, and one state school official. Practice using passive voice and parallel structure in your statements.

STEP 4: Conduct the meeting. During the meeting, all students should use the passive voice and parallel structure to make their arguments persuasive.

One student leads the meeting. This leader:

- opens the meeting by introducing the participants and explaining the purpose

- conducts the meeting by eliciting comments and questions from the participants

- asks a representative from each group to present a two-minute summary of the group's position

- closes the meeting by presenting a short summary of the meeting; asks for a vote on the issue of cutting school funding for arts

STEP 5: Summarize the issue. Write an editorial letter to the local newspaper voicing your concerns about the cuts to the arts education program. Emphasize the important role that art and music play in the lives of all children.

UNIT PROJECT

Follow the steps to conduct an experiment on the topic.

You will organize an experiment on "The Mozart Effect." The experiment will try to determine if listening to music by Mozart can increase the speed of performing simple math, logic, or spatial problems.

STEP 1: Choose four to six people to participate (or divide the class into two groups). Divide the participants into two groups: Group A: control group, and Group B: test group. Explain to the participants the purpose of the experiment, and give a little background that you have learned in this unit.

STEP 2: Direct the participant groups to go into two rooms. Group A sits in silence. Group B listens to Mozart. After 10 minutes, all participants solve math problems. You can use these sample problems below, or find or design your own:

1. Study the table of numbers below for 2 minutes. Then cover it up, and try to reproduce it yourself.

2	6	6	1
3	4	2	6
6	3	6	0
4	2	1	8

2. How many rectangles are there in the figure?

3. What is the minimum number of arrows that must be turned in some manner so that all arrows point in the same direction?

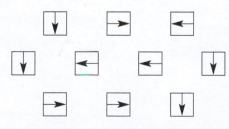

2. Answer: 9   3. Answer: 6

STEP 3: Compare the two groups' problem-solving skills in terms of speed and accuracy.

STEP 4: Report the results to the class. Then compare the results. Use the expressions of contrast and similarity and the passive voice to explain the process.

STEP 5: Work in small groups, and discuss the answers to these questions:

- Did you see evidence of the Mozart effect? Why or why not?

- If you were to repeat the experiment, how would you do the experiment differently?

ALTERNATIVE SPEAKING TOPICS

Read the quotes below by great artists and thinkers from the last three centuries or search the Internet for a few famous quotations about the arts and education. Then choose one of the activities below. Work with a partner.

1. "Art is both creation and recreation."

   —*Lin Yutang, Chinese writer and inventor*

2. "Art and the approach to life through art, using it as a vehicle for education and even for doing science is so vital that it is part of a great new revolution that is taking place."

   —*Jonas Salk, American biologist and physician*

3. "Art is a necessity—an essential part of our enlightenment process. We cannot, as a civilized society, regard ourselves as being enlightened without the arts."

   —*Ken Danby, Canadian artist*

4. "Art knows. Art sees beyond . . . . Art points us in new directions that make us think and question."

   —*Warren Criswell, American artist and animator*

5. "Music has to be recognized as an agent of social development, in the highest sense because it transmits the highest values—solidarity, harmony, mutual compassion."

   —*José Antonio Abreu, Venezuelan orchestra conductor*

Activities

1. Paraphrase the quotes (use different words to express the same ideas). To introduce your paraphrase, use one of the following phrases:

   - In other words. . .

   - What this quote is saying . . .

   - The gist here is . . .

   - My main takeaway from this quote is . . .

   - What _____ is saying is . . .

2. Select your favorite quote from the ones you chose above and explain what it means to you personally.

3. Select one of the quotes above as a slogan for encouraging arts in education. Explain your choice.

■■■■■■■■■■■■■■■■■■■■■■■■■■ *GO TO* MyEnglishLab *TO DISCUSS ONE OF THE ALTERNATIVE TOPICS,*
WATCH A VIDEO ABOUT AN ART ACADEMY, AND TAKE THE UNIT 7 ACHIEVEMENT TEST. ■■■■■■■■■■■■■

CHANGING LIVES FOR
$50

1. Three billion people—roughly half the world's population—live on less than two dollars a day. Why are so many people poor? Why is it so difficult for people to escape from poverty?

2. Many governments, organizations, corporations, groups, and individuals have tried for years to find the best way to lift people out of poverty. Check (✓) the program(s) in the box that you know about. Then working in a small group, discuss these or any programs you have heard about which are designed to alleviate poverty. Talk about how effective these programs are and why.

_____ government-based loans

_____ government-based aid

_____ global businesses

_____ microfinance

_____ campaigns led by famous celebrities

_____ private agencies and organizations

GO TO MyEnglishLab *TO CHECK WHAT YOU KNOW.*

2 FOCUS ON LISTENING

LISTENING ONE PROMISES AND PITFALLS OF MICROFINANCE

VOCABULARY

1 🎧 Read and listen to this interview with the director of a microfinance institution. Discuss your reactions to microfinance.

---

www.transformationInternational.org

An Interview with Sylvia Otero

Director of leading microfinance institution, Transformation International, Sylvia Otero discusses microfinance and her bold efforts to raise the poor out of poverty.

What exactly is Transformation International? *Edward Montgomery, Kansas City, Kansas*

Sylvia Otero: Well, like other international microfinance institutions, our mission is to provide financial services to the very poor. We believe that many people are poor because they have no control over capital—meaning money or property (buildings, equipment, machines, tools, etc.). Now, without capital, the poor do not have any way to make money and businesses can't start or grow. So, what we do is we offer loans or credit to people who have <u>no</u> access to traditional financial services. We do <u>not</u> give charity or handouts.

What is your mission? *Lida Stepanek, Czech Republic*

SO: Well, we are committed to the four themes set forth by the international microfinance movement:
1) empower women
2) reach the very poor
3) build financially stable and **sustainable** incomes and institutions
4) create positive, measurable impact

How do you respond to skeptics who say that poor people are not likely to repay a debt? *Ali Faramawi, Dubai*

SO: Well! We respond by publicizing the facts. As you know, poor people are generally excluded from traditional banking services because many are illiterate, lack collateral[1] to get a loan, or feel intimidated. Banks readily point out potential **pitfalls** of loaning money to the poor. Basically, they fear that the poor could easily get **overextended** and fail to repay their loans. Yet the fact is that the rate of global repayment of microcredit loans is between 97 and 99 percent. Those numbers are quite **compelling**. Our thousands of microcredit success stories disprove the **characterization** of poor people as unmotivated and a credit risk. Absolutely, we see success at the bottom of the economic pyramid.

---

[1] **collateral:** money or property offered as a guarantee to repay a loan

Is it true that most microcredit borrowers are women? *Natalia Bruzoni, Junín, Argentina*

SO: Yes, as a matter of fact, it is. Internationally, 85 percent of microcredit clients are women because they are the ones who usually **bear the brunt** of poverty. We lend tiny loans of $25 to $100 mainly to very poor women who use the money to open small, simple businesses, **cottage industries**, such as selling food, textiles, or dairy products. The women usually repay loans at a higher rate than men. In addition to that, if a woman's business is undercapitalized,[2] she will apply for a new loan, reinvest, and stick with the business instead of spending whatever she's made on alcohol or girlfriends. And, finally, microcredit institutions know that women are the best investment because the impact can reach **in perpetuity**, benefiting their children and future generations. In this way, we **diminish** poverty long-term.

Do you ever see a *backlash* from men who may be jealous of their wives' success?
Reka Randell, Auckland, New Zealand

SO: Well, you might think so, but actually we don't see this because it's not a zero-sum[3] situation: The wife's accomplishments don't take away from her husband's success. Most families are just happy to have food on their plates and a **safety net** in case of health emergencies.

How and why did you start the foundation Transformation International?
Eser Vural, Denizli, Turkey

SO: Well, I joined the Peace Corps in 1976 and, being of Haitian ancestry, I specifically requested to do my volunteer service in Haiti, the poorest country in the western hemisphere. Hurricane Jeanne hit Haiti in 2004, and it **wiped out** hundreds of small coastal villages and killed over 3,000 people, including some very close friends and relatives.

A week after the hurricane, I decided to quit my high-paying job as a biotech consultant to start a foundation which would provide long-term economic support to the poor in Haiti and help rebuild the devastated country. And then I became an **overnight success**, an activist for the poor as well as the founder and CEO of Transformation International. Clearly, microfinance is not an absolute **panacea**, but it is proving to be an effective tool to ease the poorest of the poor out of poverty.

---

[2] **undercapitalized:** not having enough money to operate effectively
[3] **zero-sum:** where a gain for one person means a loss for another person

> **QUOTE OF THE DAY:**
> *When asked what his strategy was in forming the Grameen Bank, Muhammed Yunus said:*
>
> *"Well, I didn't have a strategy. I just kept doing what was next. But when I look back, my strategy was: whatever banks did, I did the opposite. If banks lent to the rich, I lent to the poor. If banks lent to men, I lent to women. If banks made large loans, I made small loans. If banks required collateral, my loans were collateral free. If banks required a lot of paperwork, my loans were illiterate-friendly. Yes, that was my strategy: whatever banks did, I did the opposite."*

2 Find the **bold-faced** words or phrases in the interview on pages 216–217. Circle the best synonym or definition for the word or phrase as it is used in the interview.

1. **sustainable**

   a. able to continue   **b.** very large

2. **pitfalls**

   a. costs   **b.** dangers

3. **overextended**

   a. owing too much money   **b.** having too much money

4. **compelling**

   a. interesting   **b.** upsetting

5. **characterization**

   a. personality   **b.** description

6. **bear the brunt**

   a. suffer the worst   **b.** accept the fact

7. **cottage industries**

   a. home-building businesses   **b.** home-based businesses

8. **in perpetuity**

   a. for all future time   **b.** in old age

9. **diminish**

   a. ignore   **b.** lessen

10. **backlash**

   a. violent action   **b.** negative reaction

11. **safety net**

   a. help in times of trouble   **b.** equipment for work

12. **wiped out**

   a. cleaned   **b.** destroyed

13. **overnight success**

   a. suddenly successful   **b.** mysteriously successful

14. **panacea**

   a. solution   **b.** option

■ GO TO MyEnglishLab FOR MORE VOCABULARY PRACTICE.

PREVIEW

You will listen to a radio interview on the promises and pitfalls of microfinance. The host, Ross Reynolds, interviews three leaders in the field:

- Alex Counts, president and CEO of Grameen Foundation USA

- Raj Shah, Director of Financial Services and Agriculture with the Bill and Melinda Gates Foundation

- Matt Flannery, co-founder of Kiva.org, a website that connects lenders with people in need of microloans

Alex Counts,
Grameen Foundation USA

Raj Shah,
Bill and Melinda Gates
Foundation

Matt Flannery,
Kiva.org

People living in *extreme poverty*—less than a dollar a day—are unable to meet their basic needs for survival. Those living in *moderate poverty*—one to two dollars a day—can just meet their basic needs but have no safety net in case of misfortune. People in microfinance like to study the outcomes of the move from extreme poverty to moderate poverty.

🎧 Work with a partner. Predict what basic needs might be met when a family moves from extreme to moderate poverty. Write your predictions on the lines. Then listen to the excerpt to check your predictions.

_____

_____

_____

_____

MAIN IDEAS

Read the items. Then listen to the interview. Complete the sentences to express the main idea(s) of each segment from the interview. Add an additional sentence if necessary. Compare your sentences with those of another student.

Part One: Alex Counts, Grameen Foundation USA

1. According to Alex Counts, $60 or $70 dollars can make a huge difference in the life of a poor

person because _____

_____

Part Two: Raj Shah, Bill and Melinda Gates Foundation

2. According to Raj Shah, the biggest outcome of moving from extreme to moderate poverty is

_____

_____

Part Three: Matt Flannery, Kiva.org

3. According to Matt Flannery, microfinance is more beneficial than direct charity programs

because _____

_____

Part Four: Alex Counts

4. According to Alex Counts, the biggest impact of microcredit is _____

_____

DETAILS

Listen to the interview again. As you listen, fill in the outline with information from the interview.

I. ROSS REYNOLDS, interviewer and host of the radio show
   A. Credit has two pitfalls:
      1.
      2.

II. ALEX COUNTS, Grameen Foundation USA
   A. The poor are disadvantaged in two ways:
      1.
      2. *no safety net*
   B. The options the poor have include:
      1.
      2.
   C. Challenges originally faced by Bengali woman:
      1. *couldn't afford more than three chickens*
      2.
   D. Possible outcomes of the $60–$70 investment:
      1.
      2. *send child to school*
      3.

III. RAJ SHAH, Bill and Melinda Gates Foundation
   A. Impact on the kids when parents have benefited from microfinance investments:
      1.
      2. *better school attendance*
      3.
   B. Percentage of clients who move out of poverty: _____

IV. MATT FLANNERY, Kiva.org
   A. Microfinance is sustainable; it's "a _____ that can keep on _____."

V. ALEX COUNTS, Grameen Foundation USA
   A. Drawbacks:
      1.
      2.
   B. Examples of going from extreme poverty to moderate poverty:
      1.
      2.

GO TO MyEnglishLab FOR MORE LISTENING PRACTICE.

MAKE INFERENCES

RECOGNIZING ASSUMPTIONS ABOUT A LISTENING AUDIENCE

In Listening One, the radio host and the interviewees discuss a complex and sensitive topic—how to improve the lives of people living in poverty. The radio host and guests make assumptions about what their audience might be thinking or how much the audience might know about a particular topic. Because the host and guests are making assumptions about what the audience may or may not know, they may be less direct in their comments. Skillful listeners "listen between the lines" to infer information that speakers do not explicitly state.

🎧 Read and listen to the example. Then decide what Reynolds assumes about his audience and read the explanation.

Example

HOST, ROSS REYNOLDS: There are obvious benefits to credit, but there are also pitfalls. You can get overextended, you don't own anything, the bank ends up owning it. In some ways, paying as you go might be a better idea. Is credit always a good thing, particularly for poor people?

Reynolds assumes that the radio audience believes providing credit to poor people might

a. be very risky

b. be somewhat risky

c. not be risky

The answer is *b*. There are four clues which indicate his assumption that the audience is skeptical about credit: 1) He asks the question he thinks his audience is asking; 2) Reynolds emphasizes the words *always*; 3) He stresses *particularly for poor people*; and 4) He also says *paying as you go might be a better idea*.

🎧 Listen to each excerpt. Select the correct answer to the question that asks about the underlying assumptions the speaker is making about the audience. Provide an explanation for your choice. Then discuss your answers with your partner.

Excerpt One

1. The host, Ross Reynolds, assumes that his radio audience _____.

   a. disagrees with the concept of microfinance; i.e., that a small loan can lift people out of poverty

   b. is skeptical that a small loan can lift people out of poverty

   c. lacks the necessary information to know whether or not a small loan can make a difference

   Explanation: _____

2. The host, Ross Reynolds, asks if microfinancing is "zero sum" and brings up the topic of other charities. He assumes that his audience wants the guest to _____.

   a. compare microfinancing with direct charitable giving

   b. realize that there are enough charities already to help the poor

   c. admit that loans won't help people in extreme poverty

Explanation: _____

3. The guest, Alex Counts, assumes that the radio audience _____.

   a. believes this is a big change

   b. doesn't understand how big a change this is

   c. is aware of the impact of microfinance

Explanation: _____

EXPRESS OPINIONS

Discuss the questions in a small group. Give your opinions. Then share your answers with the class.

1. What information from the interview was most surprising? Most predictable or obvious? Most confusing? What questions do you have after hearing the interview? What information would you be passionate about sharing with a friend or relative at the dinner table?

2. Do you think that microfinance is an effective strategy to lift people out of poverty? Why or why not? Do you agree with the approach of targeting microfinance at the poorest rather than the lower middle class? Explain.

3. Many microfinance organizations and institutions focus on empowering women rather than men. Do you agree with that approach? Why or why not?

■■■■■■■■■■■■■■■■■■■■■■■■■ *GO TO* MyEnglishLab *TO GIVE YOUR OPINION ABOUT ANOTHER QUESTION.*

VOCABULARY

1 🎧 The **bold-faced** words and phrases will appear in the next listening selection. Notice them as you read and listen to what Sylvia Otero, the microfinance director, has to say about Muhammed Yunus, the founder of the Grameen Bank, the first microfinance institution. In 1996, Yunus won the Nobel Peace Prize.

I met the charismatic Muhammed Yunus in the late '70s when I was a Peace Corps volunteer in Haiti. He had just started the Grameen Bank in Bangladesh and wanted to share his crazy, revolutionary microcredit idea with the world. He told us a moving **anecdote** of how in 1976, distraught over seeing millions of **malnourished** citizens in Bangladesh, he decided to lend $27 to 42 bamboo weavers. He **had faith in** the weavers and was confident they would quickly repay the loans. He knew the risks: They might struggle, **take a hit**, and actually not be able to repay the loans. Yet, to his and many others' surprise, they succeeded. They never **hit a ceiling** and went on to create small, yet profitable cottage industries. Microfinance was born. Today the Grameen Bank and other MFIs like it serve well over five million clients—10,000 families a month.

2 Match the words or phrases on the left with the definitions or synonyms on the right. Write the corresponding letter in the blank.

—— **1.** anecdote	**a.** believed in; trusted
—— **2.** malnourished	**b.** reach the limit of success
—— **3.** had faith in	**c.** be negatively affected
—— **4.** take a hit	**d.** sick or weak due to lack of food
—— **5.** hit a ceiling	**e.** short story based on personal experience

COMPREHENSION

🎧 Listen to a microfinance expert, Will Bullard, tell the story of a woman in a village in Honduras, Central America. This real story illustrates how a local lending organization, or "assembly," works—the promises and pitfalls.

Part One: María José's Story

Check (✓) the true statements. Correct the false statements.

_____ 1. María José Perona had nine children, all of whom were malnourished.

_____ 2. The women in the assembly decide who gets the loan.

_____ 3. The women voted not to grant María José Perona the loan because they thought she would spend the loan on food, not on the business.

_____ 4. The women finally agreed and gave her a loan of $25 dollars.

_____ 5. María José Perona had to take a test to get the $25 dollars.

_____ 6. María José Perona bought flour and cooking supplies with her loan.

_____ 7. She created a small meat pie business in front of the school.

_____ 8. Although she paid her friend back, she was not allowed into the assembly.

_____ 9. She finally became successful and was then allowed into the assembly.

_____ 10. She built a concrete house and became president of the assembly.

Part Two: Non-Monetary Benefits of Microfinance

Check (✓) the non-monetary benefits (other benefits not related to money) that the speaker mentions or implies.

_____ 11. sales and marketing skills

_____ 12. education

_____ 13. confidence

_____ 14. risk-taking ability

(continued on next page)

Part Three: Business Training

Check (✓) the phrases that accurately complete the statement.

The speaker believes that business training is important because the women _____.

_____ **15.** find the loans too small

_____ **16.** don't know how to manage their money carefully

_____ **17.** sell very similar things

_____ **18.** should sell things that bring them more money

■■ *GO TO* MyEnglishLab *FOR MORE VOCABULARY PRACTICE.*

LISTENING SKILL

LISTENING FOR SUMMARY STATEMENTS

In the second listening, the interviewer clarifies what the interviewee, Will Bullard, says by briefly summarizing what Bullard has said. By using this technique, the interviewer shows that he clearly understands what Bullard has said and restates the essence of Bullard's message to help the listening audience understand. Recognizing and understanding these summary statements helps to improve listening comprehension.

🎧 Read and listen to the example. Then answer the questions and read the explanation.

Example

WILL BULLARD: She became a dynamic entrepreneur and she became very successful. She lived in a horrible grass hut and then she built a concrete house that she moved all of her kids into; it's only a one-room house, but it's a huge step up. She became the vice president of her *Adelante* assembly.

INTERVIEWER: It sounds like from that anecdote that woman got incredible benefits and was really able to change her life through the power of microloans . . .

1. According to Bullard, what were the woman's accomplishments?

_____

2. What language does the interviewer use to introduce the summary statement?

_____

3. What are the two key points that the interviewer makes in his summary of what Bullard said?

• _____

• _____

In this example, Bullard says that the woman accomplished several things:

- she became a dynamic entrepreneur and became successful
- she moved from a grass hut to a concrete house
- she became vice president of her assembly

The interviewer signals that he is about to summarize by saying "It sounds like from that anecdote . . ." He follows by restating what Bullard has said in two key points.

- the woman got incredible benefits
- she was really able to change her life through the power of microloans . . .

By summarizing, the interviewer helps to clarify for the listener the most important points of what Bullard said.

Listen to the remarks. Check (✓) the statements that the original speaker makes. Then listen to the summary statement and paraphrase the key point(s). The introductory language for the key points has been provided for you.

Excerpt One

_____ The speaker isn't sure that people are moving out of poverty.

_____ Studies show that people are moving out of poverty.

_____ There are benefits other than money.

Key point(s) of the summary: So, in short, _____

_____

Excerpt Two

_____ Women want to do better, but they just don't know how.

_____ Women want to have better lives, but they know they are limited.

_____ The majority of women will do whatever is necessary to make more money.

Key point(s) of the summary: So the gist is that _____

_____

(continued on next page)

Excerpt Three

_____ Getting the house is a direct result of selling meat in the village.

_____ Getting the house stops her from further success.

_____ There is a limit to how far a person can get by selling something such as meat in the village.

Key point(s) of the summary: _It sounds like_ _____

_____

GO TO MyEnglishLab **FOR MORE SKILL PRACTICE.**

CONNECT THE LISTENINGS

STEP 1: Organize

Review Listenings One and Two. In each listening, speakers refer to three major benefits of microfinance. Work with a partner. Complete the chart by identifying specific examples of these benefits from each listening selection.

BENEFITS OF MICROFINANCE	EXAMPLES: LISTENING ONE	EXAMPLES: LISTENING TWO
FINANCIAL CHANGES	_Increases the amount of capital to support business_	
NON-MONETARY CHANGES		_Gives confidence_
SUSTAINABILITY		

STEP 2: Synthesize

Work in groups of three. Each person will choose one of the benefits listed in the chart from Step 1. Review the related examples from Listenings One and Two.

After two minutes, close your book and present a one-minute summary to the group. Use examples from both listening selections.

GO TO MyEnglishLab **TO CHECK WHAT YOU LEARNED.**

3 FOCUS ON SPEAKING

VOCABULARY

REVIEW

A journalist for *Economic Daily*, Pedro Martínez, broadcast an "audio postcard" about his recent trip to La Ceiba, Honduras.

1 Read the transcript of Martínez's report. Fill in the blanks with the appropriate word or phrase from the box. Use the clues under the blanks to help you.

anecdote	had faith in	panacea	took a hit
compelling	hit a ceiling	pitfalls	wiped out
diminish	malnourished	sustainable	

Pedro's Audio Postcard

Greetings from La Ceiba, Honduras. First, I must tell you that this little speck on Earth is just unbelievably gorgeous—beautiful, lush, with breathtaking cloud formations hugging spectacular green mountains.

Still, on the drive from the airport to my lodge I witnessed the pervasive poverty we see the world over: skinny,

_____ children standing next to
1. (sick or weak due to lack of food)

houses and shops still not rebuilt since Hurricane Mitch

_____ much of the country in 1988. Already
2. (destroyed)

the second poorest country in Latin America, Honduras

_____ and never recovered. To research
3. (was negatively affected)

my article, I set out to visit microfinance institutions as well as

meet the microcredit client to whom I had lent money from my

laptop in Mexico City, where I live.

(continued on next page)

Kiva.org is a nonprofit microcredit organization that allows individuals with access to the Internet to fight global poverty in a _____ way by making a direct
4. (able to continue long-term)
personal loan to poor entrepreneurs anywhere in the world. On the Kiva website I came across the _____ photo and story of Julia Marta Mendez,
5. (so interesting or exciting that you have to pay attention)
a fascinating Honduran widow in her late thirties with six children, to whom I had lent $50 dollars. I

_____ her, and just knew she
6. (believed in; trusted)
would stick with her goals and use the money well.

With this tiny loan, Julia opened a small shop in which she sold delicious coconut bread made from a unique family recipe. After three months, she was able to leverage the initial investment to expand her business to include other savory Honduran foodstuffs, such as *baleadas*, special Honduran tortillas.[1] I wish you all could witness the non-monetary benefits of the loans—no challenge, no obstacle, nothing can _____ Julia's enthusiasm, sense of confidence,
7. (make something smaller or less important)
and hope for her future. But here's the real kicker, which you might find difficult to believe! In spite of Julia's outstanding success so far, she worries that her business may already have

_____. A competing shop has opened next to hers, so she now feels
8. (reached the limit of success)
she needs training in marketing and advertising to fuel future business growth. Indeed, I realize

that money alone is not a total _____. We all know that
9. (something thought to eliminate a problem)
when it comes to alleviating poverty, there is no such thing as overnight success. Truly, one of

the biggest _____ of microfinance is the need for business training.
10. (problems or difficulties)
Listen again for tomorrow's story—I'll share an _____
11. (a short story based on personal experience)
from my visit with Julia. This is Pedro Martinez reporting for *Economic Daily*.

[1] **tortilla:** a piece of thin, flat bread made from wheat or corn

2 🎧 Listen to the audio postcard to check your answers. Then work with a partner and discuss the questions.

1. What might be the pros and cons of lending money to microborrowers on a website like Kiva.org? Would you be interested in doing so?

2. Why do you think microfinancing institutions don't focus more heavily on job training for the microborrowers?

EXPAND

After hearing Mr. Martínez's audio postcard, several listeners called the radio station to voice their reaction. The following is a transcript of those comments.

Read the listener comments and match the **bold-faced** words or phrases with a similar expression on page 232. Compare your answers with your partner's.

• **Jiseon Park, barista at Starbucks, Seoul, Korea, August 20**

Wow . . . Pedro Martínez's story was so inspirational. Just amazing how this woman Julia could actually **(1) make do** with a single small loan to get her business off the ground. Raising six children alone on two dollars a day, Julia really does **(2) bear the brunt** of poverty. Loaning money **(3) as opposed to** just giving charity or a handout clearly is a better way to help the very poor fulfill their dreams of improving their lives, or at least building a **(4) safety net** in case of emergency.

• **Susana, English teacher, São Paulo, Brazil, August 21**

I heard Martínez's broadcast the other day and even though I found it interesting and moving, I have mixed feelings about microcredit. The way I see it, microcredit only tells half the story. Even if Julia repays her initial loan, reinvests future loans, and lives a slightly better life, she'll still be at the **(5) bottom of the** economic **pyramid**. Of course, she may enjoy some **(6) non-monetary** benefits from her microcredit enterprise. But, I hate to say it, ultimately her business will only generate very slim profits. Research shows it takes years for even the most ambitious microlending entrepreneurs to **(7) pull themselves up by their bootstraps**.

• **Dr. Nguyen Anh Tuan, physician, Hanoi, Vietnam, August 21**

Thank you for airing Mr. Martínez's audio postcard yesterday. It reminded me of a visit I made to a family in a small village 30 kilometers from Hanoi two years ago. I knew the family well because I had treated a poor peasant woman's son who had been fighting a very serious intestinal illness. For years, **(8) top-down aid** from international organizations had never reached this rural community. Struggling with deep debts and worry caused by her son's illness, Le Thi Tran was desperate. One day she heard about the Tao Yeu May[1] Fund, a microfinance organization with local, **(9) grassroots** support in Vietnam, and with a single loan of $40 she purchased six chickens. She reinvested her earnings, creating a business that sold the tastiest chickens in the area. Her son is doing fine now; all debts have been paid off, and Le Thi lives in a brand-new house. Truly, TYM gave her the **(10) gift that keeps on giving**.

[1] **Tao Yeu May:** I love you (literal translation)

(continued on next page)

_____ **a.** assistance from higher levels

_____ **b.** a gift that continues to grow and benefit its recipient

_____ **c.** suffer the worst

_____ **d.** not related to money

_____ **e.** manage

_____ **f.** related to ordinary people

_____ **g.** improve their situation through hard work

_____ **h.** compared to

_____ **i.** lowest economic level

_____ **j.** plan or arrangement to help in case of problems or difficulties

CREATE

Work with a partner.

Student A: Cover the right column on page 233. Read comments 1 to 6 to Student B. Be sure to look at your partner when you are speaking. Stop after each one so Student B has a chance to respond.

Student B: Cover the left column on page 233. Listen to each comment. Select one of the words from Vocabulary for Student B below. Respond to Student A with the appropriate comment from the right column on page 233, filling in the blank with the word you selected from your vocabulary list.

Student A: Give Student B a clue if necessary. The answers are in parentheses.

Switch roles after item 6.

Vocabulary for Student A	**Vocabulary for Student B**
anecdote	grassroots
as opposed to	make do
bear the brunt	pitfalls
bottom of the economic pyramid	sustainable
hit a ceiling	take the biggest hit
top-down	upward mobility

Example

STUDENT A: Microcredit loans are simply not a *cure-all* for poverty. (panacea)

STUDENT B: So, you mean that these loans are not a **panacea** for poverty.

Student A

1. It's really painful to see how some people in Lagos, Nigeria, are forced to *manage* on $2 a day. (make do)

2. Although microfinance offers a promising solution, there are still a number of potential *problems and dangers* in the approach. (pitfalls)

3. A poor, illiterate person cannot create a *healthy, lasting* business on a $50 microloan without access to job training and education. (sustainable)

4. Living in slums or tiny rural villages, many poor people do feel there's no real *ability to move to a better position*. (upward mobility)

5. When natural disasters strike, the "poorest of the poor" are the ones who *are most severely affected*. (take the biggest hit)

6. The women in the *local borrower's* group are responsible for managing and repaying the group's loans. (grassroots)

Now switch roles.

Student B

7. It is a myth that the very, very poor can leave poverty behind. The reality is that poor women in developing countries will always *suffer the worst* of poverty. (bear the brunt)

Student B

1. Yeah, some of the people have to _____ on so little.

2. Exactly. However, even with the _____, the advantages do outweigh the disadvantages.

3. Right. So, in order to ensure these businesses are _____, many organizations provide training.

4. So in other words, _____ is a dream for many of the world's poor.

5. Definitely. The people living at the bottom of the pyramid often _____ in natural disasters.

6. So, you mean that the loans are managed at a _____ level.

Student A

7. Yes and it is a sad reality that women _____ of poverty.

(continued on next page)

8. There are limits to growing a business through microcredit. It's clear that, after moving from extreme to moderate poverty, many people *reach a limit*. (hit a ceiling)

8. Uh-huh. I have heard exactly that. Many just _____ and can't grow as much as they'd like.

9. I'd say *large-scale, high-level*, government aid alleviates poverty more than microcredit does. (top-down)

9. You mean, you favor a _____ government solution over a bottom-up, grassroots one?

10. I was moved by the *story* of the Thai woman who rebuilt her peanut business after the tsunami destroyed it. (anecdote)

10. Me too. She told a powerful _____ on how she recovered from the tsunami.

11. Microfinance institutions require small, frequent loan repayments *rather than* more traditional large, long-term loans. (as opposed to)

11. Oh, I get it. So, the loans are repaid more often in small bits _____ a single, large chunk.

12. Unfortunately, women are often stuck at the *lowest economic level*, since they usually have less education than men. (bottom of the economic pyramid)

12. Yeah, it's really too bad that women end up at the _____ because they have to take care of their families instead of going to school.

GO TO MyEnglishLab **FOR MORE VOCABULARY PRACTICE.**

GRAMMAR

1 Work with a partner. Examine the statements and discuss the questions that follow.

- *If* María José **weren't** a successful micro-entrepreneur, her children **couldn't attend** school.

- *If* María José's friend **hadn't had** faith in her, she **wouldn't have given** María José her first 25-dollar loan.

- *If* María José **hadn't invested** the initial loan, she **wouldn't be** such a successful micro-entrepreneur today.

- *If* the microfinance organization **offered** job training, she **might have enjoyed** larger profit margins from the get-go.[1]

1. Which sentences express conditions in the past? In the present? Both?

2. How do the times, or tenses, in the last two sentences differ from those in the first two? What is the difference in meaning?

---

[1] **from the get-go:** from the beginning

Conditional sentences express ideas about things that happen or don't happen because of certain situations. They consist of an "*if* clause" and a "result clause." Use unreal conditionals to express ideas which are contrary to fact in the present, past, or both.

Remember:

- Not all conditional clauses use *if*.

  They wish they **could provide** more training in marketing.

- When there is an *if* clause, it can come before or after the result clause.

  If the women make enough money, the children can go to school.

  The children can go to school **if** the women make enough money.

Note: There is a comma after the *if* clause when it comes before the result clause.

PRESENT UNREAL CONDITIONALS

Use present unreal conditionals to discuss situations in the present that are contrary-to-fact.

Real Situation	Conditional	
	IF CLAUSE	RESULT CLAUSE
	If + subject + verb (past form)	subject + *could* + verb (base form) *would* *might*
She doesn't have any savings, so she can't afford medicine when her children get sick.	**If she had** some savings,	**she could afford** medicine when her children get sick.
Microcredit is not truly a panacea, so the poverty rate is high.	**If microcredit were** truly a panacea,	**the poverty rate wouldn't be** as high as it is.

PAST UNREAL CONDITIONALS

Use past unreal conditionals to discuss situations in the past that are contrary-to-fact.

Real Situation	Conditional	
	IF CLAUSE	RESULT CLAUSE
	If + subject + verb (past perfect form)	subject + *could* + *have* + verb (past *would* participle *might* form)
Mrs. Du Ying got a loan, so she could buy raw silk for her rug-making business.	**If Mrs. Du Ying hadn't gotten** the loan,	**she couldn't have bought** the raw silk for her rug-making business.
She repaid the loan, so the other women in her group weren't responsible for it.	**If she hadn't repaid** the loan,	**the other women in her group would have been** responsible for repaying it.

(continued on next page)

Changing Lives for $50   235

MIXED UNREAL CONDITIONALS

Sometimes, present and past unreal conditionals are mixed if the times of the "*if* clause" and the "result clause" are different.

- Past result of a present condition:

   If microfinance **weren't** so successful, Yunus **wouldn't have won** the Nobel Peace Prize.

- Present result of a past condition:

   If the epidemic **hadn't killed** her cows last year, she **wouldn't be** so poor now.

Real Situation	Conditional	
	IF CLAUSE	RESULT CLAUSE
	Past *If* + *had* + verb (past participle form)	**Present** subject + *would* + verb (base form) *could* *might*
	Present *If* + verb (past form)	**Past** subject + *would* + *have* + verb (past participle form)
Hurricane Mitch wiped out her home and village in 1998, so she is poor today.	**If Hurricane Mitch hadn't wiped out** her home and village in 1998,	**she wouldn't be** so poor today.
She has low profit margins, so she applied for a second loan.	**If she had** higher profit margins,	**she wouldn't have applied** for a second loan.

NOTE: The present progressive is often used with mixed conditionals: If I **had known** about the Grameen Bank 10 years ago, **I'd be working** for the bank now.

2 Discuss real and unreal situations with a partner. Imagine the opposite of the statements that follow.

Student A: Cover the right column. Read the sentence that reviews information on microfinance.

Student B: Cover the left column. Using a present unreal conditional comment about the information, talk about the opposite condition. Use the cues provided.

Then switch roles after item 5.

Student A

1. Many of the world's poor have no access to capital, so they cannot start or grow a business.

2. She has some money now, so her children are in school.

3. I have faith in Julia, so I'll lend her money.

4. Yunus listens to critics who mention the pitfalls of microfinance, so he continues to improve the system.

5. Since all women in the solidarity group need to approve, it is difficult to get a loan.

Now switch roles.

6. In general, men are not good risks as borrowers, so they are approved less often for microloans.

7. Yunus is a charismatic leader, so he is able to persuade people to believe in his vision.

8. She studies day and night so she can pass the literacy test.

9. She takes a business training class each week so she learns ways to make her sugar shop more profitable.

10. Many young people are developing innovative social business ideas, so many people's lives are improving.

11. The government outlawed street begging so many of the poor turned to crime to survive.

12. She earns 3 dollars a day so she can now save money and eat two meals.

Student B

1. That's true. If the world's poor had . . .

2. Do you mean if she didn't have . . . ?

3. Are you saying that if you (not, have) . . .

4. That's good. If he . . .

5. So, probably it . . .

6. Really? So do you think that if men were . . .

7. True. Some people think that if Yunus (be, not) . . .

8. Yes, it's pretty clear that if she . . .

9. Sounds good. I imagine then if she . . .

10. It's great! If young people . . .

11. That is a sad reality. If the government . . .

12. I see. So, if she . . .

3 Work with a partner. Discuss past unreal situations.

Student A: Ask your partner questions 1 through 3.

Student B: Answer Student A's questions using past unreal conditionals. Use the information from the unit and your own opinions and imagination.

Switch roles after question 3.

What if . . .

1. . . . Muhammed Yunus hadn't started the Grameen Bank?

2. . . . Yunus hadn't won the Nobel Peace Prize?

3. . . . the Kiva founders weren't passionate about making a difference?

Now switch roles.

4. . . . Muhammed Yunus lent $27 to 42 stool makers?

5. . . . she had more education and some job skills?

6. . . . the tsunami wiped out the palm tree population?

4 Discuss mixed real and unreal situations with a partner. Imagine the opposite of the statements that follow.

Student A: Cover the right column. Read the sentence that reviews information on microfinance.

Student B: Cover the left column. Using a mixed unreal conditional comment on the information, imagining the opposite condition. Use the cues provided.

Switch roles after item 3.

Student A	Student B
1. One microborrower didn't repay her loan, so her group members can't approve any further loans now.	1. That's too bad. If she (repay) . . .
2. I heard a compelling broadcast about Kiva on the radio last month, and now I am a microlender.	2. Oh, I see. So, if you . . .
3. Julia Mendez's husband died a year ago, and now she struggles to support her six children alone.	3. Hmmm . . . but I think even if her husband (not) . . .

Now switch roles.

4. Julia repaid her initial loan this week and is now feeling really confident.	**4.** Uh-huh. You know, if she . . .
5. Three of the five borrowers in the group failed the exam on the banking policies, so now they can't join the microfinance program.	**5.** That's unfortunate. If they . . .
6. Microfinance has not been a panacea, so now Yunus is still dreaming of a "museum of poverty."	**6.** Too bad. If microfinance . . .

■■■■■■■■■■■■■■■■■■■■■■■■■■■■■■■■ *GO TO* MyEnglishLab *FOR MORE GRAMMAR PRACTICE.*

PRONUNCIATION

COMPOUND UNITS

Meaningful units composed of two words are stressed on the first word when the unit is a noun. Pitch is also high on the first word.

🎧 Listen to the two-word nouns and sentence.

cóttage   rúg-   páth   póverty
  ìndustry   màking   wày   cỳcle

A **cottage industry** like **rug-making** can become a **pathway** to break the **poverty cycle**.

TWO-WORD NOUNS	EXAMPLES		
Noun-noun units (compounds)	cóttage ìndustry	páthwày	póverty cỳcle
Adjective-noun units	grándchìldren	lívestòck	bláckbòard
Preposition + verb used as a noun	íncòme	óutgròw	bácklàsh
Other sequences	hóusehòld	rúg-màking	mícrolòans

1 🎧 Listen to the two-word nouns and repeat them. Pronounce the first word with heavy stress and high pitch.

1. microcredit	**6.** business growth
2. interest rates	**7.** debt payment
3. aid agencies	**8.** grassroots
4. overnight success	**9.** pitfall
5. drawback	**10.** household

2 Work with a partner. The words in the box can be combined with the words under the blanks into two-word nouns that match the definitions. Read the definition. Then write the appropriate two-word noun in the blank.

back	broad	live	profit	safety

1. A negative or critical reaction to a program or policy: _____
(lash)

2. The difference between the money a business earns and the money it spends:

_____
(margin)

3. Information made public, usually by radio or television: _____
(cast)

4. Farm animals: _____
(stock)

5. A source of help during difficult times: _____
(net)

3 Look at the three categories below. Add more examples to each category. If you include a two-word noun unit, circle it. Then share your lists with the class.

Drawbacks to Microlending	Safety Nets for Poor People	Cottage Industries
high interest rates	aid agencies	selling eggs

SPEAKING SKILL

DEMONSTRATING UNDERSTANDING WITH SUMMARY STATEMENTS

As you learned in the Listening Skill section on page 226, you can demonstrate your understanding of what a speaker has said by responding with a short summary statement. With this statement, you can communicate you have understood the basic message. An effective summary statement includes these features:

- conveys the gist of the message
- is short and to the point
- does not include any new ideas or opinions
- signals the summary statement with an introductory expression

Many speakers signal these "summary statements" or "gist messages" with the following expressions:

- So what you're saying is . . .
- So you're saying that . . .
- In short, . . .
- So, the gist is that . . .
- What I understood was that . . .
- It sounds like . . .

Work with a partner.

Student A: Read Comment #1 on the next page.

Student B: Listen carefully. Demonstrate your understanding by making a short summary statement. Be sure to start your summary statement with an introductory expression from the Skill Box above.

Student A: Evaluate Student B's summary statement using the checklist below. Give Student B feedback.

Take turns reading the comments, making summary statements, and evaluating them using the checklist.

Checklist for Summary Statements

❏ conveys the gist of the message

❏ is short and to the point

❏ does not include any new ideas or opinions

❏ signals the statement with an introductory expression

(continued on next page)

Comments

1. The Grameen Bank feels it's OK to give credit to poor people without providing business training. The microfinance bankers say that people already have lots of practical skills and can be successful without training. Many of these people are natural salespeople with lots of charisma.

2. Women are the most motivated microfinance borrowers because they bear the brunt of poverty and feel the most pain. Seventy percent of people in extreme poverty are women and women represent the highest numbers of illiteracy, malnutrition, and HIV/AIDS.

3. Critics of microfinance say that microfinance isn't a panacea. According to these critics, the borrowers are overly dependent on these loans; 55% of the Grameen clients still cannot meet nutritional needs and many women feel that loans simply increase their burden. They have to make money and raise a family.

4. Microfinance institutions do not provide enough support programs. Their clients lack business training so after some time, they hit a ceiling. They never save enough money to survive if the business is wiped out by a natural disaster, for example.

5. The solidarity group, a form of "social collateral" is really an effective model. It puts pressure on the members to repay their loans. If a member in the group defaults, the group has to pay back the loan, and then the member is excluded from future loans. The system is great since it helps to minimize the bank's risk.

6. As microfinance has grown, it has become clear that capital, knowledge, and opportunity are three key items to empower the poor. We know that microfinance can provide capital. However, many poor people still lack the resources to access knowledge and opportunity.

GO TO MyEnglishLab **FOR MORE SKILL PRACTICE AND TO CHECK WHAT YOU LEARNED.**

FINAL SPEAKING TASK

In this task, you will compete for a contract to help the Brazilian Ministry of Health and Finance build a program to alleviate poverty in the country. Representing an anti-poverty agency, present recommendations for tackling this problem. Use the vocabulary, grammar, pronunciation, and listening and speaking skills that you learned in the unit.*

Follow the steps.

STEP 1: As a class, complete the first row of the chart on page 244 with information about microfinance.

STEP 2: Work in a small group. You will be assigned to one of the following agencies:

Group 1: Microfinance Institution

Group 2: World Bank

Group 3: Global Business

Group 4: Ministry of Health and Finance

Groups 1–3: Read the information in the chart. Pay particular attention to the agency you represent.

Group 4: Read the information in the chart.

STEP 3: Groups 1–3: Prepare a plan for alleviating poverty. Then decide how to present your plan to the ministry. Acknowledge the challenges of your plan, but be sure to explain how the potential benefits outweigh them. Refer to the other agencies' plans in order to illustrate how yours is superior. Be sure to use the vocabulary, grammar (unreal conditionals), and speaking skill (making summary statements) from the unit.

Group 4: Create challenging and provocative questions to assess the viability of each agency's plan.

STEP 4: Groups 1–3: Present your plan to the ministry and the class.

Group 4: At the end of each presentation, pose your questions to each agency.

---

* For Alternative Speaking Topics, see page 246.

AGENCY / DESCRIPTION	EXAMPLES	BENEFITS	CHALLENGES
MICROFINANCE INSTITUTION			
WORLD BANK			
• Wealthy member nations provide loans and grants to poor countries. • Programs aim to boost economic growth and improve living conditions by fixing major government institutions (highways, schools, public services).	• help countries create programs to stop disease • fund education • build roads, bridges, power plants	• provide long-term, low- or no-interest loans • require recipients to take steps to fight disease, grow economy, etc. • can offer huge resources	• leave countries in debt • establish programs that may not consider unique needs of that culture • may introduce corruption and bias • may cost a lot to administer program, no direct benefit to the poor
GLOBAL BUSINESS			
Provides jobs to people in developing countries	• retail stores (Wal-Mart, Home Depot) • food companies (Dole, Chiquita) • auto makers (Toyota)	• can offer factory jobs with pay to lift workers out of poverty • create competition between businesses—drives up local wages • bring wealth of developed nation, not limited by local economy • provide jobs for people who are not entrepreneurs • offer stability	• might have bad working conditions in "sweatshops" or fields • may introduce child labor • require relocation of villagers to the city • raise environmental concerns about shipping goods around the globe

UNIT PROJECT

Complete one of these projects.

Topic 1: Choose a Microborrower

Imagine that you would like to lend money to a micro-entrepreneur who is posted on the Kiva.org website. Visit the Kiva.org website and click on the link, "see all businesses in need." Read about the various micro-borrowers and choose one to whom you would like to lend money. Create a 2–3 minute presentation about your new business partner, explaining the reasons for your choice.

Topic 2: Research a Microfinance Institution

Unitus is a non-profit organization that supports and helps other microfinance institutions. Visit the Unitus website (http://www.unitus.com) and look for the Client Success stories. Read about one of their clients, then summarize and present your findings to the class.

ALTERNATIVE SPEAKING TOPICS

Discuss one of the topics. Use vocabulary and grammar from the unit.

Topic 1

Work in small groups. Read the quotes related to Listening One and microfinance. Paraphrase the quotes and then decide if you agree or disagree with the author of the quote. Explain the reasons for your opinions.

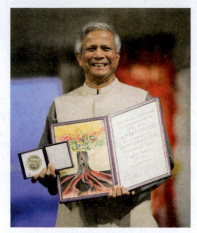

Muhammed Yunus

- *Muhammed Yunus, 2006 Nobel Peace Prize winner:*

  a. "One day our grandchildren will go to museums to see what poverty was like."

  b. "Charity is not the answer to poverty. It only helps poverty to continue. It creates dependency and takes away the individual's initiative to break through the wall of poverty."

- *Alex Counts, president of Grameen Foundation USA:*

  "I've always felt that the greatest threat to world peace was the global poverty crisis—seeing the competition for resources and how it leads to tension and violence."

- *Milton Friedman, 1976 Nobel Prize in Economic Sciences winner:*

  "The poor stay poor not because they are lazy, but because they have no access to capital."

Topic 2

Work in small groups. Discuss your answers to the question below.

One of the positive consequences of microlending is that women have gained the financial means to leave abusive husbands or relationships. They can own a home in their own name, live longer, have improved nutrition, take better care of their children, and so on.

When asked about these changes to women's status and lifestyle, Muhammed Yunus has commented, "I am destroying the culture, yes . . . culture is a dynamic thing. If you stay with the same old thing over and over, you don't get anywhere."

Do you agree or disagree with Yunus? Explain your opinion.

■■■■■■■■■■■■■■■■■ *GO TO* MyEnglishLab *TO DISCUSS ONE OF THE ALTERNATIVE TOPICS, WATCH A VIDEO ABOUT A TEEN WORKING TO END POVERTY, AND TAKE THE UNIT 8 ACHIEVEMENT TEST.* ■■■■■■■■■■■■■■■

STUDENT ACTIVITIES

Unit 2

Final Speaking Task, page 58

Ethical Dilemmas

Trading a Lemon

- A 25-year-old man bought a brand new car.
- He put the car into reverse and the car crashed into a pole across the street.
- He had the paint and dent fixed, and then he took the car to two different mechanics. Both said there was nothing wrong.
- He knows something is wrong and doesn't want to keep the car. He wants to trade it in for a new car.
- Even though both mechanics think nothing is wrong, the man is sure something is wrong.

Video Piracy

- A woman's son watches pirated, illegally recorded videos at a neighbor's house.
- Even though the neighbor has bought the videos, they are pirated.

A Doctor's Debate

- A 65-year-old man comes to his physician with complaints of persistent, but not extreme pains in his stomach.
- Tests reveal that he has cancer of the pancreas.
- The man has just retired from a busy professional career, and he and his wife are about to leave on a round-the-world cruise that they've been planning for over a year. His wife doesn't want him to know that he's dying.

Turtle Trouble

- A woman sees a man with two children walking a turtle down a path with a fishing line around the turtle's throat.
- The man's kids are dragging the turtle up and down the path.
- The woman is horrified because she feels it is cruel.
- The woman tells the man that she is a biologist at the university and that turtles are dangerous because they produce a poisonous fluid, which will make the man's children deathly ill.

Unit 3

Focus on the Topic, page 63

Quiz: Are you an introvert or an extrovert?

Check (✓) **YES** or **NO** as to whether the statements apply to you.

	YES	NO
Prefer to speak one-on-one rather than in a group		
Prefer to express myself in writing rather than speaking		
Enjoy reading, taking walks, playing a musical instrument		
Care about making money, becoming famous, or achieving social status more than my friends		
Good listener		
Risk taker		
Can concentrate deeply with few interruptions		
Like to celebrate birthdays with a few close friends or family		
People say I am "soft spoken" or "mellow"		
Wait to show others my work until it is finished		
Think before I speak		
Let my voicemail answer my calls		
Don't enjoy multi-tasking		
Prefer lectures to seminars		

How many YES answers did you have? _____

How many NO answers did you have? _____

I = Introvert. If you have the majority of "yes" answers, you're probably an introvert. You enjoy spending time alone or with a few people. You thoughtfully prepare your comments before speaking. You have an active inner life.

E/I = Ambivert. If you answered the questions evenly, yes and no, you're probably an ambivert. You are both an introvert and an extrovert since you fall right in the middle of the introvert-extrovert spectrum.

E = Extrovert. If you answered the majority of the questions "no," you're probably an extrovert. You enjoy interacting with both friends and strangers. You are assertive and can respond quickly to situations.

Unit 4

Focus on the Topic, page 93, Answers

F=Favorable / U=Unfavorable

1. **F aquarium.** If placed correctly aquariums invite the kind of chi that brings wealth.

2. **F colors red and purple.** Red is the color of energy—divine energy, the energy of the sun and life, joy, excitement, richness, and luxury. If used too much, though, it can bring destructive energy. Purple is excellent for physical and mental healing and is associated with spiritual awareness.

3. **F and U. desk facing a view.** The view should not be direct. If possible, have the light come in from the right if you are right-handed, or the left if you are left-handed. The light from the view should not cast a shadow on your work surface. It should invite creative and financial opportunities.

4. **U living near a cemetery.** Cemeteries have a "dark" energy that throws off the balance in the surrounding area.

5. **U living on a quiet dead-end street.** Living at the end of the dead-end street, or the "T" of two streets, is unfavorable because the shape of the street traps the sha (negative or low energy).

6. **F mirrors.** If placed properly, a mirror brings an energy like the calming and refreshing energy of water. Mirrors can invite beneficial chi into a space, or shift the chi in that space.

7. **F flowing water.** Flowing water is a universal symbol of abundance and helps circulate the chi.

8. **U odd number of dining room chairs.** Odd numbers represent loneliness. An even number of chairs represents balance and togetherness (pairing).

9. **F pictures of bats on the walls.** Bats invite happiness and good luck.

10. **F plants and flowers.** Live plants are best, and fake plants are fine depending on where they are placed. Plants invite good luck and wealth. Dead or dried flowers and plants are not good. They invite bad luck.

11. **U room full of windows.** There should not be too many windows in any room or office. If there are too many windows, good luck and energy can flow out easily. The proper ratio is three windows to every door.

12. **F a tiger statue outside an office door.** The white tiger is one of the best symbols of protection and guards against getting "stabbed in the back."

13. **U staircase in the middle of the house.** This is the worst position for a staircase. A staircase in the middle of a house disrupts the calm Qi. Those living with a staircase in the center will not enjoy good health, will often have bad tempers, and will be constantly anxious and irritable.

14. **F natural materials, such as stone or wood.** Natural materials distribute chi energy more efficiently than synthetic or unnatural materials.

UNIT WORD LIST

The Unit Word List is a summary of key vocabulary from the Student Book. Words followed by an asterisk (*) are on the Academic Word List (AWL).

UNIT 1

affected*
animate
astounding
authenticated
best and the
   brightest
buy into
competency
degrade
fool oneself into
   thinking

go through
incrementally
ingenuity
meticulous
perceive*
register*
renders
rewire
rigorous
skeptics
task shifting*

UNIT 2

conceal
elating
erosion*
finely honed
inflated
intrusive
mislead
mull over
pervasive
preoccupation

put one over on
put the pieces
   together
reincarnated
relentless
rule of thumb
tattling on
trivial
uncanny
veneer

UNIT 3

attributes*
carried away
come to light
colossal waste
cranky
crave
diagnosis
discounted
fill the void
groomed for
make lemonade out
   of lemons

mindful of
on the verge of
orientation*
profound
psyche
put one's stamp on
   something
run with
sea change
wallow in one's
   misery
whereas*

UNIT 4

abundance
acuteness
align
anecdote
catch off guard
circulate
digression
enhance*
frowned upon

govern
hard-bitten
quote*
sense
skeptically
transcendent
vitality
young at heart

(continued on next page)

UNIT 5

autonomy
bottom line
by virtue of
chit-chat
cubicle
day in day out
do favors of
    enduring
first hand
get right

guru
happy hour
incremental
insight*
intangibles
productivity
revenues*
worst case scenario*
setback
stalled

UNIT 6

advocate*
anonymity
capacity*
collaborate with
conscious choice
debacle
degradation
get a grip
given that
horse is out of
    the barn

impersonator
overwhelmed
persona
pseudonymity
ratchet down
seek intimacy*
throttle back
tuck away
velocity

UNIT 7

adept
affluent
alter*
core*
diverse*
drag
engaged
equipped*
fall into the trap of
get a bad rap
have access to*

have the means to
incentive*
infused
instill
persistence*
preliminary*
refining*
sense of
tangible
venture outside the
    box

UNIT 8

anecdote
backlash
bear the brunt
characterization
compelling
cottage industry
diminish*
have faith in
hit a ceiling
in perpetuity

malnourished
overextended
overnight success
panacea
pitfalls
safety net
sustainable*
take a hit
wiped out

GRAMMAR BOOK REFERENCES

NorthStar: Listening and Speaking Level 5, Fourth Edition	*Focus on Grammar Level 5*, Fourth Edition	*Azar's Understanding and Using English Grammar*, Fourth Edition
Unit 1 Verbs followed by Gerunds or Infinitives with a change in Meaning	**Unit 16** Gerunds **Unit 17** Infinitives	**Chapter 14** Gerunds and Infinitives, Part 1 14–3, 14–6, 14–7, 14–9, 14–10
Unit 2 Modals—Degrees of Certainty	**Unit 5** Modals to Express Degrees of Certainty	**Chapter 10** Modals, Part 2 10–1, 10–2, 10–3, 10–4, 10–5, 10–6
Unit 3 Adjective Clauses—Identifying and Non-Identifying	**Unit 12** Adjective Clauses Identifying or Non-Identifying	**Chapter 13** Adjective Clauses 13–4, 13–5, 13–6, 13–8
Unit 4 Discourse Connectors	**Unit 21** Connectors	**Chapter 19** Connectives that Express Cause and Effect, Contrast, and Condition 19–4
Unit 5 Direct and Indirect Speech	**Unit 11** Direct and Indirect Speech	**Chapter 12** Noun Clauses 12–6, 12–7
Unit 6 Wish Statements—Expressing Unreality	**Unit 22** Conditionals; Other Ways to Express Unreality	**Chapter 20** Conditional Sentences and Wishes 20–6, 20–9, 20–10
Unit 7 The Passive Voice and the Passive Causative	**Unit 14** The Passive: Review and Expansion	**Chapter 11** The Passive 11–1, 11–3, 11–7
Unit 8 Present Unreal Conditionals Mixed Unreal Conditionals	**Unit 22** Conditionals; Other Ways to Express Unreality	**Chapter 20** Conditional Sentences and Wishes 20–1, 20–2, 20–3, 20–4, 20–6, 20–7

AUDIOSCRIPT

UNIT 1: The Fantastic Plastic Brain

Listening One, page 6, Preview

NORMAN DOIDGE: I spoke to a gentleman Stanley Karanski, who was 90 years old, who did the program, and in six weeks he found that his trouble recognizing and remembering names and faces, his trouble being alert, his trouble driving, all reversed itself, and they have very fine studies showing that this is possible in large groups of people.

page 6, Main Ideas

KERRY O'BRIEN: What is it about the plasticity of the brain that allows it to be rewired?

NORMAN DOIDGE: Well, for the longest time, for 400 years, we thought of the brain as like a complex machine with parts. And our best and brightest neuroscientists really believed that. It was a mechanistic model of the brain and machines do many glorious things, but they don't rewire themselves and they don't grow new parts. And it turns out that that metaphor was actually just spectacularly wrong, and that the brain is not inanimate, it's animate and it's growing, it's more plant like than machine like and it actually works by changing its structure and function as it goes along.

O'B: You've given a number of examples in your book about how this has been applied in adults with some quite astounding results. Instances where people are being treated for strokes, to recover, to help them recover from strokes. One illustration: the surgeon.

ND: Yeah, I spoke to Michael Bernstein who was an eye surgeon, so he did microsurgery intervention inside an eye. He was a classical pianist and a tennis player and one day playing tennis, half of his body was completely rendered immovable. He had the usual amount of treatment which is about six weeks of rehabilitation, then sent home because the assumption was, you know, that's the best you can do, the brain doesn't grow or reorganize in any way. And, luckily, he was in Birmingham, Alabama, where Edward Taub developed a therapy for strokes which basically does the following: the assumption is that when you have a stroke, you lose cells in your brain and you try to move the affected limb, it doesn't work, so you learn it doesn't work. You stop using it and you use your good limb. Taub had the ingenuity to put the good limb in a sling or cast so you can't use it and then incrementally train the affected limb, and he was able to bring Dr. Bernstein back to the point that he practices medicine. I spoke with Taub patients who'd had strokes 50 years before, and there were children there who had had cerebral palsy who were using this treatment and recovering their independence.

O'B: Has Taub's work been authenticated, has it gone through the rigorous testing **process**?

ND: Oh, yeah. The thing about Taub is Mr. Meticulous, and they've got very, very fine studies that show that it's effective. And in fact, some of the other forms of rehab that we've been using for many years unfortunately are not that effective.

O'B: There's the claim that we can radically improve how we learn, think, perceive and remember, even in old age. Is that proven?

ND: Yes, it is proven. Michael Merzenich, who is perhaps the most important plasticity researcher alive, and who persuaded most scientific skeptics that the brain is plastic, has developed programs both for children with learning disabilities, severe reading problems, and for people in their old age which can do things like turn the memory clock back somewhere between 10 and 25 years. I spoke to a gentleman Stanley Karanski, who was 90-years-old, who did the program and in six weeks he found that his trouble recognising and remembering names and faces, his trouble being alert, his trouble driving, all reversed itself, and they have very fine studies showing that this is possible in large groups of people. And what we do is we go in and we actually rebuild the various parts of the brain up from scratch, just the way you sort of learn, for instance, how to distinguish sounds as a baby; we do this now with the adult.

O'B: Have you tried to exploit your knowledge of neuroplasticity to your own benefit?

ND: Sure. One of the easiest changes to make is the change in attitude. Once you understand that plasticity exists from cradle to grave, what it means is that a development, which most people think of as, really, child development, is something that goes on throughout the course of life. So, my own attitude towards my patients when they have issues of difficulty has changed, 'cause I know that brain change is possible, and my attitude towards myself has changed, and I do some exercises myself.

page 7, Make Inferences

Excerpt 1

DOIDGE: The thing about Taub is [that he is] Mr. Meticulous, and they've got very, very fine studies.

Excerpt Two

DOIDGE: And, in fact, some of the other forms of rehab that we've been using for many years unfortunately are not that effective.

Excerpt Three

DOIDGE: Yes, it is proven. Michael Merzenich, who is perhaps the most important plasticity researcher alive, and who persuaded most scientific skeptics that the brain is plastic, has developed programs both for children with learning disabilities, severe reading problems and for people in their old age which can do things like <u>turn</u> the memory <u>clock back</u> somewhere between 10 and 25 years.

Listening Two, page 10, Comprehension

SHERRY TURKLE: We believed for so long that multi-tasking was a 21st century alchemy, that we could make more time by doing all of these things together. And quite frankly the education community bought into this myth. Um . . . we did treat it. We said things like, "teachers would learn how to multitask so they could keep up with their students because this was such an important learning skill. And now we know the research is clear that we can multi-task. But we degrade our performance for every task we multi-task.
MAN: Well, Sherry, technically, we can't multi-task. Right? The brain is not capable of doing two kinds of . . .
ST: Yes, but you can choose to multi-task. What I mean, you can choose to do what looks to you like multitasking . . .
MAN: . . . where in fact you are task shifting.
ST: Yes.
MAN: You are moving from one thing to another.
ST: Absolutely, totally correct precision. Yes, you can fool yourself into thinking that you are doing something called . . . that looks to you that's multitasking and what is tricky about this is that the brain rewards you neurochemically when you do this . . . so that as you do this activity of shifting back and forth and getting your emails as you are writing, as you are doing your presentation as you're this, as you're that, the kind of mini tragedy here is that you feel you're doing better and better at everything even as your productivity and competency in everything is degrading. And that may be ok if you are shifting back and forth from your email to your filling in your date book, but it's really not ok when you want to get something serious done and people know that when they want to get something serious done, they have to turn it off.

So, I am saying that we really need to retrain ourselves to make it ok to do one thing at a time . . . to train ourselves to be unitaskers and I think that is the challenge for both individuals and corporations in the years ahead is to put a new value on unitasking.

page 11, Listening Skill

Excerpt One

SHERRY TURKLE: Yes, but you can choose to multi-task. What I mean, you can choose to do what looks to you like multitasking.
MAN: . . . where in fact you are task shifting.
ST: Yes.

Excerpt Two

ST: . . . you can fool yourself into thinking that you are doing something called . . . that looks to you that's multitasking and what is tricky about this is that the brain rewards you neurochemically when you do this. So that as you do this activity of shifting back and forth and getting your emails as you are writing, as you are doing your presentation as you're this, as you're that, the kind of mini tragedy here is that you feel you're doing better and better at everything even as your productivity and competency in everything is degrading.

Excerpt Three

ST: And that may be ok if you are shifting back and forth from your email to your filling in your date book, but it's really not ok when you want to get something serious done and people know that when they want to get something serious done, they have to turn it off.

UNIT 2: Is Honesty the Best Policy?

Listening One, page 38, Preview

DR. EKMAN: Well, a lie is a very particular kind of deception that lies meet two criteria. First, it's a deliberate choice to mislead another person. That one's pretty obvious. But the second, a little less obvious, is that you don't give any notification of the fact that you're going to do that. And in many situations in life, we either notify someone, like a magician does . . . a magician lies to us, a magician fools us, but we're notified.

Part One

DR. GOODWIN: I'm Dr. Fred Goodwin. As you'll hear during this show, lying can be approached from a variety of perspectives: moral, legal, interpersonal. Let me offer the perspective of one psychiatrist. People who lie more or less regularly often tend to narcissim. Absorbed as they are with an inflated sense of themselves, they are tempted to lie because they believe they can do it so cleverly that they won't get caught. But beneath this confident veneer lies a pervasive sense of insecurity that fuels the need to lie. Lacking a core, a consistent sense of who one is, narcissists must constantly define and redefine themselves through the responses of those around them. In a way, to survive, the narcissist develops a finely honed intuitive focus on the moment, but ultimately cannot see beyond it. To do so requires that internal compass, that independent, stable sense of one's true self.

Part Two

DR. GOODWIN: But what does the narcissist's preoccupation with the moment have to do with lying? It is this: Lies are usually about the here and now. They're a short-term solution to an immediate problem, a way to avoid criticism or anger, to look good, to please another. I believe that what helps most people stay honest most of the time is an awareness of the long-term impact of lies, the slow, but relentless erosion of trust. It's as if the narcissist, with his inability to see beyond the moment, is ultimately trapped in his lies, confirming for others what he deep down believes to be true: there's nothing there.

Part Three

DR. GOODWIN: Dr. Paul Ekman is professor of psychology at the University of California Medical School, San Francisco, and director of the Human Interaction Laboratory. Welcome to *The Infinite Mind*, Dr. Ekman.

DR. EKMAN: Thank you.

DR. GOODWIN: Nice to have you. Now start out with basics. Why don't you tell our listeners how you define a lie? What is a lie?

DR. EKMAN: Well, a lie is a very particular kind of deception that lies meet two criteria. First, it's a deliberate choice to mislead another person. That one's pretty obvious. But the second, a little less obvious, is that you don't give any notification of the fact that you're going to do that. And in many situations in life, we either notify someone, like a magician does . . . a magician lies to us, a magician fools us, but we're notified.

DR. GOODWIN: Is there more to the definition that that?

DR. EKMAN: That's all it requires. There are many different ways to tell a lie. You can conceal information. You can falsify information. You can even sometimes tell the truth in a mocking fashion. I call it tell the truth falsely.

Part Four

DR. GOODWIN: Have you catalogued sort of why people tell lies?

DR. EKMAN: Yes. And there are nine different reasons. The most common one for both children and adults alike is to avoid punishment for something that you've done. You know, you . . . you tell the traffic cop, 'Gee, officer, I didn't think I was going over 55.'

The second is to get a reward that you couldn't get otherwise or you couldn't get as easily, so you cheat on an exam 'cause you're more certain that you're going to get a high mark, or you don't want to put in all the time studying and preparing for it.

The third is to protect another person from being punished. That's an altruistic lie. And, in fact, we disapprove. If one . . . if a brother tells on a sister, we say that tattling. We expect kids to protect each other.

A fourth is to protect yourself from the threat of physical harm.

Another is to win the admiration of others. You know, it's—it is the name droppers. The father who says, 'Well, you know, the last time I saw George W., he said so-and-so and so-and-so.' T's . . . it's . . . it's trying to get people to admire you.

A very common one is getting out of an awkward social situation, even a trivial one, like the telephone salesman.

Another is to avoid embarrassment. You see that particularly in kids who make mistakes. Kids who wet their pants will lie about it because they're so embarrassed.

Another is to maintain privacy. This particularly occurs in adolescents who have overly intrusive parents.

And the last is to get power over other people. It's the greatest power and the most complete power in the world to have somebody believe something that you've told them that you know is untrue. You've really got control over them. Most adolescents will do this once or twice or three times. They can now put it over the old man, or they can fool their mom now. But they won't continue to do it. But there are people who continue that as a lifelong pattern. So those are nine very different reasons why people lie.

Part Five

DR. EKMAN: You lie, because life itself is more important than telling the truth or lying. The rule of thumb I think people should follow in trying to decide, 'Should I tell this lie or not?' is, 'Do I care about a future relationship with this person? And if I do, how would they feel if they found out?' Because to lie is—to be caught lying is to destroy trust, and nobody knows the step that you could take to ever re-establish trust. So it's a very high price. The loss of trust is a very high price to pay for being caught in a lie.

page 40, Make Inferences

Excerpt One

DR. GOODWIN: I believe that what helps most people stay honest most of the time is an awareness of the long term impact of lies . . .

Excerpt Two

DR. EKMAN: . . . There are many different ways to tell a lie. You can conceal information. . . . You can falsify information. You can even sometimes tell the truth in a mocking fashion. I call it telling the truth falsely.

Excerpt Three

DR. EKMAN: First, it's a deliberate choice to mislead another person. That one's pretty obvious. But the second, a little less obvious, is that you don't give any notification of the fact that you're going to do that.

Listening Two, page 43, Comprehension

Part One

POLA RAPAPORT: Many years after my father died, I had found a small photograph of a young boy that resembled him enormously in my father's desk, which had remained un—undisturbed for all those years. The picture was signed 'Pierre' on the back, and I really didn't know what to do with it, even though it looked so much like my father and he had never mentioned having—certainly never mentioned having a child before. I knew he didn't have any other relatives other than us. That was over 10 years ago. When years later my mother got a letter from Romania signed with the name Pierre, which was the same name on the back of the picture, we started to put the pieces together, and I thought perhaps this is someone who's looking to find his lost family. And, in fact, after a short exchange of letters between me and this stranger, Pierre, in Bucharest, he finally acknowledged that his father was my father.

INTERVIEWER: So that the photograph that you found in the drawer was in fact your long lost half-brother.

PR: That's who it was, I mean, the suspicion was right that he was our long lost brother or half-brother, living in Bucharest all that time. And then I had never been to Romania, but I had an opportunity to go. Actually, my husband was shooting a documentary there. So I kind of piggybacked and went along and I met Pierre for the first time. And it was an absolutely extraordinary experience to see him waiting for me at the airport with a little bouquet of flowers, and it was as though I were seeing my father reincarnated standing there because he resemble him almost identically.

INTERVIEWER: He looks a lot like the photographs of your father, in the film.

PR: Yeah. It's really uncanny.

INTERVIEWER: Your father had never told you or your sister anything about a son that he had had in Europe?

PR: No, he was really incredibly successful at keeping the secret from us.

Part Two

PR: My father was very secretive about the period in his life when he lived in Romania. In fact he was secretive about the period of his life when he lived in France prior to meeting my mother.

SISTER: Daddy was a secretive person and people who . . . people who had to run from, you know, Gestapo persecution I think became secretive, as a matter of survival.

Part Three

INTERVIEWER: So how did you as a filmmaker and as a person go into uncovering these secrets when you have a family legacy and teaching of, maybe this is not such a good thing to explore secrets. Was it scary for you? Was it elating for you? Did you have a feeling that you were trespassing on forbidden ground?

PR: Oh, all of those things, actually. But I—the feeling of trespassing was actually very elating; it was very exciting to get into this territory. I—I think I used to kind of mull over these things alone and come up with all kinds of images of what things could be and ideas of what things could be. And so actually to open it up and have a real situation where I could uncover these thing that were forbidden to me was actually very exciting.

INTERVIEWER: Do you think that there's any relationship between the family secrets and the experience of being lied to?

PR: You know, you can't blame people for lying. I think sometimes they're trying to go for a higher value, like not hurting someone else. But I must say, I think the truth is always best because, eventually it's going to come out, particularly—I—I mean, people are smart and children are really smart, and they know something isn't right when something isn't right. I think they know when something's being kept from them, on some level, often non-verbal with children. And, um, so eventually—sometimes the truth doesn't come out, but there's always going to be a hole in your experience, like an emptiness of some—something that's not right and out of order if this kind of secret—secret is kept in families.

page 44, Listening Skill

Excerpt One

INTERVIEWER: He looks a lot like the photographs of your father in the film.

POLA RAPAPORT: Yeah, it's really uncanny.

Excerpt Two

INTERVIEWER: . . . was it scary for you? Was it elating for you? Did you have a feeling that you were trespassing on forbidden ground?

PR: Oh, all of those things, actually. But I—the feeling of trespassing was actually very elating; it was very exciting to get into this territory.

Excerpt Three

INTERVIEWER: Do you think that there's any relationship between the family secrets and the experience of being lied to?

PR: You know, you can't blame people for lying.

page 55, Pronunciation, 2

ANTON: I think José's hair looks awful. I could've given him a better haircut with my eyes closed. Do you really think he looks good?

MOLLY: No, I agree, he looks terrible. He should've kept his hair long. But I couldn't tell him that.

ANTON: No, but he didn't ask you what you thought. You volunteered the compliment. You shouldn't've said anything at all.

MOLLY: But he saw me staring at him. If I hadn't said anything, he would've thought I didn't like his haircut. He knew I'd noticed, so I told a white lie. What's the harm?

ANTON: Well, first, you told a lie when you could've said nothing. But what's worse, now José thinks he looks good when he really doesn't.

MOLLY: But if I hadn't said anything, it would've been awkward. Anyway, when his hair grows, I'll tell him he looks even better.

UNIT 3: Revolution of the 50%

Listening One, page 67, Preview

SUSAN CAIN: So the idea of the book is that we live in a culture that is biased against a constellation of traits, namely shyness, seriousness, introversion, and that this leads to a colossal waste of talent and of energy and of

happiness, and that introversion really does have a uh . . . all kinds of attributes to it.

page 67, Main Ideas

Part One

JENNA GOUDREAU: Your new book, *Quiet: The Power of Introverts in a World that Can't Stop Talking*, just launched this week and it's getting a fantastic reception. Can you summarize for us the thesis of the book and how you arrived at it?

SUSAN CAIN: Yes. So the idea of the book is that we live in a culture that is biased against a constellation of traits, namely shyness, seriousness, introversion . . . and and that this leads to a colossal waste of talent and of energy and of happiness, and that introversion really does have a uh . . . all kinds of attributes to it . . . some real surprising powers to what it means to be an introvert and and yet this is not something we are mindful of and instead what we do is we encourage introverts to act more like extroverts instead of acting like their best selves.

JG: That's interesting. Can you explain for us briefly what the difference between an introvert and extrovert is?

SC: Yeah . . . good question. So introverts are people who like more quiet less stimulating environments, whereas extroverts crave more stimulation to feel at their best, and this is an important thing to see because people often assume that being an introvert means being anti-social, but it's really not that at all. It's just differently social.

So an introvert preferring less stimulation will often prefer to have a glass of wine with a close friend as opposed to going to a loud party full of strangers.

Part Two

JG: And you say that this part of your personality may be as crucial as your gender and race. Why is that?

SC: Yeah, because . . . you know, er . . . you, . . . the question of what your orientation is in general are you oriented more towards the outer world or more towards the world of your own inner riches? It's very profound, and it affects . . . it affects every day to day interaction in your life. It affects how you like to spend your time . . . you know, it . . . it . . . affects you in similar ways to the way gender does in terms of it shaping your life.

JG: And if there really is a bias against introverts then that's a bias against almost half our population.

SC: Yes yes, and this is another way in which there's a parallel to gender. It . . . . . . you know . . . I . . . I . . . I . . . often say that that the place of introverts in our culture today is very similar to where women were around the fifties or the early nineteen sixties. I mean it was half the population, and it was a piece of the population that was discounted because of something that went to the core of who they were, and I will also say it was a part of the population that was on the verge of coming into its own, and I believe that's what's happening with introverts now. I think we're we're at the cusp of a real sea change in the way we understand this personality type.

Part Three

JG: Do you think that now in workplaces and in society in general we are mistaking the person with the loudest voice and maybe the person with charisma as a good leader?

SC: Oh yeah. Yes. We absolutely do that. And, in fact, we know that extroverts are much more often groomed for leadership positions than introverts are and um this isn't to say . . . extroverts of course can be wonderful leaders, but there's also interesting new research uh . . . by Adam Grant out of the Wharton School showing that in certain circumstances introverts make the better leaders and specifically when you have employees who are really proactive and really engaged, they often do better with introverted leaders because those leaders let the proactive employees run with their ideas and implement them, whereas an extroverted leader almost without realizing what they're doing may be putting uh . . . their own stamp on things and being more dominant so that the ideas of the employees may never actually really come to light.

JG: So tell me a little bit more about the sea change. How do you actually see this going into effect? What do you hope to accomplish?

SC: Well it's a few things. I mean the first thing I would like to change is people's psyches. So many of the introverts who I interviewed for my book and many of the people they don't appear introverted uh . . . but so many of them told me about a kind of secret sense of shame that they had about who they were and how they prefer to spend their time. So, the first thing that I want to see changing is people's psyches, you know, you know for people to have a comfort level about who they are . . . uh . . . but then I'd also like schools and workplaces to really rethink how they are structured and to think about meeting the needs of their introverts as well as their extroverts.

page 69, Make Inferences

Excerpt One

Susan Cain: People often assume that being an introvert means being anti-social, but it's really not that at all. It's just differently social.

Excerpt Two

SC: The place of introverts in our culture today is very similar to where women were around the fifties or the early nineteen sixties."

Excerpt Three

SC: When you have employees who are really proactive and really engaged, they often do better with introverted leaders because those leaders let the proactive employees run with their ideas and implement them, whereas an extroverted leader almost without realizing what they're doing may be putting uh . . . their own stamp on things and being more dominant so that the ideas of the employees may never actually really come to light.

Listening Two, page 73, Comprehension

Host: If you're the sort to divide people into two groups, consider the division between those who always see the bright side and those who'd rather wallow in their misery. Julie Danis tackles the Pollyanna syndrome in today's "Tale from the Workplace."

Julie Danis: I'm Julie Danis with "Tales from the Workplace."

Arriving at the office after a visit to the eye doctor with no diagnosis for my blurred vision, I was in a grouchy mood. "No time to be cranky," a co-worker said, "we have a project due."

"Besides," she continued, "now you have a prescription to skip the mascara and rest your eyes, every two hours."

She'd done it again, I realized. She had made lemonade out of lemons. We all know people like this. They find the silver lining inside the darkest cloud . . . all the time . . . without fail . . . driving others to distraction with their "find the bright side" philosophy.

"Oh well," they say, "a stop-and-go commute is perfect for listening to language tapes while doing relaxation exercises, mais oui?"

They may emit an occasional, "Oh, no," when the computer crashes and the hold time on the 1-800-HELP line promises to be hours. But that is soon replaced by an, "Oh good, time to purge the files."

This optimistic outlook does have its merits. When you're snowed in with no hope of flying for 24 hours or more, take it as a sign you should catch up on some movies.

But don't get carried away. Nothing will take away the ache in your mouth or fill the void in your pocketbook from two root canals not covered by your company's health plan.

So, the next time someone says, "You can't cry over something that can't cry over you," assert yourself in the face of their sunny-side-up point of view. State firmly, "Yes I can, and I plan to do just that." Then go suck on some lemons and feel better in your own way. I'm Julie Danis with "Tales from the Workplace."

page 73, Listening Skill: *Identifying Creative and Effective Examples*

Excerpt One
POLLYANNA: "Now you have a prescription to skip the mascara and rest your eyes, every two hours."

Excerpt Two
POLLYANNA: "Oh well," they say, "a stop-and-go commute is perfect for listening to language tapes while doing relaxation exercises, mais oui?"

Excerpt Three
POLLYANNA: "Oh good, time to purge the files."

Excerpt Four
POLLYANNA: "Take it as a sign you should catch up on some movies."

UNIT 4: Ancient Wisdom Travels West

Listening One, page 96, Preview

SEDGE THOMSON: When you walk into a building, are you able to sort of immediately sense whether it has good feng shui or not . . . a good flow of the ch'i?

KIRSTEN LAGATREE: Yes, and so are you. You know, anytime you walk into any room, you get a feeling about it, whether you feel good about being there or not so good. So everyone has experienced good feng shui. Anytime they've walked into anybody's home, or even an office where suddenly they think, "Oh, this is pleasant. I feel good." You know, maybe their mood's a little peppier or maybe they're more relaxed . . . whatever. It's just a positive reaction that you get when you're in the midst of good feng shui.

page 96, Main Ideas

Part One

SEDGE THOMSON: So, feng shui is exactly, what, a way of ordering buildings, rooms, corridors in your life to keep out evil spirits?

KIRSTEN LAGATREE: Well, I wouldn't say to keep out evil spirits. That sounds so superstitious. But I would say, it's a system of arranging all the objects around you at home or at work in such a way that they are in harmony and balance with nature in the way that feng shui teaches us to do . . . then, therefore, you are in harmony and balance, and so is your life.

ST: Now this is something that's very important in Asia. In fact, you know, it's part of the architecture of buildings . . . how the staircases go up, where buildings are aligned, how people are . . . how live . . . what is your particular interest in it? You sound as if you have a Scandinavian background. I mean, is feng shui something important in Scandinavia?

KL: Well, there's—there's—a huge digression coming. My name is Scandinavian. I was named for a Norwegian opera singer. I identify as Irish, though. But so I don't know if there is any feng shui in Scandinavia. But their designs are so clean. I would suspect so. Yes, feng shui is huge in Asia, Taiwan, Singapore, Hong Kong. I believe it's practiced widely in mainland China, even though it's officially frowned upon as a superstition. But it's also huge here in the U.S., no less than the Donald. Donald Trump doesn't make a move without it. He would no more start working on a building project without a feng shui master than he would without, you know, if it was L.A., without . . . a seismologist to tell him that the building would stay up in an earthquake. Umm . . . that's because . . . these observations that amount to feng shui have developed over thousands of years and they work—as Donald Trump says. I do love to quote Donald Trump, not that I've ever talked to him, but . . .

ST: A famous feng shui expert, as we all know. I know for instance that people in San Francisco, if a one-way street sign is put up pointing toward a house where there are some Chinese living, they can approach the city traffic sign department and have the sign removed . . . . not necessarily pointed back in the opposite direction, but have the sign removed or at least not pointing at their house.

KL: You know, I didn't know that. But thanks, that's a great little anecdote for the rest of my book tour.

ST: Did you choose your home because of feng shui? How did you set it out?

KL: We didn't choose our home because of feng shui . . . I arranged my office at home according to feng shui . . . and it's a real basic example that illustrates a couple of principles. I am lucky enough to have a great view out the window at the far end of my office. And I was going to put my desk facing out the window, and . . . uh . . . but I would've had my back to the door which is such . . . you know . . . it's not just old west saloons and feng shui, it's also a bad idea to sit with your back to the door. Anybody who comes into your office can surprise you. They surprise you with the things they have to say. You're constantly off guard. So I turned my desk, so that I still had the view at one hand, and I had the door and the rest of the room at the other hand, and then I kind of put the other furniture in the office where it worked around that. I've got a better floor plan than I would've figured out for myself.

Part Two

ST: What's the role of mirrors?

KL: Well, mirrors in the bedroom. That's about the only room where mirrors are not wonderful. You don't want a mirror to reflect your bed in the bedroom because that could scare the heck out of you when you wake up at night. It also could frighten your spirit. You know, there's always a common sense and, uh, the transcendent explanation. So, it'll either scare your spirit, or if you prefer, it'll scare you. In every other room in the house, mirrors are terrific. They reflect ch'i, which is the basic principle of feng shui . . . this energy. It's like electricity. We can't see it, but boy is it there doing things. So, mirrors will reflect ch'i, help it circulate in a more healthy way, and they also say in the dining room or the kitchen they double your abundance. Suddenly, you have twice as much food, twice as many friends sitting at the dining room table.

ST: That is true . . . Um . . . how did you develop your interest in feng shui?

KL: I came at this topic pretty skeptically as a journalist, hard-bitten journalist that I was. I did a piece for the Los Angeles Times a few years ago on feng shui as a real estate phenomenon, because major deals rise or fall on good or bad feng shui. That was kind of that. And, so then, I really got more deeply into it, started to study it. I was still at the . . . you know . . . my friends would sort of lean in, look at me with one eyebrow up, and say, "Yeah, but do you believe this stuff?" And I would say, "Well, no, but don't quote me." Now, based on just simple things I've done and also lots and lots of people I talked to for the book, I'd have to say, it works and at the very least, it couldn't hurt.

ST: When you walk into a building, are you able to sort of immediately sense whether it has good feng shui or not . . . a good flow of the ch'i?

KL: Yes, and so are you. You know, anytime you walk into any room, you get a feeling about it, whether you feel good about being there or not so good. So everyone has experienced good feng shui. Anytime they've walked into anybody's home, or even an office where suddenly they think, "Oh, this is pleasant. I feel good." You know, maybe their mood's a little peppier or maybe they're more relaxed . . . whatever. It's just a positive reaction that you get when you're in the midst of good feng shui.

page 98, Make Inferences

Excerpt One

KIRSTEN LAGATREE: Well, I wouldn't say to keep out evil spirits. That sounds so superstitious.

Excerpt Two

KL: Umm . . . that's because . . . these observations that amount to *feng shui* have developed over thousands of years and they work—as Donald Trump says, I do love to quote Donald Trump, not that I've ever talked to him, but . . .

Excerpt Three

SEDGE THOMSON: a famous *feng shui* expert, as we all know . . .

Excerpt Four

KL: . . . my friends would sort of lean in, look at me with one eyebrow up, and say, "Yeah, but do you believe this stuff: " and I would say, "Well no, but don't quote me."

Listening Two, page 102, Comprehension

STEVE SCHER: Kirsten Lagatree is our guest. Her book is *Feng Shui: Arranging Your Home to Change Your Life—A Room by Room Guide to the Ancient Art—to the Ancient Chinese Art of Placement.* OK, so, I would like to walk into our newsroom, if we can, and you just quickly kind of look at it and figure out what we can do for some of the people here who need a little help in their careers or their happiness. Any initial thoughts you have looking at this room?

KIRSTEN LAGATREE: Umm . . . There are some very good things about this newsroom. For one thing, some of the writers are facing northeast. Northeast is the direction that governs mental ability, acuteness of thinking, scholarly success. So, those people in this newsroom, who are facing this, they not only get an extraordinarily peaceful and beautiful view out the window, they are facing in the direction that's going to make them sharp, and make their writing better.

SS: OK, so this is my desk, over here, scattered with a barrel of monkeys, and they're red, so that's good . . . I'm facing east here, right? I'm facing—yeah—east, almost to the southeast. Am I blocked up a little bit?

KL: Yeah, well, facing east, actually . . . when you face east you are facing the direction of growth, vitality, the color green. Health, vitality, youth: Those are the things that come with the direction. So, maybe that's what makes you so peppy, Steve, and so young at heart. I'd like to say something about this southeast wall right here. That is your money corner. Southeast is the direction that governs money. You haven't done anything with this direction. You've got lots of equipment there . . . what you should have is the color purple, the number 4.

SS: And a fish tank.

KL: Well, one thing at a time. The color purple and the number 4 go with that one direction, with the southeast. I'm glad you mentioned a fish tank . . . water flow symbolizes cash flow. There's a lot in feng shui that does word play, both in the Chinese language and in the English language, and so, water flow equals cash flow. You walk in to some major corporate buildings nowadays, in New York or Los Angeles or Hong Kong, you are going to see fountains in the lobby. A lot of that. The fish that are in the tank . . . they symbolize abundance, as in "there are always more fish in the sea." What's your goal? You know . . . if your goal is to be a better writer, talk somebody into changing places with you here so that you can face northeast. If your goal is to become wealthy, do some enhancement there on your southeast wall, or do it at home. Say you want to get in a relationship in your life . . . at home, enhance a southwest wall with the color yellow and the number 2. The southwest corner governs marriage, partnerships, motherhood. You pay attention to what, umm, you know, what you can do to make something happen, and then you work with these outward symbols.

page 103, Listening Skill

Excerpt One

SCHER: I'm facing—yeah—east, almost to the southeast. Am I blocked up a little bit?

Excerpt Two

LAGATREE: That is your money corner. Southeast is the direction that governs money. You haven't done anything with this direction.

Excerpt Three

LAGATREE: You've got lots of equipment there . . . what you should have is the color purple, the number 4.

page 112, Pronunciation, 1

Kung Fu Master Meets *Feng Shui* Disaster

So this is the story of a true tragedy that occurred in Hong Kong, involving *feng shui*. Of course, you've heard of Bruce Lee, the famous kung fu actor. Well, he decided to buy a house in a valley that got a lot of wind. And wind can destroy *ch'i*. Actually, people couldn't understand why he chose that area. He was wealthy and could have lived anywhere in Hong Kong. Anyway, he bought the house. And then, to change his *feng shui*, he put a mirror on a tree in his backyard. However, a storm destroyed the tree, and he never replaced it or the mirror. Now, doctors concluded that he died

of a cerebral edema. But a lot of people believe that unfavorable *feng shui* also played a role.

UNIT 5: Business Not as Usual

Listening One, page 123, Preview

INTERVIEWER: They came here? The Atlanta Refrigeration Company?

TONY HSIEH: Yup, they came here. And they went back and really focused on building a strong company culture, focused on delivering better customer service. And now they are reporting back that customers are happier, employees are happier, revenues are up, profits are up.

page 124, Main Ideas

Part One

KAI RYSSDAL: Today on Conversations from the Corner Office, a trip to see Tony Hsieh, the CEO of Zappos, the online shoe retailer.

CUSTOMER SERVICE REPRESENTATIVE: Alright Monica, I'm looking at your order for a pair of Donald J. Pliner Seemas. Is that right?

KR: The main Zappos offices—is mostly its customer call center, really—are in a generic office park, just outside Las Vegas. Dozens of employees sit in cubicles, fielding calls about styles and sizes, purchases, returns, all of that stuff. In a way, it's probably like most every other call center. Except here, each pod of cubes is wildly decorated, each with a different theme. There's a space alien motif over there. An homage to surfing over here. The 1950s live on down the way. You turn the corner, and between rows of desks and telephones, there's a group of people in party hats cheering on a co-worker playing what looks a whole lot like ring toss.

ZAPPOS EMPLOYEES, CHANTING: Ingrid, Ingrid, Ingrid . . .

And that is just the way CEO Tony Hsieh wants it.

Part Two

TH: For us, our number one priority as a company is company culture, and our whole belief is that if we get the culture right, then most of the other stuff, like delivering great customer service or building a long-term enduring brand will just happen naturally on its own.

To see that culture firsthand, we went out to Vegas and went along on one of the 16 tours that Zappos gives of its offices every week.

TH: This is our nap room. It's been proven that a 20-minute nap makes people more effective during the day.

KR: As we make our way through the maze of cubicles and conference rooms, different departments introduced themselves with different noise-makers. Western wear rang some cowbells for us; dinner bells announced the clothing team; and the travel team, for some reason, happily squeezed rubber ducks. Down the hall, in the lunchroom, a woman was singing karaoke, pretty well too, actually.

At some point, you figure they are getting work done. But one thing you won't find is an office with Tony Hsieh's name on it. He works at a regular desk in a cluster of cubicles decked out in dark plastic jungle vines. It's known as "Monkey Row."

Part Three

KR: I have to ask you the productivity question, because we are here surrounded by people who are, many of whom are working, but there's another sizeable group that's standing around chit-chatting. There's a party down the hallway that's been going on for an hour. How does all this affect actually day-in and day-out selling shoes?

TH: Probably the easiest example to give is when we do new manager orientations, we encourage new managers to spend 10 to 20 percent of their time outside the office, and so what you are seeing now, consider that . . . maybe "away from their desk" might be a better term. But a lot of that is actually outside the office, whether it's going bowling with your team or happy hour with the people you work with and so on.

And the initial reaction we get from new managers is "OK, that's great, sounds like fun, but there's a lot of work to do. What about productivity?" And then we ask the managers that have done it, how much more productive and efficient is your team, because there's higher levels of trust; communication is better; people are willing to do favors for each other 'cause they are doing favors for friends not just coworkers. And the answers we get back range anywhere from 20 percent to 100 percent more productive. So kind of a worst-case scenario, you break even and you're having more fun doing it.

KR: They're definitely having fun. Zappos has been ranked among the best places in the country to work. All the high jinx don't seem to be hurting the bottom line either. Zappos took in more than a billion dollars in sales last year. It's actually been growing at a time when a lot of other shoe retailers are struggling.

Maybe because of that, Tony Hsieh has become something of an accidental management guru. People and companies pay thousands of dollars to come and learn the ways of Zappos corporate culture. Hsieh's

even written a book about it a New York Times bestseller in fact called *Delivering Happiness.*

Part Four

KR: It does seem, though, that what is being created here by virtue of your role in this company and your public profile is sort of a two-headed operation. You have this website that sells shoes and now clothing and cosmetics and all kinds of other things, and you have you.

TH: Well, we actually have a separate entity called Zappos Insights, and we help other companies figure out their own values and develop their own strong cultures. 'Cause one of the reactions we get sometimes is, "OK, glad you have this strong culture, Zappos. Happy for you, but this would never work in another industry, in a non-Internet company" and so on. But companies from all over the country, or world even, fly in, and, for example, the Atlanta Refrigeration Company does refrigeration repairs out in the field, so in some ways you can't think of a more opposite company.

KR: They came here? The Atlanta Refrigeration Company?

YH: Yup, they came here. And they went back and really focused on building a strong company culture, focused on delivering better customer service. And now they are reporting back that customers are happier, employees are happier, revenues are up, profits are up. It's just really neat seeing that this type of philosophy of using essentially happiness as a business model working in other companies and other industries.

page 127, Make Inferences

Excerpt One

KR: At some point you figure they ARE getting work done.

Excerpt Two

KR: I have to ask you the productivity question, because we are here surrounded by people who are, many of whom are working, but there's another sizeable group that's standing around chit-chatting. There's a party down the hallway that's been going on for an hour. How does all this affect actually day in and day out selling shoes?

Excerpt Three

KR: You have this website that sells shoes and now clothing and cosmetics and all kinds of other things, and you have you.

Listening Two, page 130, Comprehension

Kai Ryssdal: The cover story of the latest issue of Fortune Magazine is its annual list of the 100 best places to work. Salary, benefits, perks, intangibles—all the standard measurements. But Commentator Teresa Amabile says there's something missing from the data.

TERESA AMABILE: The list might make you conclude that the best workplaces have fantastic perks and lots of fun every day. Sure, the techies at Google love the free gourmet food, and Zappos employees get a kick out of playing Nerf Dart war. But all of that misses the most important element of employee engagement: helping them succeed at work that matters.

My research team and I analyzed nearly 12,000 work diaries from professionals in seven different companies. We discovered something we call the progress principle. That may sound like "management speak" to you, but here's the thing: It really is all about management. The single most important thing that can keep workers deeply, happily engaged on the job is moving forward on work they care about—even if the progress is an incremental "small win." And the event that most often makes for a bad day at work, feeling like you are being stalled. The negative effect of these setbacks, on motivation and emotion, is two-to-three times stronger than the positive effect of progress.

Your bosses—and how they manage you—make all the difference. The best managers in our study paid attention to progress and supported it every day. They set clear goals and gave people autonomy in meeting those goals. As a result, their employees stayed committed, productive and creative. Sure, cool perks are great. Who doesn't want gourmet food and game time? But it's the feeling of getting somewhere that keeps people jazzed about what they do at work.

And that takes work.

page 130, Listening Skill

Excerpt One

TERESA AMABILE: We discovered something we call the progress principle. That may sound like "management speak" to you, but here's the thing: It really is all about management.

Excerpt Two

TERESA AMABILE: Sure, cool perks are great. Who doesn't want gourmet food and game time? But it's the feeling of getting somewhere that keeps people jazzed about what they do at work.

UNIT 6: Together Alone

Listening One, page 156, Preview

JOHN MOE: We had friends over the other night. They had never been to our house before, and they were surprised that it was so low-tech given that I host this show. There's an old typewriter, an old camera sitting out. The computer's tucked away. After talking tech all day, I come home and unplug, except for the iPhone hidden in my pocket.

page 156, Main Ideas

Part One

JM: We had friends over the other night. They had never been to our house before and they were surprised that it was so low-tech given that I host this show. There's an old typewriter, an old camera sitting out. The computer's tucked away. After talking tech all day, I come home and unplug, except for the iPhone hidden in my pocket. We all must manage the tech in our own lives. But Sherry Turkle thinks that as a society we are not doing a very good job of it. She's the founder and director of MIT's initiative on technology and self. Her new book is *Alone Together: Why We Expect More from Technology and Less from Each Other*. It's about how we use tech to seek intimacy in things that can't provide it, and how we are going to manage a world where computers are always with us.

SHERRY TURKLE: It's not a question of saying "the horse is out of the barn" or "we're addicted." I mean this is with us to stay. And we have to learn to be a partner with it in a way that we get it right.

Part Two

JM: Is that a natural process, or is that a conscious choice we're going to have to make? I mean, is it sort of like the boom of these communications comes out and then we recognize a natural throttling back, or is it going to have to be you know like the information equivalent of going on a strict diet.

ST: I think it's going to be combination of things. What I think is very important is that we start the conversation. When people, you know, give a tagline to my book, or give a tagline to an appearance I make, they'll say things like, "Turkle says unplug." And I am not saying that.

It's not Turkle says unplug. It's Turkle says, "Get a grip. Think." It's Turkle says "reflect." I am not suggesting anybody unplug. It's not like you are for or against technology. It's just that we just need to create a partnership where our human values come first.

JM: Well, I am on Twitter. I am on Facebook and if I wasn't [sic] on those two social media platforms, I would interact with maybe four people a day other than my family. There would be my producer and a couple of people I see at work and that's pretty much it.

But instead I have tons of interactions. They aren't face to face. I've helped people get jobs. I've introduced

friends. I collaborate on things. And in large part, it's because I am sort of connected as the day goes along.
ST: That's great. That's not what I am talking about. If you don't have a problem, I'm not talking about you.

Part Three

JM: So how do you know you have a problem?

ST: If your social networks are increasing your capacity for meaningful relationships, if you feel you have a balance in your life. I am not talking about you. I am saying that I have done field work, a lot of field work, a lot of time, a lot of families, a lot of professionals who say, "I am so on my email. I am so overwhelmed with messages that I am too connected to think. "That is the story that I'm getting from the research. And more than that they say: "People send me an email and they are expecting an answer by the end of the day." And because they're expecting an answer by the end of the day and because they're expecting some kind of response, we're all starting to kind of ratchet down the quality of the questions and the quality of the answers. In other words, people are asking simpler questions in order to the get the answer. And I am starting to give simpler answers in order to be able to give an answer.

So, we are all starting to get used to a sort of degradation in performance in order to respond to the volume and the velocity.

page 158, Make Inferences

Excerpt One

ST: What I think is very important is that we start the conversation. When people, you know, give a tagline to my book, or give a tagline to an appearance I make, they'll say things like, "Turkle says unplug." And I am not saying that. It's not Turkle says unplug. It's Turkle says, "Get a grip. Think." It's Turkle says "reflect." I am not suggesting anybody unplug.

Excerpt Two

ST: That's great. That's not what I am talking about. If you don't have a problem, I'm not talking about you.

Excerpt Three

ST: If your social networks are increasing your capacity for meaningful relationships, if you feel you have a balance in your life. I am not talking about you. I am saying that I have done field work, a lot of field work, a lot of time, a lot of families, a lot of professionals who say, "I am so on my email. I am so overwhelmed with messages that I am too connected to think." That is the story that I am getting from the research.

Listening Two, page 162, Comprehension

A: Who should control your identity on the Internet? Should you be free to pick and choose among multiple personas? Or should you be expected to adhere to a single, authentic identity online, as you would offline?

In an age when bills are paid via PayPal, relationships are forged over Facebook, and revolutions are fueled by Twitter, these questions are taking on new prominence. How we answer them may define the Internet for years to come.

The deactivation of Salman Rushdie's Facebook account recently revived debate over Internet Identity. Facebook mistook the well-known, controversial writer for an impersonator. After forcing the author to prove his true identity, Facebook demanded that Rushdie call himself by his legal name, Ahmed.

Though Salman Rushdie's Facebook account soon reappeared online, the debacle points to a vibrant debate long brewing in the blogosphere: the conflict over Internet Identity and who should control it.

Advocates of Internet "pseudonymity" argue web users should be free to craft identities that reveal some, but not all, of who they are. Twitter, for example, allows its users to adopt identities of their choosing. The company says such anonymity is vital to free speech and democracy. Had Egyptian activists been forced to reveal their names in their Tweets, many more would have faced arrest. But as advocates cite politics, critics cite civility. Companies like Google and Facebook say that web authenticity is key to an open, safe, and accountable Internet experience. If users don't stick to their real names, no one will trust the social medium and we all lose out.

As Internet heavyweights decide the fate of Internet anonymity, where do you stand? Who are you when you're on the Web?

page 163, Listening Skill

Excerpt One

A: But as advocates cite politics, critics cite civility.

Excerpt Two

A: Advocates of Internet "pseudonymity" argue web users should be free to craft identities that reveal some, but not all, of who they are. Twitter, for example, allows its users to adopt identities of their choosing. The company says such anonymity is vital to free speech and democracy. Companies like Google and Facebook say that web authenticity is key to an open, safe, and accountable Internet experience

Excerpt Three

JOHN MOE: Is that a natural process, or is that a conscious choice we're going to have to make? I mean is it sort of like the boom of these communications comes out and then we recognize a natural throttling back, or is it going to have to be, you know, like the information equivalent of going on a strict diet?

page 176, Pronunciation, 2

1.
A: Remove your phone from the table.
B: Do I have to?

2.
A: I didn't hear her. What did the professor say?
B: She said we need to put away our cell phones during class.

3.
A: I think you'd better check your identity by Googling yourself daily.
B: Daily? Are you kidding?

4.
A: We can't hire him. He's not who he says he is.
B: Seriously? We spent so much time interviewing that guy. What a waste of time.

5.
A: What's wrong?
B: I just read an article about how to manage our online identities. Yet another thing I have to worry about!

6.
A: Hey. Check out this text from my grandmother.
B: Your grandmother texts? She's nearly 100!

UNIT 7: Learning Through the Arts

Listening One, page 187, Preview

MARCIE SILLMAN: Researchers have a lot of theories to explain that success. Elizabeth Whitford directs Seattle's Arts Corps, an organization that sponsors after school art classes. Whitford says the arts are fun, they engage students. And they can instill certain character traits.

ELIZABETH WHITFORD: Persistence. Any artist has to show extreme persistence to learn that skill, and discipline related to that. And courage and risk taking.

page 188, Main Ideas

Part One

MS: If you took an informal poll, most kids would probably tell you that school is a drag.

I'm Marcie Sillman. Why does school get a bad rap? And what can be done to change that reputation? That's what educators want to know. Some recent studies show that kids who are involved in the arts do better in school. Researchers have a lot of theories to explain that success.

Elizabeth Whitford directs Seattle's Arts Corps, an organization that sponsors after school art classes. Whitford says the arts are fun, they engage students. And they can instill certain character traits.

EW: Persistence. Any artist has to show extreme persistence to learn that skill, and discipline related to that. And courage and risk taking.

And some scientists believe that making art can actually alter your brain. The data that link the impact of the arts on learning are preliminary. But they've convinced some experts to venture outside the box when it comes to classroom teaching.

Part Two

MS: As Carmela Dellino strolls through the halls of Roxhill Elementary School, she seems to know every child she sees.

For the past two years, Dellino has been principal of this southwest Seattle school. She oversees a wildly diverse student body. More than 30 percent of Roxhill's 310 kids are bilingual, from Latin America, Africa, or Asia.

CARMELA DELLINO: "About eighty five percent of our kids qualify for free and reduced lunch, so they live in pretty extreme poverty."

MS: Dellino says most Roxhill families don't have the means to take their kids to the ballet or the symphony. And Roxhill's PTA can't raise enough extra money to hire a special art or music teacher, the way they do at more affluent schools. So when the Seattle School District asked if Roxhill wanted to take part in a pilot program that uses the arts to teach literacy skills, Dellino didn't hesitate to say yes.

CD: Especially in a school like Roxhill, where our students don't have that access to the arts that other students might have, what a wonderful way to be able to use the arts to develop literacy.

JENNY DEW: "Snakes, stand up, move around like a snake. I see zigzagging, hungry snakes. I hear hissing sounds."

MS: Twenty first graders slink across a brightly patterned rug in Jenny Dew's classroom. They hiss at each other, and thrust their heads forward, like pythons ready to strike. Actor David Quicksall videotapes the action, and occasionally throws out a word of advice.

DAVID QUICKSALL: "Remember, we're going to stay on our feet."

Part Three

MS: Roxhill is one of four Seattle elementary schools involved in this literacy project. It's a partnership between the Seattle School District and a nonprofit called Arts Impact. A classroom teacher from each grade in the participating schools is paired with an artist mentor. The teachers study dance, theater, and visual arts during intensive summer training sessions. During the school year, they use specially developed lesson plans that infuse those art forms into the basic curriculum. In Jenny Dew's class, they're using theater to build vocabulary.

JD: How can you move like a snake? Are you going to slither, are you going to flick, are you going to zig zag, or swim or rattle or shake?

FIRST GRADER: "I'm gonna flick."

MS: The Arts Impact project is only in its first year at Roxhill, but Principal Carmela Dellino says already, the kids are pretty engaged in what they're doing.

CD: And when we can have student engagement increase, then we're going to have student learning increase. We know, and research tells us, when the body and the brain and creative spirit are all engaged, then learning is going to really happen."

MS: The U.S. Department of Education wants more hard data about how the arts affect learning. So the Department awarded Arts Impact 241 million dollars to fund this particular project. Arts Impact Director Sybil Barnum says art making has very tangible connections to the core academic subjects kids study in school.

SYBIL BARNUM: The artistic process involves gathering information, developing ideas, refining your work, self-reflection, and revision. And all those things are also part of many other discipline processes—the scientific process, the writing process. Having the students see this process that they're working through with the arts is also a process that they use in another subject area, which is also very helpful.

page 190, Make Inferences

Excerpt One
MS: . . . For the past two years, Dellino has been principal of this southwest Seattle school. She oversees a wildly diverse student body. More than 30 percent of Roxhill's 310 kids are bilingual, from Latin America, Africa, or Asia.

CD: "About eighty five percent of our kids qualify for free and reduced lunch, so they live in pretty extreme poverty."

Excerpt Two
JD: Snakes, stand up, move around like a snake. I see zigzagging, hungry snakes. I hear hissing sounds.

Excerpt Three
SB: The artistic process involves gathering information, developing ideas, refining your work, self-reflection, and revision. And all those things are also part of many

other discipline processes—the scientific process, the writing process. Having the students see this process that they're working through with the arts is also a process that they use in another subject area, which is also very helpful.

Listening Two, page 192, Comprehension

Part One
DIANE ORSON: This is *Where We Live*. I'm Diane Orson in for John Dankosky. No, it is not the Boston Symphony or the NY Philharmonic. You are listening to the Simón Bolívar Youth Orchestra of Venezuela, a performance of Leonard Bernstein's Mambo from *West Side Story* that—that's been viewed hundreds of thousands of times on YouTube.

So explain to us. What is "El Sistema"? How does it work?

TRICIA TUNSTALL: Well, you gave a good introduction. *El Sistema* is an extraordinary program that's been going on in—in Venezuela for many years. And it is a program for youth development through orchestral education, as you said. And it involves hundreds of programs throughout the country—in the mountains, in the plains, on the shore, even in remote, sort of, uh, islands that are very difficult to get to, there are these programs which they call *núcleos*.

And in these programs children come and they play in youth orchestras—first children's orchestras, and then as they get older and more adept, uh, sort of middle level orchestras and then the advanced high school level orchestras.

Children usually come to the *Sistema* when they're young, and they usually stay there throughout their formative years, playing in orchestras every single day, sometimes for many hours a day, uh, until they graduate from high school. This program, as you said, produces many extraordinary musicians. But most of the graduates of *El Sistema* do not become musicians. What they do is go out into the world equipped both mentally and psychologically and emotionally to be productive, uh, contributing citizens and to have flourishing lives.

Part Two
DO: Let's talk a little bit more about that. What does playing a musical instrument offer these children, especially these children, uh, who come from very disadvantaged, uh, living situations?

TT: Yes, well, you know the founder of the *Sistema*, uh, José Antonio Abreu, often is quoted as saying that, "A child who has a clarinet in his hands will not pick up a gun." It's uh, I think it is almost literally true, especially in the case of Venezuela where there is so much poverty and where the poverty is so linked to gang warfare, violence, and drugs. What that child with that instrument in his hands is doing when he comes to the program is much more than just learn to play an instrument. He is, uh, he's participating in a community of his peers, all of whom are learning to play instruments. He is learning in ensemble which is very important because in the orchestral ensemble you learn not only how to harmonize musically, but how to harmonize socially—how to become a contributor, how to cooperate with other people, how to work together for one common goal. Those are extraordinary lessons for small children and for, uh, growing children to learn.

Part Three

TT: Playing an instrument also and learning and getting better at the instrument also really gives a child a sense of self-esteem, a sense of mastery, a sense of accomplishment that he or she may not have gotten anywhere else in, uh, in his or her life either at school or in the home. Um, and finally, the experience of being in these orchestras teaches every child that he is a teacher as well as a learner. There's a great deal of back and worth, uh, peer learning going on. That's one of the principal things that goes on in the Sistema. And when a child feels that he not only is learning something valuable, but that he has something valuable to teach. That's a tremendous incentive to teach, to be a contributing member of society, to be really part of a community. What these programs do, really Diane, is to offer children, uh, an alternative world to the streets, and a world that's so attractive, and so appealing, so much fun, uh, and so comforting that it really is a preventative for many of these children to, uh, fall into some of the traps of poverty.

page 193, Listening Skill

Excerpt One

TT: He is learning in ensemble, which is very important, because in the orchestral ensemble you learn not only how to harmonize musically, but how to harmonize socially—how to become a contributor, how to cooperate with other people, how to work together for one common goal.

Excerpt Two

TT: Playing an instrument also and learning and getting better at the instrument also really gives a child a sense of self-esteem, a sense of mastery, a sense of accomplishment that he or she may not have gotten

anywhere else in his or her life either at school or in the home.

Excerpt Three

TT: What these programs do, really Diane, is to offer children, an alternative world to the streets, and a world that's so attractive, so appealing, so much fun, and so comforting that it really is a preventative for many of these children to fall into some of the traps of poverty.

UNIT 8: Changing Lives for $50

Listening One, page 219, Preview

RAJ SHAH: In very poor environments, you see improved height and weight outcomes, which are signs of basic human nutrition. You see improvements in school attendance and in paying school fee. One of the mot important things I learned by visiting so many of these programs is wherever you go, anywhere around the world, you ask people what they do with the expanded income they've earned from their business activity—buy a sewing machine, make a little bit more money—what's the first thing they do with that money, and nine times out of ten it is pay school fees for their children and provide better opportunities for their children.

page 220, Main Ideas

Part One

ROSS REYNOLDS: There are obvious benefits to credit, but there are also pitfalls. You can get overextended, you don't own anything, the bank ends up owning it. In some ways, paying as you go might be a better idea. Is credit always a good thing, particularly for poor people?

ALEX COUNTS: Well, see for poor people who don't have access to jobs and don't have a safety net, the only alternative are to starve or to work for yourself. For most of the poor, they have so little money that their businesses are highly undercapitalized. So the option of doing the same things they're doing but having them at a more reasonable capital level, that's an option that people should have. They shouldn't, obviously, be forced to take it, but many of them are extremely happy to be able to take 60 or 70 dollars which triples the capital of their simple, rural business doing trading or a cottage industry of some kind, and that becomes then a pathway to break the poverty cycle.

RR: Tell us how 60 or 70 dollars can make a big difference.

AC: Well, again, just to take a very simple example that I saw many times when I was living in Bangladesh was a woman who knew how to raise chickens and she would sell the eggs and that was how she would meet her daily needs. But she never had enough capital to have more than three chickens at any given time and every so often they would be wiped out by disease. By taking 60 dollars she would be able to have 12 or 13 chickens and do it on a larger scale and generate enough income to send her child to school, to treat illness with modern medicine. And, again, this is a very small amount. Some of the women who do that ultimately end up four years later having a poultry farm of 500 chickens.

Part Two

RR: Raj, how big a part do you think these microloans and microfinancing can be to raise people out of poverty?

Raj Shah: Well, it clearly plays a very important role over time. As Alex points out, it' also not for everyone. What I thought it's important for your listeners to get a picture of is that the idea of moving someone from extreme poverty to moderate poverty, while that may not sound like a lot, actually means quite a bit to both that household and the children in those households, and so some of the most compelling data around impact has been what happens to the kids of women who are participating in these microcredit or microfinance programs. In very poor environments, you see improved height and weight outcomes, which are signs of basic human nutrition. You see improvements in school attendance and in paying school fee. One of the mot important things I learned by visiting so many of these programs is wherever you go, anywhere around the world, you ask people what they do with the expanded income they've earned from their business activity—buy a sewing machine, make a little bit more money—what' the first thing they do with that money, and nine times out of ten it is pay school fees for their children and provide better opportunities for their children. So it is important to get a characterization of what we mean when we say move from extreme poverty to moderate poverty—that can have very important outcomes for children and for the next generation. And then, as Alex points out, maybe a third to 40 percent of all clients who stick with the program for a significant period of time will move out of poverty in some sustainable manner, so it's an important tool, but its not the only tool.

Part Three

RR: Is there a zero sum here? I'm wondering whether money that goes into microfinancing is money that might go to another program that might help people in poverty and whether it diminishes some of these other programs. For example, if I go to Kiva.org, Matt, I could make a loan to someone or I could, say, you know, I think I'd rather write a check to CARE or in some other way provide support to people in developing countries who are in deep poverty. Is it taking away from other services to open up this line, or is it . . .

Matt Flannery: Well, the great thing, I think, about microfinance is that it is a sustainable way of helping people in poverty, so unlike other development aid programs it is a gift that can keep on giving. The poor can borrow and that loan can be recycled and another person can borrow it, so I think of it as a contribution that is more leveraged and can help more people over time and can go on into perpetuity and help one entrepreneur after another.

Part Four

RR: Alex, you mentioned the backlash. Do your critics have any good points?

AC: Well, of course, I'm, again, having interviewed hundreds if not thousands of microfinance clients, you don't, uh, there's no overnight success even for those who succeed; it does take years and these things are not . . . is not a panacea but what I think your listeners should keep in mind—there are really two things; one is a shift from extreme poverty to moderate poverty, while you might think it sounds like a failure—you've not crossed the poverty line—it's probably a bigger life change financially and socially than any of your listeners are ever going to have over the course of their entire lives.

RR: Give us an example of what that actually means.

AC: Well, what it means is being able to have to make choices every nine or 10 months out of the year about which two members of the five member family will eat as opposed to almost every month of the year having some minimal basic foodstuff for everyone in the family, or having to make choices of which one of three children will go to school or being able to send all three of them to school.

RR: Thanks to all of you. And doubtlessly, with the involvement of the organizations such as Kiva.org and the Bill and Melinda Gate Foundation, we're going to see microfinancing developing quite a bit more in the coming years. We'll check in on it and tell you how it is developing.

page 222, Make Inferences

Excerpt One

RR: Tell us how $60 or $70 dollars can make a big difference.

Excerpt Two

RR: Is there a zero sum here? I'm wondering whether money that goes into microfinancing is money that might go to another program that might help people in poverty and whether it diminishes some of these other programs.

Excerpt Three

AC: . . . there are really two things: one is a shift from extreme poverty to moderate poverty, while you might think it sounds like a failure—you've not crossed the poverty line—it's probably a bigger life change financially and socially than any of your listeners are ever going to have over the course of their entire lives.

Listening Two, page 225, Comprehension

Part One

INTERVIEWER: Thank you for joining me today, Will.

WILL BULLARD: It's a pleasure.

INTERVIEWER: I was wondering if you could tell me a specific story of one woman whose life was changed with the help of a microloan that she got from Adelante?

WB: I'll tell you about a client that I went and visited maybe four or five times. She was the client who had nine kids and, the world over, when you have a malnourished child, that child's hair is going to turn a reddish tint, and she had . . . her ninth child had that reddish tint hair and everyone in the village knows what that meant and so when Maria Jose went to the assembly in her village to ask to be allowed to join the assembly there, one of the major components of microcredit is that the women themselves get to decide, or have to decide, who they allow in their assembly and who they will not allow in because they are going to co-sign for her loan. And the women in this community voted not to allow her in because they felt that she was going to eat the loan—and that's a very literal term here—that you'll get your 50 dollars and you'll go out and have a good meal that you only can dream about, so they said no. But there was a very nice woman who was another client and who had faith in Maria Jose and she gave Maria Jose, I think, 25 dollars just kind of as a test loan, and Maria Jose went out and invested the 25 dollar in flour and some cooking supplies, made some little meat pies that she sold in front of the school and she paid her friend back and that was enough evidence that she could handle her money that she was then allowed into the assembly. She became a dynamic entrepreneur and she became very successful. She lived in a horrible little grass hut and then she built a concrete house that she moved all of

her kids into; it's only a one-room house but it's a huge step up. She became the vice president of her Adelante assembly.

Part Two

INTERVIEWER: It sounds like from that anecdote that woman got incredible benefits and was really able to change her life through the power of microloans, but you were saying that you think the real benefits are not monetary. Could you elaborate on what you mean by that?

WB: I'm not sure that many people are leaving poverty behind and the impact studies are kind of suggesting the same, but there are other benefits—non-monetary benefits as well as the woman I just mentioned. So she gets that house because she's been able to sell meat in her village but then, you know, things are kind of stopped, how much further can you go? You don't have a third grade education. You don't have a big market in your community. To be quite honest with you, that woman I just told about, she had such confidence in herself—that non-monetary benefit—that she sold her bicycle that she had bought, and she did what a lot of people here do; she went to the North, she tried to get to the States. She didn't make it; she came back and took a huge hit in the process. It's a very complicated world down here.

Part Three

INTERVIEWER: It sounds like the power of microloaning kind of hits a ceiling at a certain point. And you were saying how you think the next step would be to bring in business training—how would that work exactly?

WB: Women here do want a better life; they want to do better and they know that selling used clothing and they know that selling little meat pies and sweetbreads are only going to get them so far. It might not even be the majority, but a good percentage of them would do whatever they could to make more money, and to do that, like in any country in the world—developed or developing country, you need skills, you need training to advance. So surely there's a way to go to women and to say, "Well, your sweetbreads are good, but what if you sold this kind of sweetbread or this kind of cake?"—and that would have a little bit higher margins, that other people aren't selling, or "You're selling things nicely but what if you targeted this particular niche market where the revenues are . . . " that's being neglected and the whole kicker is there are only so many sandals, and so many plastics pots and so many things you can sell in a village after you meet that very small pie . . . what do you do? How do you grow that pie? How do you start producing things that add value? It's a sort of tricky thing.

Interviewer: Well, thank you so much for talking with me today.

page 226, Listening Skill

Excerpt One

WB: I'm not sure that many people are leaving poverty behind and the impact studies are kind of suggesting the same, that there are other benefits—non-monetary benefits as well as the woman I just mentioned.

Interviewer: So, in short, research shows that microfinance fails to lift people out of poverty; however, there might be other benefits not related to money.

Excerpt Two

WB: Women here do want a better life; they want to do better and they know that selling used clothing and they know that selling little meat pies and sweetbreads are only going to get them so far. It might not even be the majority, but a good percentage of them would do whatever they could to make more money.

Interviewer: So the gist is that most women will sell clothing and food stuff because they do want to improve their lives, but they know their success will be limited.

Excerpt Three

WB: So she gets that house because she's been able to sell meat in her village, but then, you know, things are kind of stopped, how much further can you go?

Interviewer: It sounds like the power of microloaning kind of hits a ceiling at a certain point.

UNIT 1

Kerry Obrien speaks with Norman Doidge[Brain Plasticity]. Reproduced by permission of the Australian Broadcasting Corporation and ABC Online. © 2008 ABC. All rights reserved.

Merits of Unitasking © The Economist Newspaper Limited, London (October 14, 2011)

UNIT 2

"Lies, Lies, Lies," The Infinite Mind. "Lies, Lies, Lies" broadcast May 1, 2007 c/r 2007 Lichtenstein Creative Media Inc.

UNIT 3

"So Begins a Quiet Revolution of the 50%: The Secret Power of Introverts: A Quiet Revolution," from *Forbes*, January 30, 2011 © 2011 Forbes. All rights reserved. Used by permission and protected by the Copyright Laws of the United States. The printing, copying, redistribution, or retransmission of this Content without express written permission is prohibited.

"Tales from the Workplace: Making Lemonade—'The Pollyanna Syndrome'" by Julie Danis, courtesy of Marketplace®, © (p) 1996, American Public Media, Used with permission. All rights reserved.

UNIT 4

Interview with a Feng Shui expert. Courtesy of West Coast Live, a division of Flexous LLC. All rights reserved. Reproduced by permission.

"Feng Shui in the Newsroom." Interview with Kirsten Lagatree and Steve Scher on KUOW Public Radio on 2/6/1996. Reprinted by permission of KUOW Public Radio, KUOW Puget Sound Public Radio.

UNIT 5

"Zappos CEO on corporate culture and happiness" [Interview with Tony Hsieh]. Conversations from the Corner Office: "Zappos CEO on corporate culture and 'Happiness,'" from American Public Media's "Marketplace" © (p) 2010. Used with permission. All rights reserved.

"Are 'The Best Places to Work' really the best?" from American Public Media's "Marketplace" © (p) 2012. Used with permission. All rights reserved.

UNIT 6

"Does technology alienate us from each other?" from American Public Media's "Marketplace Tech Report" © (p) 2011. Used with permission. All rights reserved.

"Global Ethics Corner: Privacy and Responsibility on the Internet: Who Should Control your Identity on the Web?" Used with Permission of Connecticut Public Broadcasting Network.

UNIT 7

"Brain Waves: This is your brain on Art." KUOW Puget Sound Public Radio.

"Where We Live: El Sistema." Used with Permission of Connecticut Public Broadcasting Network.

UNIT 8

"Microfinance, Interview with Alex Counts, Raj Shah, and Matt Flannery," by Ross Reynolds on KUOW Public Radio on 7/17/2006 on Weekday. Reprinted by permission of KUOW Public Radio, KUOW Puget Sound Public Radio.

THE PHONETIC ALPHABET

Consonant Symbols			
/b/	**b**e	/t/	**t**o
/d/	**d**o	/v/	**v**an
/f/	**f**ather	/w/	**w**ill
/g/	**g**et	/y/	**y**es
/h/	**h**e	/z/	**z**oo, bu**s**y
/k/	**k**eep, **c**an	/θ/	**th**anks
/l/	**l**et	/ð/	**th**en
/m/	**m**ay	/ʃ/	**sh**e
/n/	**n**o	/ʒ/	vi**s**ion, A**s**ia
/p/	**p**en	/tʃ/	**ch**ild
/r/	**r**ain	/dʒ/	**j**oin
/s/	**s**o, **c**ircle	/ŋ/	lo**ng**

Vowel Symbols			
/ɑ/	f**a**r, h**o**t	/iy/	**we**, m**ea**n, f**ee**t
/ɛ/	m**e**t, s**ai**d	/ey/	d**ay**, l**a**te, r**ai**n
/ɔ/	t**a**ll, b**ou**ght	/ow/	g**o**, l**ow**, c**oa**t
/ə/	s**o**n, **u**nder	/uw/	t**oo**, bl**ue**
/æ/	c**a**t	/ay/	t**i**me, b**uy**
/ɪ/	sh**i**p	/aw/	h**ou**se, n**ow**
/ʊ/	g**oo**d, c**ou**ld, p**u**t	/oy/	b**oy**, c**oi**n